CHILD POVERTY

CHILD POVERTY

Love, Justice, and
Social Responsibility

Pamela Couture

CHALICE
P R E S S
ST. LOUIS, MISSOURI

© Copyright 2007 by Pamela Couture

All rights reserved. For permission to reuse content, please contact Copyright Clearance Center, 222 Rosewood Drive, Danvers, MA 01923, (978) 750-8400, www.copyright.com.

Biblical quotations, unless otherwise noted, are from the *New Revised Standard Version Bible*, copyright 1989, Division of Christian Education of the National Council of the Churches of Christ in the United States of America. Used by permission. All rights reserved.

Cover art: Getty Images
Cover and interior design: Elizabeth Wright

Visit Chalice Press on the World Wide Web at
www.chalicepress.com

10 9 8 7 6 5 4 3 2 1   07 08 09 10 11 12

Library of Congress Cataloging–in–Publication Data

Couture, Pamela D., 1951-
    Child poverty : love, justice, and social responsibility / Pamela D. Couture.
    p. cm.
    ISBN-13: 978-0-8272-0509-3
    1. Church work with poor children. 2. Church work with children. 3. Poverty—Religious aspects—Christianity. 4. Poor children. 5. Child welfare. 6. Social justice. 7. Church and social problems. I. Title.
    BV639.C4C685 2007
    261.8'325—dc22   2007037335

Printed in the United States of America

This book is dedicated to my four new grandchildren who arrived during its writing and editing,

Brenden Thomas Conrad,
Ethan Liam Peet,
Nolan Patrick Conrad, and
Patrick Brady Ford.

It is also dedicated to another grandmother who was a stellar member of the apostolate for children and poverty,

Hannah Meadors.

Hannah never let an opportunity pass to teach, involve, or advocate for children. I remember Hannah as she fought her last battle with breast cancer. Her ill health did not stop her from unloading potatoes for the Society of St. Andrew or from marching toward the United Nations, ignoring all the family and friends who tried to stop her, in the Stand for Children in 2002. She died in March, 2003, a stalwart role model whose dedication humbled us all.

Contents

With gratitude...

This book would not exist had I not had the unusual opportunity to work for nine years with the task force for the United Methodist Bishops Initiative on Children and Poverty. In so doing I enjoyed the rare privilege of working with the United Methodist Council of Bishops, liaisons from United Methodist boards and agencies, and academic representatives to the Initiative. Bishops Jack Meadors, Kenneth Carder, Ann Sherer, and Don Ott, as leaders of the Initiative, pushed my thinking and my understanding of the relationship between the academy and the church on the subject of children and poverty. Jim Winkler and the General Board of Church and Society offered me the opportunity to engage in conversations with European church people about United Methodist social principles in light of social and ecclesial change in Eastern Europe in 2003. Bishop Ntambo Nkulu Ntanda hosted me in Kamina, North Kantanga Province, the Democratic Republic of the Congo, in 2003. Bishops Susan Morrison, Gregory Palmer, and James King invited me to lead Bible studies at the Troy, Iowa, and Kentucky Annual Conferences.

I am grateful to them, to all of my colleagues in the Initiative, and to the bishops and conference representatives whose efforts deepened the life of their Annual Conferences in relation to children and poverty. I am personally grateful for the spiritual renewal, companionship, and hope for the church that the Initiative brought to my life and to the lives of so many.

I am also grateful for the support of colleagues who became intrigued with my work on women, children, and poverty and invited me to speak about children and poverty at academic meetings. Jean Stairs, principal of Queens Theological College at Queens University, Kingston, Ontario, initiated this work when she invited me to deliver the lectures for the alumnae gathering at Queens in October 2002. Mary Elizabeth Moore invited me to address the spirituality of the caregiver at the Practical Theology group of the American Academy of Religion in 2002. William Storrar furthered the work by inviting me to lecture for the book launch of Kathleen Marshall and Paul Purvis's *Honouring Children* at Edinburgh University in 2003, and colleagues responded to ideas about children and poverty at the International Academy of Practical Theology in Manchester, England, in 2003. Colgate Rochester Crozer Divinity School allowed me to present many of these ideas as the Wynn Lectures in 2004. John Swinton gave permission to reprint here portions of one chapter, which had been part of materials previously published in *Contact*.

I have been graciously helped with the writing style by Larry McEnerney of the University of the Chicago Professional Writing Program and by Nancy Barry and my writing group at the Iowa Summer Writing Festival.

Ann Kemper, Molly McNulty, and Ashley Cheung assisted with interviews of the Area Coordinators of the Bishops Initiative on Children and Poverty. Respondents from the German Annual Conference, the Baguio Episcopal Area in the Philippines, and the South Congo Episcopal Areas of the United Methodist Church helped me understand the efforts on behalf of children and poverty in other parts of the world. Colleagues at Saint Paul School of Theology Warren Carter, Harold Washington, Tom Haverly, Shannon Jung, and Hal Knight responded to ideas and to drafts of the manuscript. Patti Jung of Loyola University in Chicago assisted with chapter 12 on apostolic spirituality, and Leah Evison, environmental scientist at the Environment Protection Agency in Washington, D.C., read and responded to chapter 8. Guy Mande, Rob Allen, Bonnie Miller McLemore, and my daughter, Meredith Ford, read and responded to the manuscript. Ruth Gantt, Amy Hopmann, Charity Goodwin, and Carla Gunn assisted with manuscript preparation. Thanks also to Rob Perry, who prepared the Index, and public services librarian John Oyler.

While I researched and wrote this book, my husband, Art Wells, served as helper, activist, and educator on behalf of children against poverty. He has been a willing mentor for several teenagers and young people and for many years dedicated himself to the cause of eliminating lead poisoning in children.

Pamela Couture
Kansas City

Children and Poverty Timeline

Circa 1100 B.C.E.–circa 150 B.C.E.: Writings that now comprise the Hebrew Scriptures/Old Testament circulate, reflecting the norm of care for the "widow, orphan, and resident alien."

Circa 50 C.E.–100 C.E.: Writings that now comprise the New Testament circulate, establishing knowledge of Jesus' concern for the poor and for children.

Circa 100 C.E.–400 C.E.: Early church traditions demonstrate that the church offers particular care for the poor and for orphaned children.

Circa 400 C.E.–1500 C.E.: Christian religious orders establish institutions, including hospitals and monasteries, which care for the poor and for children.

1349 and 1601: England enacts the first national poor laws.

Born 1703, died 1791: John Wesley inspires the Methodist movement, offering special care for the poor who were alienated from the Anglican church. He insisted that his preachers care for children.

1890s: Denmark becomes the first Scandinavian country to enact comprehensive family policies.

Born 1897, died 1980: Dorothy Day (with Peter Maurin) leads the Catholic Worker movement, living in voluntary poverty and giving hospitality to poor persons without distinction.

1933: Dorothy Day and Peter Maurin publish the first Catholic Worker newspaper, with columns for and about poor persons and children. *The Catholic Worker* is still published today.

1936: United States' Congress institutes Aid to Dependent Children (ADC), the first entitlement program for poor mothers with children. Aid to Dependent Children later became Aid to Families with Dependent Children (AFDC).

1948: The United Nations adopts the Universal Declaration of Human Rights, charter document of the United Nations.

1950s and 1960s: Martin Luther King Jr. (1929—1968) serves as key leader in the civil rights movement.

1963: Michael Harrington publishes *The Other America,* drawing attention to the problem of poverty.

1963: The Department of Agriculture establishes the United States poverty calculation, based on three times the cost of food for a nonfarm family.

1964: President Lyndon Johnson declares the "War on Poverty."

1979: The United Nations declares the International Year of the Child.

1988: United Methodist Women begin the Campaign for Children.

1990: The United Nations sponsors the World Summit for Children, adopting the *Convention on the Rights of the Child.*

1993: United States's young child poverty rate peaks at about 26 percent for children ages 1–5.

1995: Congress significantly increases the Earned Income Tax Credit (EITC)

1996: The World Bank and the International Monetary Fund establish the Highly Indebted Poor Countries (HIPC) program, to reduce debt among very poor countries.

1996: United States Congress passes the Personal Responsibility and Work Opportunity Reconciliation Act of 1996 (PRWORA), commonly known as "welfare reform."

1996–2004: The United Methodist bishops develop the Bishops Initiative on Children and Poverty.

1997: Temporary Assistance for Needy Families (TANF) replaces Aid to Families with Dependent Children (AFDC), ending entitlement aid to poor families and imposing work requirements on single mothers.

1999: Spending on children in the United Kingdom increases 75 percent, to 1 percent of the GDP, between 1997 and 2004. Tony Blair declares child poverty a priority.

2000: Churches engage in Jubilee 2000 debt reduction campaign for poor countries with significant national debt.

2000: United States's child poverty rate declines to about 18 percent, before climbing again.

2000: The United States signs and ratifies the *Convention on the Rights of the Child (CRC) Optional Protocol on the Sale of Children, Child Prostitution, and Child Pornography,* which the U.S.A. signed on July 5, 2000, even though it has never ratified the original Convention.[1]

2001–2011: Presbyterian Church (PCUSA) declares the Decade of the Child.

2002: United Nations General Assembly Special Summit on Children, scheduled for September, 2001, is held in May, 2002.

2006: The National Center for Children in Poverty reports that of the 73 million children in the United States, 39 percent live in low-income families and 18 percent live in poor families.

Seeing and Hearing All Children Despite the Layers That Obscure Them

Christelle, Christiane, and Brenden

Guy Mande is a bright, handsome Congolese ministry student, studying at Africa University in Mutare, Zimbabwe. In 2003 Guy began his second year of theological studies while his wife remained in Lubumbashi, the Democratic Republic of Congo, to give birth to twin girls, Christelle and Christiane. When they were born, Guy proudly sent pictures over the Internet to church friends around the world. A few months later, the family rejoiced when Guy's wife and the children moved to Mutare, reuniting the family. Then tragedy struck—an epidemic of diarrhea swept through Mutare, sickening both of the children. With little money, the parents took the first sick child to a public, government-supported hospital. "With the political instability in Zimbabwe the government hospitals are not very good anymore, and Christelle died. She did not receive good care," Guy mourned. When the second child, Christiane, became ill, her parents were able, with financial aid of the church, to take her to a private hospital, where she survived. "I am grateful for her life—though we are very sad; when I look at her, I think of Christelle." Guy, despite his tragedy, is a father graced not only by his faith but by the church's willingness to step in and help.

Half a world away in California, U.S.A., my own daughter, Shannon, prepared to give birth to my first grandson. Because of a difficult pregnancy, she was ordered to remain on bed rest for seven of the eight months she was pregnant. Advanced medical care made it possible for Brenden to enter the world five weeks early, but only in the presence of a neonatal physician and nurse who could handle any emergency. As is common with premature babies, Brenden ate frequently and slept little. Shannon decided not to return to employment. "What do mothers do who must go back to work?" she wondered. Negotiating the medical insurance transfer for mother and child became challenging. "What do families do who can't pay these kinds of bills, these kinds of premiums?" she questioned. The well-being of her child, my grandson, was made possible only by circumstances not available to many children in the United States, much less the rest of the world. Three beloved children, each equally valuable in God's sight, yet with incomparable life chances: How are their lives related to one another? Children who are economically poor face many of the same problems as children with more economic means, yet poverty concentrates problems in the lives of poor children, and their families have fewer resources with which to respond. Problems, such as diarrhea, that should be inconvenient become life threatening.

Childhood and poverty always intersect: children comprise the largest subset of persons who are poor, and poverty shapes the lives of children and their families, chronically and for short "spells" of poverty. Despite this deep interconnection, societies, faith communities, and educational institutions tend to treat childhood and poverty as two separate issues rather than conditions that always point toward one other. Love, justice, and responsibility for children and poverty urge us to consider them together.

Love, Justice, and Responsibility

Through analysis of concrete cases and ministries, this book demonstrates that the flourishing of poor children and all children is best supported by interdependent conditions of love and justice. *To flourish children need both love—the direct interpersonal, familial, and community relationships surrounding a child—and justice—the conditions of peace and security, health, and human rights that indirectly and directly shape a child's life.* When the church relegates children's concerns to the private sphere of "love" and ignores the impact of social conditions on children associated with "justice," the church reduces the potency of each. The dependency and agency of children demonstrate that love and justice are organically interrelated. Love *and* justice ground the visions and norms that guide ministry, grow in the social contexts that promote children's flourishing, and thrive in successful ministries that meet the needs of poor children and all children.

Several conditions of global society in 2006 make it important to think about the way that caregivers can assert Christian love and justice for children. The United Nations Children's Fund (UNICEF) estimates that, in 2002, a half billion children lived on less than a dollar a day and 30,000 children *per day* died of preventable causes.[1] Even the United States has had a consistently dismal record in child poverty. Our young child (ages 1–5) poverty rates peaked at about 26 percent of all children in the 1993[2] and declined to about 18 percent in 2000,[3] but they have begun to rise again. Even at 18 percent our child poverty rates remain significantly higher than the rest of the industrialized world and significantly higher than they were in 1964 when the "War on Poverty" was originally declared.[4] Yet as the world's superpower we expect—sometimes, insist—that poor countries will follow our lead in economic, social, and family policy. Will the export of our social policies reduce or increase the poverty and abject destitution that many of the world's children experience?

Policy makers and churches in the United States believe that faith communities should play a significant part in reducing poverty. Within the United States, Christian churches have interacted with governments in trying to shape family policy since the late 1800s. Evangelical women in the Women's Christian Temperance Union (WCTU) joined their voices to that of other organizations of women, such as the National Congress of Mothers, to persuade government officials that church and club women could not care for children and the poor by themselves.[5] Government had to be part of the solution. Beyond the United States, Christian churches have spread their beliefs in a Christian response to poverty through various forms of global mission movements. The Christian churches' abilities to be a church, first, that *includes* persons who are poor and, second, that *cares* for persons who are poor regardless of membership, has ebbed and flowed in particular congregations; but the overall belief in the church's responsibility for responding to poverty has never been abandoned.

The Agents of Love, Justice, and Responsibility: Helpers, Activists, and Educators

The persons who are agents of love, justice, and responsibility for children against poverty are citizens and members of faith communities who respond to children in the roles of "helpers," "activists," or "educators." This book is written specifically for those persons who are already engaged or who are considering becoming active in such ministries.

Helpers assist parents such as Guy and Shannon to bring their children to good hospitals, to respond to their emotional and medical needs, and to support them as they care for their children. Helpers include tutors, mentors, medical and social workers, godparents, family members, and friends whose efforts are focused on direct, day-to-day interaction. When we are acting as helpers, we engage in "hands-on" care with poor children. We generally want to know that something we are doing makes a difference, at least to one child. Helpers find meaning in primary relationships with children, within and beyond their biological families.

Activists, in contrast to helpers, create pressure on those who have political clout to rearrange social policy. When we are acting as activists, we seek to "change the system" to reduce poverty. In response to parents such as Guy and Shannon, we lobby for development aid for Africa and medical insurance for children and families in the United States. We use a variety of means to channel power toward worthy ends: we form coalitions, organize letter-writing campaigns, make speeches, and walk in protests. We persuade others to boycott certain products, to invest their wealth in socially responsible ways, and to protest the inaction of governments in response to critical issues. If we are part of the church, we join our efforts to those of denominational representatives. We use these means to promote policies that we believe will prevent children from becoming poor in the first place, and we hold governments, churches, and other institutions accountable for adequate support for children where poverty exists. Activists reorganize power in an effort to change the social arrangements that hurt, rather than help, children.

Educators, in contrast to helpers and activists, engage in research; teach classes; make speeches; put on workshops; and write articles, books, letters to the editor, or Web site blogs. When we are acting as educators, we study a wide range of subjects, from the effect of poverty on child development and behavior to the social systems that require that poverty exist in the world. In response to the disparity of care available to Guy and Shannon and their children, we analyze the relationship between the distribution of wealth in the world and poor health outcomes. We seek to understand the root causes of politically unstable situations: whether war in Africa is rooted in ethnic strife among African tribes or colonization of Africa by Euro-Americans. We explore the world of ideas because we believe that ideas shape behavior.

As educators, seminary professors make up a special case. While religious educators usually teach about ministries to children within congregations, seminaries might include children *and poverty* in classes on mission, evangelism, or pastoral care. In classes on mission educators examine the church's history: mission movements of the Christian Church of the nineteenth century contributed to colonization, but mission agencies of the church also built some of the most important educational and medical institutions in Africa. Whether the turmoil is in an African country or a declining inner city, we affirm that the agencies and congregations of the church are the last to leave when a crisis breaks out and the first to arrive when stability reemerges.

In classes on evangelism, educators debate what comes first in spreading the good news of Jesus Christ: material care or spiritual care. We recognize that the mainline Protestant church is blossoming in the Southern Hemisphere, even as it changes and seems to decline in the North. As the church in Africa grows, Africans and African Americans have different evangelistic strategies. African Christians often renounce the practices of their religious traditions, especially the practice of witchcraft, while American Americans seek to retrieve, renew, and integrate African communal values in attractive festivals such as Kwanzaa.

In classes on pastoral care, educators question, for example, whether patterns of crisis intervention that have developed in the church in North America can be adapted for Africa, or whether

Africa needs to develop a modality of care that emerges from its own practices and traditions. We discuss ways to bring the resources of faith to suffering and bereaved parents.

My husband, Art Wells, is one of the rare persons who integrates the helper, activist, and educator roles. He is equally at home testing a child's home for lead-based paint and advising parents on how to make the home safer, persuading City of Rochester officials to adopt lead-safe policies, and presenting a PowerPoint lecture to a community group who want to be informed about the problem of lead poisoning. Most people, however, find one role more comfortable than others and need to work with persons of diverse interests and talents to challenge children's poverty. This book seeks to help helpers, activists, and educators work together in one community so that children may be well, children may be flourishing.

We See through a Glass, Darkly. . .

Helpers, activists, and educators contribute a great deal to reducing the unnecessary suffering and premature death of children. Even so, while we listen, while we agitate, while we study, children are sick, children are dying. How can this be when so many people have concern for all children and great intentions?

Consider Ed, who responded to an appeal in his church bulletin to mentor a child through a community mentoring program. Ed attended the first session with excitement. He read school books with Tom, his mentee. But Tom's interest in reading waned. Ed decided to take Tom for a coke after school; the next week Tom wanted to go for a coke and talk. So each week, Ed took Tom to a local restaurant for a snack and a talk. Tom's mother thanked Ed and supported their weekly time away. When Tom got his grades at the end of the term, he had raised his C's and D's to A's and B's. Then Tom's mother lost her job and her telephone was disconnected. Ed had to drive to Tom's house to make or cancel appointments. Ed's church also taught a "safe sanctuaries" principle, that no adult should be alone with a child who was not his or her biological child. Even though the community program allowed Ed to take Tom on outings, Ed began to have misgivings. At the same time, Tom often wasn't at home at the appointed hour. The meetings between Ed and Tom became more sporadic.

One day Tom moved, not even saying good-bye to Ed. Ed was disappointed and, the next year, refused to take a mentee.

Practical Compartmentalizing

Usually, those who are newly learning about children and poverty experience an initial period of enthusiasm—a honeymoon period—before disappointment sets in. To counter discouragement, a new helper, activist, or educator says, "OK, I will at least do this one small thing." Initially, that response is helpful—it allows us to go on. But in the long run, if we do not consider this "one small thing" in the context of a larger whole, we compartmentalize the problem. Our one problem becomes the only problem. In tutoring, in campaigning, in studying, we lose sight of the complex web of issues that intersect in the lives of children who live with poverty.

Compartmentalization has individual, social, and ecclesial effects. As individuals our compartmentalization leads us to dig in our heels and avoid new information that might "confuse" the situation. As social and ecclesial groups our compartmentalization causes us to conflict with those who ought to be our partners on behalf of children against poverty. The "hands-on" types and the "social justice" types criticize one another; the "spirituality" types and the "social action" types promote their own causes independent of one another; the "ivory tower" types and the "real world" types talk past one another, if they talk at all. We lose the ability to be partners in one community working on behalf of children—instead, we center the problem on ourselves: our identity, our commitment, our cause.[6]

An example of such compartmentalization occurs in seminary.

Children and poverty can be studied anywhere in the seminary curriculum—biblical, theological, and ethical texts on children and poverty abound; practical action to resist poverty on behalf of children might originate in any course on ecclesial practice. However, because the concerns related to children and poverty can be taught anywhere, they are frequently taught nowhere. As a result, in the formative time of their preparation for ministry, clergy may not have been asked to either think about or engage in any practice that leads them to competently preach about or relate to children and persons who are poor.

As seminary educators we have important subjects to teach, important issues to discuss, many of which lead us away from focusing on those persons who are most vulnerable.

While we justify our compartmentalization, children are sick, children are dying.

Compartmentalizing Love and Justice

Such compartmentalization pervades our daily theological thinking as well: we separate love and justice. Despite the fact that the entire biblical story and the history of the church would collapse if either justice or love were removed, Christians tend to prioritize them as if we could focus on one and ignore the other.

A parishioner asks a pastor, "What do you think about the great commandment—to love God and your neighbor?" The pastor answers, "I don't do much with it—justice 'trumps' love." A parishioner asks a different pastor about a concern for justice. The pastor replies, "I don't think much about it—the character of the Christian and the quality of Christian community is what really matters." Neither love nor justice can be achieved, however, without the other. Both love and justice require relationships, social analysis, and accurate information—the interdependent domains of the helper, the activist, and the educator.

Can the activist know what to advocate from ideas and theories alone? Or does the activist need a deep and abiding relationship with children and people who are poor to know what to advocate? And at what point does the helper, seeing a similar pattern of distress in child after child, begin to realize that the child's distress arises from the conditions of his or her school or community, rather than the aptitude of the individual child? When does the helper address the pattern of distress as a way of mitigating the individual's suffering? And how does the researcher know what to study, if he or she does not listen to individuals in distress *and* discern patterns in the lives of distressed individuals? Helping without justice disintegrates into individualism; activism without love accelerates into attack; research without love and justice begins and ends in ideological bias.

For this reason, the helper, the activist, and the researcher need to attend to love and justice. The helper may be motivated primarily by the meaning he or she finds in interpersonal relationships, but the helper needs also to recognize and intervene in social power relationships. The activist may be primarily stimulated by challenging current power relationships, but the activist needs to listen interpersonally to know how those power arrangements need to be reshaped. The knowledge generated by the researcher may well inform, guide, and strengthen the work of the activist and the helper, but the researcher needs to listen interpersonally and to evaluate patterns of social power to construct and test the knowledge the researcher produces. Research on human beings and the human community is not benign; the researcher must also anticipate how his or her research might be used. The meaning sought by the helper, the power sought by the activist, and the knowledge sought by the researcher—each of these need the moderating and liberating effects of love and justice.

But Then Face to Face...

John Wesley, Dorothy Day, and Martin Luther King Jr. were religious leaders who challenged compartmentalization. For each of them, the interpersonal relationships created by love were necessary for justice-oriented social change. Social change, especially in economic relations, race relations, and peace-making, provided the context for greater understanding and opportunities for individual and community flourishing. Such change allowed love for the neighbor to flourish and to become the norm rather than the exception. For each of them, meaning, power, and knowledge played a significant role, though in different ways. Their religious experience dispelled social compartments and promoted integration. Their witness provides a model for the helper, the activist, and the educator in each of us. For that reason, I explore their work in this book.

John Wesley

The Anglican Church in eighteenth-century England separated people by religious affiliation, by social rank, by slave or free. Wesley broke open these compartments by challenging certain prohibitions that helped to retain these distinctions. Most prominently, Wesley preached in the fields and other places where he could bring the gospel to people who were excluded from Anglican sanctuaries because they were poor. The Wesleyans, as a movement arising from Oxford, brought education to the people— they sought to unite "those two so long divided—knowledge and vital piety."[7] Working without the benefit of the human sciences or the analysis of power that emerged in the history of ideas with Marxist thought, the Methodist movement challenged arguments that sustained the benefits to a few by the pauperization of many. Such tracts as "Thoughts on the Present Scarcity of Provisions" revealed the unjust economic structure of eighteenth-century Great Britain; "Thoughts on Slavery" challenged the growing economic dependence of Great Britain and the United States on slave labor; and "The Doctrine of Original Sin According to Scripture, Reason and Experience" argued that militarism and war are incompatible with Christian love.[8] These examples demonstrate that, for Wesley, the actions of love provided a foundation for social justice by giving worth to persons who were marginalized from society.

Dorothy Day

Industrial societies of the early twentieth century separated people economically as industrialists and workers, racially as black and white, and religiously as clergy and lay. As she developed the Catholic Worker movement, Day transcended these compartments, especially as she redefined the meaning of the apostolate. A former common-law wife with a child, as a young woman she became Roman Catholic and lived, still raising her child, as if she were the founding mother of a religious order who had taken vows of poverty and chastity. She found meaning in the love of her biological family and in hospitality to all, welcoming the destitute to Houses of Hospitality. The Catholic Worker movement provided education through roundtables for clarification of thought and *The Catholic Worker* newspaper. Much like Wesley's tracts and treatises, the newspaper records the legacy of the *Catholic Worker*'s challenge to hierarchies based on class and race and to false hopes placed in military might.

Martin Luther King Jr.

North American society and the former British Empire were deeply divided in the twentieth century by race. Racial hierarchies reinforced the inordinate burdens borne by persons of African descent. As the son of a Baptist preacher, King was able to lever the benefits of education on behalf of meaning and power. King led the civil rights movement as it challenged the power exerted by racial division, but again, did so on the foundation of love. For

King the constant search for "brotherhood and understanding" was borne of the deep knowledge of the destructive power of hate on both the racially oppressed and racial oppressors. King sought to transcend the compartmentalization of racial division, but he also taught his followers to love when and where false compartments exist. Vernon Berry, an African American leader in the liberation of Italy, experienced enormous racial hatred in the United States military. Only belatedly did President Clinton give him the Medal of Honor. Berry has spoken often of the importance of his father's teaching him as a child not to hate. In the words of Bishop James Thomas, a leader of African American Methodism both in segregation and after the integration of African American Methodism in the twentieth century, "If you can learn not to hate while segregated..."[9] So King taught about the power of love to overcome compartments even while they exist.

My Assumptions

I come to this study with a set of assumptions that shape this work. My primary academic interest is poverty, and children are a significant subset of poor people. Academic interests inevitably emerge from personal history. Conflicts over poverty, ethnicity, gender, and colonialism are set in my bones.

I was raised knowing that six of my eight great-grandparents came to the United States between 1880 and 1910 as economic refugees, fleeing poverty in their home countries of Switzerland, Hungary, and England. My Hungarian grandparents, who were likely "black" Hungarians whose ethnicity derived from the region that is now Turkey,[10] hid their nationality in order to assimilate into society. To get ahead, they "passed" for a more privileged race. As my great-grandmothers and grandmothers assimilated, they developed new understandings of their gender. They had the courage as women to make strong, independent decisions and actively participate in family business ventures in farming, entrepreneurship, and real estate, even as they demurred to a feminine domestic role as part of their embrace of upward mobility in the newly emerging "family wage society."[11] The son of my remaining two great-grandparents, my grandfather Couture, emigrated from French-speaking Canada also at the turn of the century. He likely descended from Guillaime Couture, who came to Canada in 1647 as a translator between the French military and the native Iroquois.[12] Any potential self-righteousness about the fact that I am not descended from a southern, slave-holding family is wiped away by the knowledge that my Couture ancestors undoubtedly were of a time, place, occasion, and viewpoint to contribute directly and indirectly to Native American genocide. Class, ethnicity, gender, and colonial strategies drove the "family story" as we negotiated unresolved conflicts over these aspects of North American culture.

This personal history sets the stage for a number of "academic" assumptions: (1) that narrativity, or "the way we tell the story," is critical; (2) that the story needs to record certain strengths of both the modern search and the postmodern critique; (3) that a perspective from persons living in involuntary and voluntary poverty may offer both clear and partially obscured insight about the world; (4) that the people who live with poverty, establish families, and raise children in its restrictions and its possibilities bear the image of God and are of equal worth in God's sight to those more economically fortunate. These assumptions and the unresolved conflicts from which they are borne will reappear in the chapters to come.

In a previous book, *Blessed Are the Poor? Women's Poverty, Family Policy, and Practical Theology* I chose the life and experience of African American women as a contrast to my experience as a white woman.[13] In *Seeing Children, Seeing God* I focused on mapping the terrain of studies of children and poverty and internationalized my work.[14] In this book I include stories of children, their families, and those who care across biographical lines of various races, ethnicities, and nationalities. Racism continues to extend its tentacles in subtle ways in the United States and internationally; and in some places I report others' analysis of statistics based on race. However, I do not analyze racism in relation to children and poverty in this book. My small step toward challenging racism in this book is to espouse the theology of Martin Luther King Jr. as one that contributes theological insight and practice that can guide the lives of all people.

In previous work I spoke as a feminist scholar analyzing gender. In this book I report rather than analyze the presence of gender as a distinctive category. Dorothy Day did not consider herself a feminist, and feminists have struggled with the breadth of her insight and activism and the dearth of her recognition of the gender oppression in the religious tradition she adopted. In this book my primary feminist work has to do with guiding theological metaphors.

I give my primary attention in this book to voluntary and involuntary poverty. Wesley, Day, and King model ways of resisting poverty, in theology and practice.

The language of scholars simultaneously reflects and hides our personal worlds, and I incorporate into my methodology a check against work that is simply an abstraction of my own experience. I use case studies from multiple cultures as recognition that the conclusions I may come to on the basis of my local experience may not hold true for another's local experience. Emmanuel Lartey's contention that in intercultural experience we are "like all others, like some others, and like no others" bears out in the examples taken from the United States, Africa, the Philippines, and Europe.[15] In as many cases as possible, persons from those parts of the world who have provided vignettes have read and collaborated with me on the way their thread is being woven into the story.

Development of the Argument

The first section of this book, "Culture, Ethics, and Ministry with Children and Poverty," defines the phrase "children and poverty," as used in this book. United States' culture quickly judges parents who are poor and their children as either "deserving" or "undeserving" of considerations of love and justice. I argue that all persons are so deserving. Love and justice connects children's private lives and the public contexts in which children live, where lives and social conditions impinge on one another. Turning to Christian resources for creating love and justice, I suggest that a spirituality of engagement, dignity, and hope undergirds the caregiver's loving and just activities in both private and public contexts. Loving and just ministries of care, evangelism, and mission seek to imitate Jesus' example.

The second section of this book, "The Unnamed Children's Issues," demonstrates ways that large social systems shape children's lives. In a search for "justice" we frequently look to reshape systems that create injustice. Though denominations provide some good examples of how to think about larger social systems in relationship to children,[16] most Christians do not think about the impact of these systems—the international law that constructs human rights, the global economy, the natural environment, war and peace—on children's lives. To most Christians even "welfare reform" was not about children, only adults. When Christians do think systemically, they are more inclined to recognize the impact of policies related to health and welfare, education, and family support as children's issues. The larger public systems that shape children's lives are often neglected as "children's issues" by ministries of spirituality, pastoral care, mission, and evangelism that the church promotes. This section helps to fill the gap of this neglect.

The third section, "Rhizomatic Ministry: Engaging Disciples and Apostles," presents the ministries with children and poverty of mainline denominations. Rather than simply arguing that the church should "do something," it behooves us to uncover *what the church is actually doing* and *how ministries with poor children are actually renewing the church.* This section focuses on how ministries with children and poverty link the church and the world and renew the church. Using the categories of rhizomatic ministry, discipleship, and apostolate, this section analyzes what Christian groups who are concerned about poor children might learn from the results of one Protestant denomination, the United Methodist Church, after a decade of intensive focus on ministry with children and poverty. This analysis suggests much to be celebrated: poor children are being ministered to, and poor children are in turn changing the church. These ministries are well worth celebrating, *and* there is potential for further growth in understanding "issues related to children."

Culture, Ethics, and Ministry with Children and Poverty

CHAPTER 1

Deserving or Undeserving Children?

Joyce

"In the months around the birth of my twin sons, I was unemployed and received public assistance in the form of food vouchers from a nutrition program for women, infants, and children known as WIC," writes Joyce, about a time in her life when she was in transit from graduate school to theological teaching in the Philippines. "One day at the grocery store I got in line with my basket full of all the things to which I as an anemic new mother of twins was entitled in this program—cheese, cereal, carrots, lots of milk. I decided at the last minute to add a small bag of corn chips to my purchases along with a few other items, such as disposable diapers, for which I would pay cash.

"Two women in line behind me, seeing my WIC vouchers, began to talk about my groceries and me. 'Look at that. They just don't know how to spend their money. That's why welfare doesn't work. You give these people money for food, and they buy potato chips with it.' Neither of the women said anything like, 'Oh, look, that good mother has a basket full of fine nutritious foods that will contribute to her health and the health of her babies.' Instead, their attention went directly to that which to them was evidence of poor choice by a person they deemed poor, relegated to the ranks of 'these people.'"[1]

What Is Poverty?

Children who live in poverty rattle our settled notions of love and justice. Usually we think that if families are poor, their children are poor, and if families have enough, their children have enough. A closer look at children's lives confounds these definitions, however.

Our society has long distinguished between the "deserving" and "undeserving" poor.[2] By fact of association with their families, many children are doomed to become part of the "undeserving poor"—undeserving of community or social assistance for their development. Ideas of love and justice that are tested by the lives of children, especially poor children, confuse such distinctions.

"Poverty" has many different meanings for many different people. *Language about poverty is "socially constructed"—in other words, poverty is whatever we say it is.*[3] In Christian language "widows, orphans, and resident aliens" are "the least of these"; and the community is enjoined to care for these persons as a part of God's law. In popular speech "poor people" may be a generalization that connotes certain qualities of people—"poor people are lazy." In social policy language in the United States, "poverty" is a measure by which some people are "targeted" for social benefits and others are not—"families of three or more who earn less than $15,000 a year are poor." In international social policy language "indebtedness" and "poverty" may become a measure by which some countries receive development aid and international investment while others do not—for example, the "Democratic Republic of Congo is a Highly Indebted Poor Country." Speaking about "poor children" using each of these frameworks for language is complicated because, sometimes, children are poor because their families, communities, or countries are poor; and, sometimes, as a result of violence, disease, neglect, or abuse, children are poor even when their families, communities, or nations are not.[4]

We tend to resolve our conflicts about poverty by creating categories of "deserving" and "undeserving" poor. In the storyline of Hebrew Scriptures and the New Testament, however, we do not find such distinctions—rather, we find a consistent message that individuals and society are tested by the way they treat persons who are poor or displaced.

Poverty and Poor Children in Biblical Language

In the biblical story, the emphasis is not on the qualities of individuals but on the gift of generosity and freedom God gives to all people. All people then are expected to extend these same gifts to one another. Biblical law also commends as normative the community's generosity toward those who may be socially and economically vulnerable. Biblical law recommends penalties for specific acts, but these acts are not associated with a particular social or economic status. Jesus comes to fulfill the law (Mt. 5:17) that he summarizes as love of God and love of neighbor (Mt. 22:36–40).[5]

Biblical law originates with the Ten Commandments, upon which all other law is based. The first commandment in both Exodus and Deuteronomy reads: "I am the LORD your God, who brought you out of the land of Egypt, out of the house of slavery; you shall have no other gods before me" (Ex. 20:2–3; Deut. 5:6–7). Too often, Protestants have omitted the significant phrase "who brought you out of the land of Egypt, out of the house of slavery" when they have learned this commandment or written it on their church walls. This phrase and another like it, "God redeemed you," refers to God's liberating generosity in freeing the Israelites from Egypt. As God treated the Israelites when they were vulnerable, the Israelites are to treat vulnerable people in their midst. Therefore, a person who has employees or slaves must treat them with the same liberating generosity that God treated Israel in the exodus. Slaves and laborers are to be freed in the seventh year and provided for:

> And when you send a male slave out from you a free person, you shall not let him go empty-handed. Provide liberally out of your flock, your threshing floor, and your wine press, thus giving to him some of the bounty with which the LORD your God has blessed you. Remember that *you were a slave in the land of Egypt, and the LORD your God redeemed you;* for this reason I lay this command upon you today. (Deut. 15:12–15, author's emphasis).

When the Decalogue is interpreted more fully in the Deuteronomic law, this directive is often associated with care for those most likely to be vulnerable, "the least of these" in Israel: widows, orphans, and resident aliens. A person shall not use his or her power in a way that takes a livelihood from those who are most vulnerable, because the ancestors of that person were also once the same as these (Deut. 24:17–18). Tithes are offerings brought to the temple for the care of the priests and the care of "the resident aliens, the orphans, and the widows" (Deut. 14:28–29). The community is enjoined not only to feed widows, orphans, and resident aliens, but to include them in their worship and festivals (Deut. 17:9–12).

God liberated the people from their bondage in Egypt simply because they were vulnerable, not because the Israelites had done anything to earn God's favor. God simply heard their cry for help and acted. Throughout the Hebrew Scriptures, however, the people lose sight of this basic teaching. They begin to believe that attention to religious practices absolves them of any need to care for the poor and marginalized, especially the widow, orphan, and resident alien. Isaiah charges that the community has lost its way—that people now prey upon the poor (Isa. 10:1–2). Jeremiah proclaims that if people return to the care of the poor, God will look with favor upon them (Jer. 7:3–7).

Many of the famous and romanticized passages about Jesus with children need to be read in light of this tradition. In Matthew 19:13–14 the disciples try to keep children from Jesus. William Herzog, a biblical scholar whose work pays particular attention to the social strata that are reflected in various biblical passages, claims that Jesus, as a rabbi, was expected to instruct children. The disciples should not have given a second thought to children in Jesus' presence—unless they were *ptochos* children, children of the destitute, the orphans, or street children, who wandered from place to place in search of food. Jesus and his disciples were *penetes,* of the poor but slightly better off than beggars. The *ptochos* children were the untouchables of society, those with whom *penetes* would not associate. Herzog believes that the only meaning to this passage could be that the disciples were trying to keep *ptochos* children from Jesus, but Jesus is urging *all* children, *ptochos* and *penetes,* to come to him.[6]

The passages of the Bible associated with children reflect the biblical law that commands care for the poor. Indeed, the category of "the orphan" reminds us that children are often among those most despised by their communities, whom God specifically identifies as ones who can be lost or exploited as the community goes about its business.

Poverty and Poor Children in Popular Speech

In contrast to religious language, our popular speech tends to divide the poor population between the "deserving" and "undeserving." This dichotomy developed as notions of poverty evolved. The poor of Europe in the Middle Ages were serfs who owned no land and worked the feudal estates. The lord of the estate was expected to provide for his serfs, and the church provided support in cases of extreme need. In the transition between the social organization of the Middle Ages and Industrial England, the first poor laws were enacted in 1349 and 1601, creating a new era and class of people deemed poor.[7] Over time, poverty became a crime for which people were imprisoned.

In colonial America the "deserving" poor were those people known to have conformed their behavior to community norms of having large families, living in one community, working hard, being sexually faithful, belonging to the church, dressing and behaving properly—but in some way they fell on hard times, largely because of the death of an adult or drought. Their children might be considered part of the "deserving" poor.

The "undeserving" poor were those who flaunted community norms, failed to reproduce, drifted from community to community, were lazy or drunken, were enslaved or female and had sex outside marriage, failed to attend or were banned from church, and conducted themselves improperly. Their poverty was considered their own fault, even criminal, and their children were part of the "undeserving" poor.

Although people in the United States spend time and energy distinguishing deserving and undeserving poor, these categories are not strict. Groups facing common economic hardships may benefit from claiming "poverty" as language that applies to them. For example, Martin Luther King's "Poor People's Campaign" and Dorothy Day's "voluntary poverty" dignify poverty as a condition that promotes moral agency and spiritual insight. The language of poverty may be useful when a group movement develops that raises the self-esteem of people who have been systematically denied. Other times, people may oppress others by calling them "poor" because they have limited incomes, relationships, or institutional connectedness. Such rhetoric reduces dignity and self-respect. Instead, we can think that all people have various strengths and weaknesses. Here, theological language becomes important: each person, regardless of economic attribute, is made in the image of God. How do *we* see that image?

Poverty and Poor Children in United States' Social Policy

In 1963 the United States set a poverty line by trying to determine the income a family needed to feed itself and multiplying by three, as families usually spent about one-third of their income on food. Social policy in the United States continues to establish the "poverty line" in this way, recognizing that those determined to live "in poverty" may fall short of minimal income needs by as much as 100 percent. Social policy largely depends upon programs "targeting" people below a certain income level, who also meet certain behavioral requirement. For example, people "deserving" of "Temporary Assistance for Needy Families" (TANF) must be employed at far less than minimal income requirements and may not have a criminal record. Those who do not qualify may be poor and "undeserving." Social policy in European countries, in contrast, promotes "universalized" child entitlement programs. "Universalized" programs (Social Security and Medicare in the United States) are inclusive: everyone pays something into the fund, and every one receives a benefit, regardless of income. Many countries in Europe provide universally available child allowances, child care, child support recovery, health care, and maternity leave. In most cases these policies helped a country increase its population, though legislators and citizens in Europe have also argued for universal programs on principle.[8]

Being "officially" poor becomes very important, not only for the purpose of receiving benefits, but also for statistics that guide policy decisions.

Poverty is not just about the absence of money—it is also about the absence of networks that connect people to society. In *Seeing Children, Seeing God* I called this "the poverty of tenuous connections."[9] In some cases relationships are stretched thin in poor communities where stable families and community institutions have broken down. In other cases extended families are spread across the country and the employment of adults has reduced many of adults' previous commitments to civic engagement. This time and work crunch invades not only the relationships between parents and children but the possibility of adult friends as part of a child's relationship network. When these factors are compounded by inadequate community institutions, children and youth are left without adequate opportunities for supervision and adult friendships.

Clearly, strong institutional relationships in communities support fragile families while weak institutional relationships leave fragile families to fend for themselves. Children in all family structures can be supported by strong and accessible child care, schools, activities for children, mentors, and job opportunities. Many of these relationships and opportunities are provided by religious congregations.

Poverty and Poor Children in International Policy

The categories of "deserving" and "undeserving" poor carry over into our attitudes toward poor countries and their people. Why do we get news of war and genocide in some countries and not others? Why is the United States willing to make a case for international intervention and development aid for poverty in some countries and not others? What accounts for the timing and scale of international intervention?

The inequity of our response to international disaster, war, and famine suggests that a sense of "deserving" and "undeserving" nations exists in international relationships, just as it does in our national attitude toward poverty. "Deserving" poor nations—the ones who get media attention and development aid—are usually defined as those who have governments that are strategic military allies of the United States (regardless of whether they are democratic governments or dictatorships) and those who are moving toward globalized market economies.

In 1998 at lectures at Colgate Rochester Crozer Divinity School, Bishop Ntambo Nkulu Ntanda, the United Methodist Bishop from the Democratic Republic of Congo (DRC), compared the attention given to the war in Bosnia to the lack of attention given to the simultaneous war in the DRC. "The Bosnians are the lucky ones, because they have the world's attention," he claimed. "More people will die in Congo because the war has little publicity." A February 2004 MSN Internet Search confirmed his point about disparity in publicity: "War in Bosnia" found 400,850 Internet items, but "war in the Democratic Republic of Congo" found only 87,033 items. In February 2005, the same search yielded 550,384 items for "war in Bosnia" and 262,583 for "war in the Democratic

Republic of Congo." The war in Bosnia claimed an estimated 25,000–200,000 lives[10]; at that time the war in the Democratic Republic of Congo had claimed an estimated 3.3 million lives.[11] Most recently, the point of the "deserving" and "undeserving" nations was made in the movie *Hotel Rwanda*, as the Rwandan elite and UN Peacekeepers realized that the Western nations would not intervene in Rwandan genocide.

"Undeserving" nations are militarily and economically weak nations that may be deemed "undeserving" for a wide variety of reasons, depending upon political circumstances. The taint of coming from an "undeserving" country has decreased the hope and well-being of families and children who cannot afford to wait for their country to improve its international reputation. For example, the HIV-AIDS crisis is a children's crisis in Africa. It threatens to kill a generation of adults in the young adult and middle-aged population, who are most likely to be responsible for children.

Who are the international "deserving" and "undeserving" poor? Who gets the media attention? Who gets the development aid? Which children and populations are considered expendable? These are political, economic, ecclesiastical, and theological questions that must be debated.

Deserving and Undeserving, or Loving and Just?

Rather than thinking about whether people who are poor are "deserving" or "undeserving," biblical norms call Christians to consider that all people are valuable in and of themselves. All people, regardless of economic means, are at times "loving" and "just"—and all people at times fall short of that aim. If we focus on ourselves and what it means in our individual and collective lives to be loving and just, judging others as deserving and undeserving might become less important.

The integrated ideas of love and justice found in the work of three practical theological voices and their partners will help ground an understanding of love and justice in relation to children and poverty. These persons communicated through primary practical theological genres: sermons, prayers, liturgies, essays, journals, articles, and treatises. I use the title "theological voices" as two figures, John Wesley and Martin Luther King Jr., would identify themselves as theologians, but the third, Dorothy Day, explicitly did not claim to be a theologian—though her writing and editing qualifies her as a "practical theologian" as defined above. The dialogue with these figures demonstrates the value of drawing from diverse ecumenical, gender, race, and class sources who might guide our practices of care.

John Wesley

John Wesley, with his brother Charles, was the theologian of the eighteenth-century Methodist movement. As an Anglican priest seeking evangelical reform of the Church of England, Wesley birthed the religious revival that became the Methodist movement. "Methodist" referred to strict habits of worship and charitable works that marked the lifestyle of the early Wesleyans. The Wesleys and their associates spread the gospel in all social ranks, but particularly cared for the poor and the outcast. Many of those who joined the early Methodist societies were the destitute or the working poor of Great Britain's industrial revolution.

The Wesleys believed that works of piety and works of mercy were "means of grace" through which God's love could be known and experienced by humankind. Works of piety include reading and studying the scriptures, praising God in worship and hearing the Word preached, partaking of the sacraments, praying, and fasting. Works of mercy include feeding the hungry, giving drink to the thirsty, welcoming the stranger, clothing the naked, visiting the sick, and visiting the imprisoned—the actions enjoined in Matthew 25:34–36. They understood justice, God's judgment and righteousness, to be wielded against those persons and groups who built their lives without regard for God or for those who were poor and exploited in society. They focused attention on the poverty of Great Britain as a primary religious expression of justification and sanctification, not only in evangelism and mission but in care.

Dorothy Day

Dorothy Day, who publicized the thought of Roman Catholic lay philosopher Peter Maurin, was the journalist/theologian of the Catholic Worker movement, a lay Roman Catholic movement of the middle twentieth century that endures today. In 1933 Day and Maurin founded *The Catholic Worker* newspaper and sold it for one penny a copy, a price they thought anyone could afford. The newspaper specifically addressed the concerns of working people, such as labor rights and race relations, interpreting them through the lens of Catholic social thought and practices. Day and Maurin scheduled "roundtables" for conversations about such issues. They opened their first house of hospitality—a place where all in need of food and shelter were welcomed—in New York City.

Like Wesley, Day and Maurin emphasized "the spiritual and corporeal works of mercy" as a central means toward knowing God. Their expression of the means of grace differed from the Wesleys, in that Day and Maurin emphasized clarification of thought, houses of hospitality, and farming communes. The practice of clarification of thought brought people of diverse opinions and backgrounds to a common conversation through which they could deepen their understanding. Houses of hospitality provided homes for people who otherwise would be homeless. Farming communes allowed residents to live in direct relationship with God, who is the focus of the life of prayer, earth, and creation. The regular practice of prayer and sacrament bound these three practical expressions together. The combination of these expressions of spiritual and corporeal works of mercy engaged the Catholic Worker movement with social issues of the twentieth century—race relations, labor rights and healthy working conditions, nuclear disarmament, and peacemaking. They paid attention to children in the context of these issues.

Martin Luther King Jr.

After World War II, the civil rights movement strengthened the resolve of African Americans to claim their equality, and Martin Luther King Jr. was the primary theologian of the movement. After earning the Master of Divinity degree at Crozer Theological Seminary and the Doctor of Philosophy degree at Boston University, he became the pastor of the Dexter Avenue Baptist Church in Montgomery, Alabama. He was pushed to the forefront of the civil rights movement when he was asked as pastor to be the spokesperson for the participants in the boycott of the Montgomery bus system. Thereafter he became a prominent leader and the foremost theological interpreter of the civil rights movement until his assassination in 1968.

For King, the primary expression of love was *agape*, or self-sacrificial love, as exemplified by Jesus on the cross. Such love explicitly showed itself in active love of the enemy. This love proclaimed the equal stature of the poor and those denoted by society as racially inferior, and it provided a balm and defense against the injury society wreaked on them. It also provided a proactive force for love that, through natural and supernatural means, sought to transform the hatred of the enemy into love. In that effort it created power for good that was internal to the interpersonal relationships between persons within the civil rights movement and to the social transformation it sought, as it faced the evils of racism, poverty, and war.

Although the three theologians and movements differ in many ways, they have in common the understanding that people are unified in acts of love and justice rather than in stereotypes of deserving and undeserving. These theologians responded to people of all economic means, including people and children who are poor. The lives of children in the Democratic Republic of Congo and the United States, despite their extraordinarily different conditions, are equally gifts of God, and equally deserving of the loving and just responses of individuals and communities. Indeed, their lives depend on it.

CHAPTER TWO

Love, Justice, and Children
in Public and Private

Dong Yangnan

The New York Times, August 25, 2002:

Donghu, China – Neighbors remember when young Dong
Yangnan was a "xiao pangzi," or little fatty, the kind of
husky, moon-cheeked child that Chinese grandmothers
adore. Today, at 12, he is orphaned, stick thin, and dressed
in tattered clothes. Last summer, his mother died of AIDS.
His father, coughing and feverish, succumbed to the
disease in May. Yangnan lives with an elderly grandfather,
surviving on rice gruel and steamed buns. "Before, I had a
happy life, and my parents took good care of me," he said
listlessly, his eyes staring away to a lost past. "Now I have
to look after myself and often have no money." [1]

Dong Yangnan, in the eyes of the world, is "undeserving." He
lives in a remote section of China and is infected with HIV-AIDS.
What do love and justice mean for children such as Dong Yangnan?
Does practical theology have anything to offer to the way we think
about such children and what we do on their behalf?

I approach the issue of children and poverty as a practical
theologian, a professor whose primary "practice" is pastoral care.

Pastoral care is often thought of as visiting the sick in the hospital and counseling the conflicted in the pastor's study. It is often understood as promoting love and having little to do with justice. However, in my view and in the view of many of my colleagues, pastoral care at its best promotes love *and* justice in private *and* public realms. Pastoral care is one of the arts of ministry reflected upon by practical theology. Practical theology is concerned with norms and values that lie at the intersection of smaller and larger systems. *By identifying these norms and values, practical theology helps us keep our moorings as we are pushed and pulled by the practical arguments of the world.*

What can I affirm, as a practical theologian, about Dong Yangnan? I do not know his religious practice, but my Christian understanding of his life begins with my understanding of God. I believe that God is a good God who created the whole world as a place of care for life. The earth, air, water, vegetation, and animal life of the world create an abundant, lush environment. When we use that environment wisely, we have enough natural resources to sustain life for all of us – enough for Dong Yangnan. God is good, and God provides.

Dong Yangnan is a person of infinite worth and value in God's eyes, yet he is particularly vulnerable because of the social conditions that surround him. He is one of the children whom the disciples would probably try to keep away from Jesus, but of whom Jesus would say, "Bring him to me." He is one in whom we see Christ, one who is thirsty, hungry, and unclothed, of whom Jesus said, "when you do it for the least of these, you do it for me." He is as valuable as the children to whom I gave birth, the ones for whom I feel most responsible.

Even as I affirm all of this, another voice nags at me from underneath, saying, "There are many children like Dong Yangnan. His situation is hopeless. I am powerless. I can do nothing. It will not matter that much if he and the children in situations like his dies." What is that voice? It is the voice of sin, the voice of evil—a blasphemous voice that denies the presence of God in Christ and the Holy Spirit, a presence I routinely and overtly affirm.

This voice of sin and evil cannot be equated to the voice of the world. The world has important voices with whom theologically minded people can join to value Dong Yangnan's life as an individual and to affirm the society in which he lives. In both the church and the world, however, we can also find people who act as if Dong Yangnan's life is hopeless and to be forgotten, and systems that tend to reinforce our sense of inadequacy in making a difference.

We may confront sin and evil by focusing on love and justice. Many of us are used to thinking about love in interpersonal terms and justice in institutional terms. These distinctions suggest that our primary response to Dong Yangnan will be to show God's love to him through Christian *charity*. We would exercise the virtues of kindness, generosity, and compassion. We could, through Christian love, literally feed and clothe him, acknowledging that, in so doing, we are feeding and clothing Jesus himself. We could organize our churches to send assistance to his community, perhaps through the Red Cross or through our own mission agencies. We could send notes of encouragement along with medical kits, and we could pay school fees for the community's children. Or, people might be motivated to adopt him and others like him. Through neighbor love and charity—the ancient tradition of Christian *caritas*—we seek immediate relief from the effects of the situation that Dong Yangnan finds himself in.

But to show God's *justice* we would expect ourselves to address the "root causes" of the situation in which Dong Yangnan and his community find themselves. *The New York Times* article states that Donghu developed the high death rate from AIDS because rural peasants relieved their poverty by the sale of their own blood. Some sold their blood occasionally for emergency cash, and others sold their blood as often as daily as a regular means of income. Blood collection stations, including Red Cross stations, were set up in Donghu and other rural communities to facilitate collection of blood from peasants. Officials reassured the peasants that these practices were safe, but these blood collection stations actually became particularly efficient vehicles for spreading HIV in the early 1990s. At the time of the writing of the article, October, 2002, as many as half of the adults in the village were infected or dead. This form of blood collection was banned in the mid-1990s; but we, seeking justice, could still provide active, public awareness of the situation through watchdog nongovernmental organizations or the World Health Organization. We could challenge the economic system in which the adults in his community saw the sale of their own blood as a means out of poverty, an economic benefit that was, according to the article, particularly efficient in spreading HIV. We would argue for conditions that foster the ability of people to achieve a sustainable, dignified livelihood. In many Christian circles this kind of ministry of justice is considered more important than a ministry of charity, which often is viewed as partial and patronizing.

Love and Justice in Three Practical Theological Voices and Movements

The life work of John Wesley, Dorothy Day, and Martin Luther King Jr. demonstrates the integration of love and justice in Christian tradition.[2] For each of them, love of God and neighbor was a primary, interpersonal practice that was necessary for justice and social change. They developed ideas of love and justice in sermons, speeches, prayers, articles, and treatises that were accessible to large groups of people, both the educated and the illiterate. They were concerned with love as the center of direct relationships among people who are poor, and between the poor and wealthy. They recognized children as objects and subjects in the world they were trying to transform. They were grounded in a deep sense of Christian theology and relied heavily on seeking a direct experience of the grace of God for support—especially in times when each felt a sense of failure pervade their spirits and the movements they led.

Though the ecclesial authority for their lives differed—Wesley was an Anglican priest, Day a Roman Catholic laywoman, and King a Baptist preacher—each of them thought Jesus' Sermon on the Mount (Mt. 5—7) held special significance. Wesley believed Matthew 5:1–12 (the Beatitudes) provided "the *spirit*...the quintessence...indeed the *fundamentals* of Christianity."[3] For Day the Catholic Worker movement was an effort to live out the precepts of the Sermon on the Mount and the works of mercy outlined in Matthew 25.[4] For King the critical moment of being called to be the spokesman for the Montgomery bus protest drove him to "the Sermon on the Mount and the Gandhian method of non-violent resistance."[5] For each the ideal laid out in Matthew 5:1–12 fertilized the Christian soul; it nourished them with courage and perseverance. The Beatitudes became not an external ethical obligation but an inner truth from which to live. Christianity needed this infusion, like oxygen, into the body of Christ. As the individual or the community lived out these ideals, righteousness would be attained. The means of love and the end of justice were inseparably married to one another. From this source Christian action sprang.

The qualities of character these theologians promoted would be categorized today as "virtue ethics," though Wesley specifically cautions that understanding these qualities as human virtues leads us erroneously to be "proud of knowing that we deserve damnation."[6] Rather, just as faith is a gift of God, the ability to live as outlined in the Beatitudes is also God's gift. It may not be "achieved" by the believer, but may be sought through the practice of the means of grace How might we discern the components of love and justice, as related to the gifts of the God outlined in the Beatitudes?

Love and Justice in Wesley's Sermons on "The Sermon on the Mount"

Wesleyans helped children of all social and economic classes learn to love God. They visited the poor, including children, at their own homes, ate with them, and got to know them. They insisted on a well-rounded education for both boys *and* girls. They provided children with food, medical care, financial assistance, and clothing. Methodist preachers were expected to spend an hour a week specifically with children in care and instruction.[7]

This care for children grew out of Wesley's commitment to love and justice. Wesley tells us in his thirteen sermons on the Sermon on the Mount that living in love and justice is not a human achievement; rather, it is a gift of God.[8] Even though the specific gifts that make ethical living possible cannot be earned, they may be sought through the practice of the means of grace, works of mercy, and works of piety. Child advocates who feel they have never done enough should take note: what they have done, they have done by God's grace; what they will do, will come through discernment of God's Spirit. In a series of sermons Wesley interprets the famous section of the Sermon on the Mount, the Beatitudes.

"Poverty of the spirit" allows humans to recognize their own propensity for sin and evil so that they may cooperate with God as God seeks to renew them after God's likeness.[9] "Mourning" the absence of God leads one to "to grieve over the state of the world, and to wonder, 'Where is God in this?'"[10] The meek respond to evil in the world by transforming their own impulses toward anger and retaliation to offer the love of God to the world. Only meekness, Wesley suggests, provides a secure route to gaining the necessary provisions of life, particularly food and shelter—the gifts of the earth.[11]

The first three beatitudes seek to "remove hindrances" to the Christian life, but the fourth introduces the human soul to its genuine longings. The "hunger and thirst" for God— a metaphor evoking an image of the primal drive for necessary nourishment—motivates religion: doing no harm, doing good, and using the means of grace. "Merciful" souls are already filled with God and have genuine concern for others who are without God. They respond to others with love and charity, as described in 1 Corinthians 13, not with malice. Such mercy not only applies to interpersonal relations but also to "Christian" kingdoms, which, Wesley suggests, contradict "the Prince of Peace" by waging war on one another.[12] The "pure in heart" are those who, having received the gifts of the earlier beatitudes, "now love the Lord their God with all their heart, and with all their soul, and mind, and strength." They "see all things full of God," talk with God "face to face" as with a friend, and "see the Creator in the face of every creature, and look upon nothing as separate from God."[13]

The peacemakers "endeavor to calm the stormy spirits of men, to quiet their turbulent passions, to soften the minds of contending parties, and if possible reconcile them to one another." Peacemakers seek to bring resolution to conflict not only among family and friends but with neighbors, strangers, and enemies. Peacemakers engage in works of mercy, feeding, sheltering, and visiting, according to the commands of Matthew 25.[14]

Those "persecuted for righteousness sake" follow the tenets of the Sermon on the Mount and fail to conform to the ways of the world. They may suffer not only "torture or death or bonds or imprisonment" but also the far more ordinary persecutions of "estrangement of kinsfolk, loss of friends who were as their own soul."[15] Persecution seeks to destroy the earlier gifts of God, particularly the gift of meekness, but Christians need to be strong in meekness to love their enemies and pray for their persecutors.

These fundamentals summarized the Wesleyan life. As the evangelical revival spread across England, people who were newly converted through field preaching were organized into societies.

Societies met for mutual support in homes, barns, and various other available sheltered places. Eventually, the societies needed structures in which to conduct worship and live out their beliefs regarding love and justice. Chapels began to emerge—large and famous chapels that had extensive ministries in urban centers, and small chapels in remote areas that served as centers of worship and provided for occasional needs, such as housing for local preachers or widows, or schools for children.[16] These chapels helped distressed people: food, clothing, medical care, education, and a loan program for new businesses were among other types of assistance. Methodists were taught to provide these services with an intimate, personal touch. Rather than giving relief at a distance, Wesley taught a love ethic that guided personal relationships with those who were in need: "Give none that asks relief either an ill word or an ill look. Do not hurt them if you cannot help." And, he insists, "Expect no thanks from any man."[17]

The chapels did all of this within the context of preaching and worship, yet at some political peril. The Wesleys insisted that Methodists belonged to the Church of England. They were not Protestant Dissenters.[18] As Methodists gathered to pray and hear the Word in homes, barns, and fields, they were legally challenged by their neighbors. They were fined by the courts and licensed, sometimes as Dissenters and sometimes not, depending on how magistrates applied the letter of the law and how Methodists valued their relationship with the Church of England.[19]

The Methodist movement was largely a movement of the poor learning to be "good neighbors" to one another as a result of their faith.[20] They responded to the distress of their neighbors. For example, sick mothers died peacefully when the Methodists agreed to care for their dependent children. "To have waited for parliamentary legislation or revolution, bloody or bloodless, would have been a tragedy," Leslie F. Church claims.[21] The early Methodists did not have methods of social change such as "direct action" or "nonviolent resistance" available to them. They did publicly challenge the practices of enclosure, slavery, and extremes of wealth and poverty.[22] The pursuit of justice in their radical religion consisted of going wherever their faith led them, to love God in Methodist worship and love neighbor in the most dire of circumstances, regardless of the persecution that sometimes awaited them.

Dorothy Day and "The Sermon on the Mount"

Dorothy Day and other participants in the Catholic Worker movement regularly refer to the Sermon on the Mount as the basis for their actions, though Day does not as neatly describe her interpretation of that text as does Wesley. Still, we can read Dorothy Day's actions through Wesley's interpretation of "the counsels of perfection" (Mt. 5:48) to see how the Sermon on the Mount might have been operative in her life.

Day engaged in self-examination in daily prayer, the sacraments of eucharist and penance, and regular times of retreat—Wesley's understanding of spiritual poverty. For Day, an equally important form of spiritual poverty was living in "voluntary poverty" with the destitute. She practiced corporeal and spiritual works of mercy not only as an ethical obligation but also as a way of "mourning the absence of God" and seeking the presence of God in everyday life. While God was sought directly in practices of piety, God was seen most visibly in the face of the distressed neighbor. But neighborly relations were difficult. To find God in others Catholic Workers transformed their impulse to respond to others with coercion and force by practicing what Wesley understood as full-bodied "meekness"—they sought to respond to the distress of others with love.

Day early became interested in mystical experience and read Wesley and Thomas á Kempis as guides to that experience.[23] The more mature form of her "hunger and thirst after God" developed in the total orientation to God in three central locations of Catholic Worker activities: roundtables for clarification of thought, houses of hospitality, and farming communes. Emphasizing "spiritual works of mercy," these locations incorporated into daily life the insights of the Catholic retreat experience. Emphasizing "corporeal works of mercy," the houses and farms took literally the commands of Matthew 25 to feed the hungry, give drink to the thirsty, shelter the homeless, clothe the naked, and console the sick and imprisoned. During World War II and the Cold War, Catholic Worker "works of mercy" witnessed with nonviolent methods. In a sentiment close to the heart of John Wesley but in a method very different than his, Catholic Workers refused to participate in civil defense drills in the 1950s that supposedly prepared the United States population for nuclear attack. Day herself participated in the peace movement, though diversity of opinion existed among

Catholic Worker leadership about war as an instrument of national foreign policy. For these actions the leaders of the Catholic Workers were at times the focus of derision, if not outright persecution for their beliefs. Catholic Workers sought to respond with respect and love by responding to the image of God in the persecutor.

"Peacemaking" became a central part of the Catholic Worker experience in interpersonal relationships and in society. In houses of hospitality and in farming communes, the experience of welcoming all in need necessitated developing the skills of interpersonal conflict resolution as a form of peacemaking. Actions such as these on behalf of peace and against the building arms race were understood as "instructing the ignorant," one of the spiritual works of mercy in the Roman Catholic tradition. The direct focus on God in the iterative relationship between contemplative and active life aimed toward "purity of heart" in Christian perfection.

Secondary literature refers to Day's newspaper *The Catholic Worker* as "a labor newspaper," but its articles understand "labor" in a broad perspective. Its first volume ran regular articles that criticized both communism and capitalism, supported the claims of workers as they negotiated with employers, denounced crimes against African Americans, promoted equal race relations, supported women's right to employment, and described the sexual vulnerability of women who took employment in households. *The Catholic Worker* regularly reported on the progress of laws against child labor and the effects of the Great Depression on children. It ran "The Children's Corner," a column for and by children. Articles on social issues were interwoven with reminders of the actions of a personal lifestyle of traditional Roman Catholic faith—woodcut images that depicted the works of mercy, selections from the writings of Saint Thomas Aquinas and other saints (especially on virtues and vices, liturgies and prayers), and reports on papal encyclicals that were developing Catholic social teaching.

The interdependence of love and justice and the deep connection of the private and public life epitomized by the Catholic Worker movement is summarized in Maurin's "easy essay" describing his idea for "houses of hospitality."[24] Hospitality, as practiced by the early church and the Catholic Worker movement, understands the poor and unemployed as bearers of Christ. It treats the poor with dignity rather than disdain. It offers the poor hospitality from the individual's heart rather than from the distance of taxes paid. It offers the rich the opportunity to serve the poor as the Bible dictates. The house of hospitality provides room and board—but more: vocational training, religious education, and roundtable discussion. Maurin concludes his "easy essay":

6. In a word, they could be
   Catholic Action Houses
   where Catholic Thought
   is combined with Catholic Action.[25]

Martin Luther King Jr. and "The Sermon on the Mount"

Similar to Dorothy Day, Martin Luther King Jr. does not provide a sustained interpretation of the Sermon on the Mount. However, Wesley's interpretation of the Beatitudes offers a window to King's most important themes. The "poor in spirit" recognize that we live in a society riddled with poverty, racism, and militarism. Genuine self-knowledge involves knowing that we are complicit when we participate in lifestyles and unjust laws that uphold these evils. Genuine self-knowledge also reveals that human beings have inherent dignity because they are made in the image of God. Self-knowledge transforms the "nobodiness" of the oppressed into "somebodiness." Self-knowledge and dignity that leads one into noncompliance with unjust laws brings "mourning"—the search for a personal God who helps God's children face outer dangers with an inner calm. With God's help one can respond to these dangers with nonviolence, what King called the "mass political application of the ancient doctrine of turning the other cheek,"[26] a refusal not only "to shoot" but also "to hate."[27] Such "meekness" seeks peace, righteousness, and justice with the "weapons of truth, noninjury, courage, and soul-force"—with means that are as pure as the ends.[28]

Such action is only possible when one is convinced that the "universe is on the side of justice," that the world ultimately arches toward the good, and that "the hunger and thirst for God" will be satisfied. Such action seeks not humiliation of the oppressor but his or her understanding, friendship, and brotherhood—ultimately it finds the mutual involvement of the oppressed and the oppressor in "the beloved community."[29] It recognizes that those who engage in violence do violence to their own internal spirits, and so it fans the desire for "purity of heart," as self-purification is a step in nonviolent training.[30] Peacemakers sustain themselves with this purity in the midst of tension and conflict. Nonviolent direct action dramatizes the evils of society by meeting them head-on, bringing to the surface the tension that is already simmering below so that it can be resolved. This process will bring persecution—in King's case it brought death threats, bombing of his residence, an unsuccessful assassination attempt, and finally his death. People are persecuted because they are "maladjusted" to an evil society; though they are persecuted, their spirituality allows them to overcome desperation and the fear of death.[31]

Suffering by children and youth, and the adversity they would face in the future if conditions did not change, were at the center of the civil rights movement. King was quite aware that "creating a crisis so that communities would have to negotiate" put children and youth at immediate risk. Most poignantly, four little girls died when the 16th Street Baptist Church in Birmingham was bombed, and King preached their funeral sermon.[32] Children and youth were jailed during demonstrations and treated roughly by police and prison officials. They suffered for the benefit of other children's futures, as well as their own. Maintaining the status quo, however, would have meant that children were physically assaulted and lynched, and racism and segregation destroyed children's self-esteem and spirits. The immediate, short-term suffering of children and youth newly attending formerly all-white schools as they desegregated was a lesser evil than the long-term suffering of children and youth without good schools and adequate educational opportunity.[33] King's famous "dream" articulated the hope that children would one day be able to play together, go to school together, learn from one another, and enjoy society's benefits side by side.[34]

The youth and student movements were a significant part of the struggle for civil rights and revealed the potential of the movement and the continuing work that needed to be done, even among people of good will. King was heartened by the willing engagement of Chicago gang members, who were otherwise committed to impulsive violent response. Under King's influence, these gang members trained for nonviolent resistance and demonstrated peacefully. Furthermore, he noted that in areas where peaceful demonstrations occurred, the crime rate actually declined.[35] He was sobered by the hard work yet to be done when northern white students tried to join with less educated southern black youth on the side of struggle. The white youth failed to recognize that the experience of racism in the black youth was expressed in terms different from those of white intellectuals. Even people of good will needed to grow toward mutual relationships.[36]

These values and practices were enacted not in a structure, as in the Methodist chapels or Catholic Worker houses of hospitality, but in demonstrations and marches. A march dramatized injustice, bringing to the forefront the tension over segregated schools, segregated housing, intimidation, and the ballot box. Marches had the short-term effect of giving people the opportunity to express pent-up frustration. Over the long term, marches created the "pressure and power for change."[37] The symbol of the military march, as extolled in the *Battle Hymn of the Republic*, was transformed into a peaceful march for the purpose of justice. It also served as a God-image: through the people, "God was marching on."[38]

Children and Poverty: Methodists, Catholic Workers, the Civil Rights Movement

These three movements arose in different contexts from different ecclesiologies and offer three different lenses toward a common aim: the necessary integration of love and justice in ministries with children and poverty. The early Methodist movement, rooted in the Church of England, separated from the mother church as it spread in England and the United States. The Catholic Worker movement has remained an independent lay movement within the Roman Catholic Church, though its actions at times created tension with the Roman Catholic hierarchy. King's portion of the civil rights movement entered the stream of larger currents of civil independence already afoot, gathered ecumenical strength, and experienced schism among African Americans and Baptists who charged that the movement either pushed too hard or did not push enough. The Methodists, the Catholic Workers, and King's activists expressed their central religious convictions by joining their love of God with love of neighbor in the common aim of concern for people who are oppressed and impoverished. All three groups understood that children are among the oppressed and impoverished. They included children as members of their organizations.

What might a child such as Dong Yangnan have found within the communities and practices of these groups? In his distress, the Wesleyans would have responded to his direct need and the need of his village with care in the form of food, shelter, medical care, and education. The Catholic Workers would have helped him rebuild his life and saved other children from the same fate. Civil rights activists would have worked to change the systems and environments that caused his deadly situation. In other words, had these groups been operative within proximity, they could have intervened in love and justice, offering help in the present need and hope for the future, individually and collectively.

CHAPTER 3

Love, Justice, and the Spiritual Persistence of the Caregiver

Three Spiritual Challenges

What spiritual challenges face an adult population that wants to remember that the future of the world lies with the health and happiness of all the world's children—children of the wealthy *and* children of the destitute? And what is involved in growing a spirituality of engagement, dignity, and hope, grounded in love and justice, of those who will fight for the welfare of all children?

In the previous chapter I argued that children are best served by *an integrated understanding of love and justice.* In this chapter I suggest that *an integrated understanding of love and justice is grounded in a spirituality that is engaging, hopeful, and dignified.*

Let us consider three different spiritual challenges.

Distance or Engagement?

In Rochester, Monroe County, New York, the county legislative room has the dignity of a court—tall ceilings supported by Grecian columns, leather-backed chairs and long tables behind a bar, and a large citizens' gallery opening onto an elegant hall. On a Tuesday evening in early 2004, the gallery was packed with people who wanted to speak; more waited in the hall. After the chaos of the terrorist attacks in September 2001, legislators had

40

increasingly struggled to balance the county budget. In 2002 the county executive proposed cutting the subsidies of child care for 1300 children; a legislator shamed him by spontaneously offering $50,000 of his own money to begin a fund to reduce the cuts. In 2003 the county executive suggested cutting 24 percent of children's services, including protective services, foster care, and social work. The legislature passed a bill that raised taxes and restored some services, which the executive vetoed, though the legislature overrode the veto. In 2004 the county cut the state-mandated school nurse program from its budget, making the program into a political football among different sources for funding. Meanwhile, the county and city wanted to build a new underground bus terminal and a sports stadium. The people's priorities and tax dollars were being torn in two.

Rochester was experiencing a trend the *New York Times Magazine* called "The Backlash Against Children."[1] The backlash reveals our cultural disengagement from vulnerable children. In the renewed energy of townspeople fighting for children's services, however, Rochester was experiencing the benefit of an engaged spirituality of townspeople on children's behalf.

Despair or Hope?

In Prague, the Czech Republic, a single bulb lit the cellar so that we could peer into its tunnels and caves, where in an earlier day one could have easily hidden. It smelled damp from the whitewash that was not yet dry. The cellar was being remodeled, Rev. Joseph Cervenak proudly explained, so that youth could gather away from the drug traffic on the streets. The church was responding to the social problems that had developed since the transition from communism. But all this social work was new and overwhelming. Under communism social work had been illegal. Opening the Czech economy to integration with Europe also opened the society to social dysfunctions affecting children and youth. Now the church was trying to respond to prostitution, alcoholism, and drug trafficking. Increasing numbers of Czech people were looking to the church for assistance in their life crises. Rev. Cevernak was in the position of needing to respond from faith, but without traditions, resources, or trained personnel.

Czech church members face spiritual challenges with such rapid change. Older Christians whose faith endured communism were learning to become a church in the world, rather than a

church surrounded by and separated from the world. They hoped
for the strength to do the social work needed. Young adults who
have been attracted to the church since 1993 shared sentiments
bespeaking of a different spiritual challenge. Their parents, who
were teenagers when the Prague Spring was crushed on August
20, 1968, pulled inside themselves, unable to trust, even to trust
the church. They say their own generation, the one that came of
age during the transition toward a more open society, is more
hopeful.

Dependence or Dignity?

Kamina, North Katanga Province, the Democratic Republic
of the Congo (DRC), awakes at dawn. As the sun rises, women
dressed in bright blue, green, and orange print wraps gather in
front of the former brewery to fill their large yellow plastic barrels.
The brewery closed when war raged from 1996 through 1999;
the war surrounded Kamina but never fully engulfed it. Still, the
economy collapsed. Refugees arrived, so more bellies needed food.
In 2003 the dilapidated brewery was one of two sources of clean
water in Kamina. So, the women wait for the doors to open.

Some women will take water to the United Methodist Center
for Abandoned Children. Widows, who otherwise would have
no home or livelihood in Congolese society, will boil the water to
make rice or beans for the children's noon meal. The church has
employed the widows to feed the children orphaned by war and
disease—and their numbers have grown from an initial thirty-five
to over eight hundred children.

Men employed by the church walk briskly down a dusty,
rutted high road to an old Belgian farm the church has bought.
A Congolese man with a university degree in agriculture is the
overseer. Most of the men will hoe the fields by the river where
the dirt is brown and rich. Some of the men will clean and repair
the brick pigpens so they will again be suitable for animals. They
will raise enough food to feed the orphans and a community of
refugees who live in mud huts on the edge of Kamina.

In this context a third set of spiritual issues emerge. The
Congolese bishop can engage these men and women in these
projects because he is a persuasive fundraiser who garners
significant financial support from the United States and Europe.

When visitors from the U.S. and Europe arrive, the Congolese know that they are being examined. They know that they are not fully trusted—the Northerners want to know whether the Congolese have spent the Northerners' money well. They also know that Northerners' hearts are motivated by poor, black children's faces—children whom the Northerners want to help. Yet it is the Congolese who are caring for their own children. "Do not come here to see poor children," they will say to those who ask, "but come here to see our community caring for our children." The spiritual issue in this case is not so much disengagement or despair but a sense of paternalism and dependency that wears away human dignity. Though the feeling of humiliation sears into the soul of many Congolese pastors, they and their leaders at the same time find dignity in their relationship with God.

An engaged spirituality, a hopeful spirituality, a dignified spirituality: How might God's love strengthen people in different contexts facing different challenges to care for children and youth?

Caring for the World's Children as a Spiritual Issue in the United States

Let us assume that we *do* care about children who are not biologically "ours." We *want* to live the great commandment: "Love God with all your heart, mind, and soul; and love your neighbor as yourself." We *know* the world's children as our neighbors whom we are called to love as we love ourselves. We try to love children—we serve soup, we tutor, we lead a Sunday school class or youth group. We seek justice—we want to change the systems that entrap children in unhealthy practices and environments.

Then real disappointments hit. Most people who work with children experience some form of disillusionment.

"I made time to tutor a child who didn't show up."

"I got stuck in traffic, was late for our appointment, and the child wouldn't speak to me when I arrived."

"I served soup at a shelter, a fight broke out, and I got frightened."

"After three years of my weekly mentoring, my charge became a teenager and hit the streets, doing drugs and prostitution."

"I went on a mission trip to repair a hospital and got an exotic parasite that the doctor couldn't diagnose."

These kinds of experiences deflate the enthusiasm of people with generally good intentions. Sometimes, people react by distancing themselves from children—"I buy toys at Christmas for children I don't know, and I write checks to the church. I don't get personally involved." Other times people dig deep into their spiritual well to find sustenance that allows them to develop spiritual persistence.

Responding through a Spirituality of Engagement, Dignity, and Hope

The children, youth, and those who care for them, whether in our own communities or globally, need sustained, trustworthy relationships—relationships that transcend disappointment. Such spirituality holds together acts of spiritual nurture, such as prayer, reading scripture, and hymn singing, and acts of compassion and justice, such as feeding the hungry, clothing the naked, visiting the sick and imprisoned. These acts are two expressions of the same spiritual consciousness. Janet Parachin calls this work in the world "engaged spirituality." When we become disillusioned with our relations with children, a deeper relationship sustains us.

Spirituality, according to Parachin, roots our relationship to God in the present conditions of life but also looks "beyond personal concerns" to "that which transcends"—which various people call God, Allah, Divine Mystery, wisdom, love, service, the Great Chain of Being, etc. Engaged spirituality draws from "the springs of living water that sustain the human soul" and participates "in actions that meet the needs of a suffering world."[2]

A great cloud of twentieth-century witnesses have lived a powerful testimony to this insight: Mahatma Gandhi, Martin Luther King Jr., Howard Thurman, and Thomas Merton are examples. Their lives reveal the potential for ecumenical and interfaith cooperative practice. They are role models as persons who developed deep wells from which to draw spiritual persistence in which both love and justice were integrated. Their way of thinking about spirituality contradicts current trends that narrow spirituality only to building one's relationship with God through practices of prayer and other acts of piety, leaving out the essential element of works of justice.

The Spirituality of Dorothy Day

Dorothy Day's writings articulate the relationship between care of God and care of the world. For Day, engaged spirituality incorporated Christian contemplative practice and social action. Day's Christian contemplative practice included the daily practice of eucharist, recitation of the rosary and prayer book, fasting, studying scripture, the discipline of living in community, personal reflection and journal writing, discussion and instruction, and participation in retreat. Day's retreat notes, edited by William D. Miller in *All Is Grace: The Spirituality of Dorothy Day*, reveal her single-minded attention to the direct love of God.[3] Her focus on God's love allowed her to see God in all creation, to transform sensual life into the spiritual, to contemplate Christ's sacrifice, to grow in the love and likeness of God, and to cultivate in herself a peaceful, nonviolent spirit. This direct attention to God in retreat was taken into Day's daily love of neighbor in houses of hospitality and farming communes. Indeed, the practice of a loving, nonviolent spirituality was tested regularly in the houses of hospitality. As communities open to all who come, people occasionally became aggressive. To maintain their ideals, the participants developed nonviolent means of conflict intervention. The practice of love and nonviolence in houses of hospitality demonstrate God's grace and love; prayer in the midst of conflict is a necessary part of the intervention.[4] Day's spirituality considers a spiritual response to persons in the most difficult of circumstances. Day's kind of engaged spirituality draws upon traditional practices of spirituality in ecclesial life to build the child caregiver's strength in reliability, resilience, compassion, and deep listening, especially as obstacles arise when adults are called to provide care to children beyond their biological families.

Wesleyan Spirituality

John Wesley's "engaged spirituality" has much in common with Day's. For Wesley, both works of piety and works of mercy are means of grace. Listening to God through prayer, reading the scripture, remembering our baptism, and receiving eucharist may call us to various acts of compassion and justice; conversely, acts of compassion and justice may be the means through which God calls us into a deeper practice of listening to the transcendent God.

In his sermon "On Visiting the Sick," Wesley writes that works of mercy are a necessary means of grace, the neglect of which lessens one's faith.[5] Furthermore, in the same sermon Wesley complains about the effect of a disengaged spirituality on the opinions of the powerful:

> One great reason why the rich in general have so little sympathy for the poor is because they so seldom visit them. Hence it is that, according to the common observation, one part of the world does not know what the other suffers. Many of them do not know because they do not care to know: they keep out of the way of knowing it--and then plead their voluntary ignorance as an excuse for their hardness of heart.[6]

In other words, the rich—those in congregations who limit their acts of mercy to Christmas presents, those in mentorship programs who are discouraged at the first sign of disappointment, those who fail to provide proper safeguards in congregations so that healthy adult-child relationships can grow, those who use children to their political advantage, and those who exercise decision-making power far from the daily concerns of the poorest and most vulnerable—have not spent enough time carefully listening to the world's children, receiving from them the grace that God would impart.

Furthermore, the Wesleys (John and his brother Charles) stressed the importance of children as part of the communal means of grace. All preachers visited and instructed children in their homes, and the Wesleyan mission established schools and orphanages.[7] The Wesleys wrote poetry and hymnody for and about children, including *Hymns for Children* (1763) and *Hymns for the Use of Families* (1767). Hear the affirmation of engaged spirituality in the third and fourth verses of Charles Wesley's short hymn, "Jesus, the Gift Divine I Know":

> O God, on me the grace bestow,
> unblamable before thy sight,
> whence all the streams of mercy flow;
> thy mercy, thy supreme delight,
> to me, for Jesus' sake, impart
> and plant thy nature in my heart.

Thy mind throughout my life be shown,
while listening to the sufferer's cry,
the widow's and the orphan's groan,
on mercy's wings I swiftly fly
the poor and helpless to relieve,
my life, my all for them to give.[8]

Charles Wesley is commending the practice of building relationships across the lines of culture and class from a social position of social privilege. Though the Wesley family was materially poor—in fact, some of the siblings were destitute—John Wesley had what would now be called the "social capital" of education, reputation, and connections within the Anglican church. These nonmaterial assets gave him significant advantages. He used and risked this advantage on behalf of persons who suffered.

The Spirituality of Martin Luther King Jr.

A different emphasis emerges in the engaged spirituality of Martin Luther King Jr. Similar to John Wesley, King has the advantage of education, reputation, and connections with the Baptist church. Though his family was not materially poor, King was writing as a person whose privilege was relative to the race to whom he belongs. As an African American in U.S. society, he knew the dynamics of his own oppression.

King understood the importance of building relationships—King's word is "brotherhood." King struggled to make such relationships possible. He articulated a method, a practice of spirituality, to bring white and black, poor and rich people to friendship and understanding—to open them to the kind of "visiting" and "listening" that Wesley commended. He saw it as his job to make it comfortable for people with privilege to visit and listen and to make it uncomfortable for them to remain ignorant of the circumstances other human beings endured. Therefore, his work focused on the practice of spirituality as nonviolent resistance.

The practice of nonviolent resistance seeks to face evil and injustice, transforming it to justice and mercy. Nonviolent resistance is possible through love, an idea that appears frequently in King's sermons, speeches, and writings. Wesley, speaking to his aristocratic Anglican audience, emphasizes love of the poor, and speaking to his poor congregants, emphasizes love for one another after the example of Christ. King, speaking to an oppressed African American population and to those from all races who would stand with the African American community, concentrates on love of the enemy. This love of the other who may be caught in the evil and unjust cycle of racism is the means of transformation. The practice of love as nonviolent resistance has several goals: it seeks not to shame and humiliate the racist, but to seek his or her friendship and understanding. It also seeks to avoid what King calls "internal violence of the spirit" in those who do resist racist practices.[9] Retaliation through physical violence harms the spirit of the one who gives in to physical aggression.

King avoided physical violence and violence to the spirit because he rooted nonviolent resistance in *agape*—the kind of love exemplified by Jesus Christ which requires nothing in return. *Agape* is love as a gift without strings attached. As King emphases the priority of agape, he seems most concerned in transforming the retaliation and revenge that are easily released when rage surfaces. The moral power of agape confronts, exposes, and transforms the distortion and alienation of oppressive power.

Agape love invites people to develop commitments that transcend Christmas charity. It counters the many disappointments that occur in caring for children when we are social caregivers—mentors, club leaders, teachers, nurses, or court appointed advocates. It is tested in the cycle of abuse, victimization, and healing that occurs in caring for those involved with child sexual abuse. It sustains international relationships when cultures conflict and communication fails. It intercedes in conflicts between social caregivers and primary caregivers—parents, grandparents, and guardians. Increasingly in our world, war, AIDS, and poverty leave children without sources of agape love. Who, then, will care for these children with godly self-sacrifice? And what kind of support do such caregivers deserve from their societies?

Agape calls us to "love our enemies." Societies have great difficulty separating those they perceive as adult enemies from their vulnerable children who need care. In the United States our so-called enemies include parents who make war, other than those who fight for the United States; parents who contract HIV-AIDS; and parents who are poor. Society cannot distinguish these adults from other perceived "enemies": children who are conscripted as soldiers or children who are fighting for survival on the streets. King's practice of spirituality as loving the enemy through agape provides a different route than needing to distinguish parent from child—agape calls for loving parent *and* child. It provides an example of the extent and range of love required for children and their families who must live in a variety of horrifying conditions. It is love that transcends the political process in Rochester, a love that sees its way through overwhelming social conditions in the Czech Republic, a love that allows Congolese and Ugandan seminary roommates to see each other as persons at Africa University in Zimbabwe. Agape can provide the basis for an engaged spirituality as it reengages us in the face of extreme difficulty.

This love seeks justice. Justice, for King, bends the world toward good in the future. It creates a path on which the good in the world seeks its eschatological fulfillment, against evil that deters it. Justice is also a creative force that acts from future justice upon the present. We imagine a future world in which children are free from violence, disease, oppression, and poverty; and that vision of the future shapes the present. Justice, as the end, is consistent with love, its means. Present and future, love and justice offer hope.[10]

Furthermore, nonviolent spirituality maintains human dignity. Only dignified resistance truly resists. In "Love, Law and Civil Disobedience," King writes:

> If the Negro stayed in his place and accepted discrimination and segregation, there would be no crisis. But the Negro has a new sense of dignity, a new self-respect and new determination... Now this new sense of dignity on the part of the Negro grows out of the same longing for freedom and human dignity on the part of the oppressed people all over the world; for we see it in Africa, we see it in Asia, we see it all over the world.[11]

This kind of self-esteem and dignity in the present, regardless of circumstances, and hope for the future, even in the face of enormous obstacles, are important aspects of the spirituality of child care givers. The United States underrewards those who provide care for children. We in the United States may well admire the efforts of poor widows who care for the orphans of their

African communities, even as we ignore the women and men who work tirelessly in schools, child protection services, and child care agencies in our own communities. In the United States we may consider a poor mother to be "not working" and limit the time of her benefits if she cares for her children on a welfare check. But we applaud her "welfare to work" behavior if she is employed by caring for other people's children in a child care service, meager though her pay may be. People in the United States who engage in unpaid and paid care for children usually do so because of a combination of intrinsic and material rewards in the present and despite obstacles, such as precarious funding, that threaten the future. They need a spirituality that gives value to their efforts, regardless of cultural messages to the contrary.

And yet, the direct Wesleyan emphasis on building relationships fills out an implicit portion of King's message that loses its emphasis as King undergirds nonviolent spirituality with agape love and justice. King defines *philia* and *eros,* but does not develop these understandings of love in relationship to other aspects of his message. Still, ideas akin to these play a large role in King's spirituality. The agape of the nonviolent resister is always seeking other ends—the understanding, friendship, and the "brotherhood of man." Yet King gives *philia* or "friendship" short shrift.[12] He says that he is not really seeking affection or active love from others. But agape love is not enough. *Philia*—friendship and care that has warmth, affection, and direct concern—is exactly what children need. It is exactly what many children are missing. A reciprocal friendship between an adult and child makes room for the child's response, participation, and partnership. Just as we learned in British studies after World War II that orphaned children without adult affection die, we will learn in African orphanages that food and housing are not enough. Warm relationships with parental surrogates are necessary for human development—without them orphans die.

Such friendship is also what is needed in international relationships to support the African caregivers of children and to right the history of paternalism and colonialism. Paternalism and colonialism developed through the types of relationships that incorporate a particular form of distant affection—one that leaves the paternalist or colonialist far less vulnerable than those who receive benefits from him or her. Mutuality is absent. Africans who are trying to build new relationships with Northerners remind us that direct, heartfelt, mutual affection is as important as the dollars the church is so good at raising. Agape is rarely sustainable on an ongoing basis, and at times is not healthy for either party.

Feminist theologians criticize agape, suggesting that wholly self-sacrificing love may reinforce subordination rather than create self-respect and dignity. In international ecclesial relationships a strictly "self-sacrificing" ethic may deteriorate into counterproductive relationships of paternalism on the side of the "self-sacrificing" contributor and dependence on the side of the "self-sacrificing" recipient. I say "self-sacrificing" recipient because the international recipient may indeed subordinate himself or herself in an undignified way to get his or her needs attended. To counteract this tendency, direct, mutual friendship—where love as *philia* is present—can be the vehicle of engagement, dignity, and hope. Friendship provides a depth in international human relationships that makes visiting and listening and mutual participation possible.

Practicing Engaged Spirituality

How does a person or congregation grow an engaged spirituality? God gives people ministries with children, youth, and their caregivers; but God gives people different strengths and sensibilities in this work. Some people gravitate more naturally to ministries of prayer; others find ministries of caregiving in the world the easier place to begin. People who are engaged in work with children of all economic standings deserve the opportunity to interpret this work as God's work through sermons, prayers, Sunday school classes, the study of scripture, and communal support with one another. People who are drawn first to these practices also need a chance to discern how those practices may be calling them to work in the world. Whether one's new and somewhat uncomfortable practice reflects the work of mercy or piety, the beginning principle is the same: *Start with a small commitment that can be regularly sustained.* A half an hour of tutoring weekly is more important than a large donation of toys once a year at Christmas. A short time of devotions sustained regularly will grow our spiritual life more than full-length liturgies that may wear us out quickly. When we think about care with children beyond our biological families in this way, our spirituality helps us respond to disillusionment, despair, and humiliation with engagement, dignity, and hope.

CHAPTER 4

Poverty, Love, Justice, and Integrative Understandings of Pastoral Care, Mission, and Evangelism

Poverty in the Seminary Curriculum

In the previous chapter I argued that spiritual formation often ignores practice of care with persons who are poor; similarly, *most seminary curricula that form clergy leaders for ministry in local congregations offer no permanent home for studying involuntary poverty and practicing ways to resist it.* As a result, ministry has suffered. If you are a layperson in a local congregation who is interested in expressing your Christian faith through ministries with people who are poor, your pastor may have had little or no training or experience that helps him or her help you find your vocation. Worse yet, if you are a member of a congregation and you are poor, your pastor may have little idea of what your life is like.

The study of poverty in professional training for ministry might be covered in social ethics classes; practices of responding to poverty might be included in courses on pastoral care, mission, or evangelism. Professors may also teach these subjects without attention to poverty, assuming that another subdiscipline "has it covered." Worse yet, professors may consider poverty "not essential" for theological studies. As a result, even though practices in response to poverty are central to biblical heritage and the theology of the church, in their most formative years the future clergy of the church have little opportunity to study that which would help them lead congregations to respond to poor children in their communities.

This chapter is designed to help theological educators of all stripes—in seminaries and in local congregations—find new ways of connecting the traditional arts of ministry with practices of poverty.

Is It Pastoral Care, Evangelism, or Mission?

Jamaa Letu, in Lubumbashi, the Democratic Republic of Congo, is a orphanage run by the South Congo Conference of the United Methodist Church. The secretary of Jamaa Letu writes:

> We are happy and thankful for what has been realized... enabling us to erect the orphanage "Jamaa Letu" (in Kiswahili "Our Family") here in the Ruashi-township of Lubumbashi. The very well-built complex, built on church-owned ground, offers a comfortable home for 80 girls, aged from 0–18. While we are, of course, happy for our orphan girls at "Jamaa-Letu," we also know that besides them there are hundreds of boys and girls—street children—much less fortunate. In the last few years the number of street-children has increased dramatically. While the Southern part of Katanga Province, including Lubumbashi, is not directly in a war-zone, nevertheless thousands of displaced families have had to flee their villages and now live here in camps just outside of town. For years already our Church has a small Feeding Centre for street-children, where, according to funds available, 2 to 3 times weekly, simple meals are served. We, the UMC of Southern Congo/Zambia Area, are well aware that there is a purpose in this street-children situation around us, and that "God, who is in the least of these" wants us to respond to their needs. We are also conscious that these children are the Church of Tomorrow, and we are therefore most willing and able—provided the means—to do much more for them.[1]

In Pennsylvania, U.S.A., Tina Whitehead, who identifies herself as a "pastor's wife," describes her efforts to build relationships across race and class in her own local congregation: a white, middle-class church in a neighborhood that is now black and low income. She calls herself "the gopher" who makes connections between kids, camp, and congregation. She says:

> What it's done to the community and to our role as a church in the community...[has] been very powerful...
>
> We had an incident Christmas Eve where a boy was shot and killed by the State Police. He was twelve years old and shot in the back. He was a member of our program. The black community asked if they could have the funeral in our church and asked my husband if he would do the service. They asked me to do the eulogy. Our women of the church, and some of them are very well-to-do, were in the kitchen serving the community after the funeral... That was just incredible from this one tiny little hour-and-a-half ministry. It's nothing, but God has just used it... If the people can catch the vision of how powerful this is, it would be incredible.[2]

As they reach out to street children, the Congolese United Methodists and the Pennsylvania congregation are engaging in pastoral care, evangelism, *and* mission. The Congolese are transforming the image of themselves as objects of mission into an understanding of themselves as caregivers, evangelists, and missionaries in their own right. In love they reach out to the street children of their city of Lubumbashi; in justice those who were formerly "recipients" of ministry become self-determining agents who participate in the rebuilding of their society. Love and justice form the center of their ministry that is at once a form of pastoral care, evangelism, and mission. The "pastor's wife" has led the congregation in mission, evangelism, and pastoral care. She has crossed boundaries of difference, as in mission, and shared her faith, as in evangelism, but she has also established relationships of care that can be called upon in the midst of a crisis.

How are mission, evangelism, and pastoral care related to the worship setting of this funeral? In love she was the "gopher" who crossed the boundaries of income and race to care for children. Love became justice through relationships of respect and trust within which it was acceptable for the less vulnerable community in her husband's congregation to care with the suffering in their time of need. When love and justice interrelate, these ministries function well together. Relationships that are established in the course of these ministries inform the reflective theories that pastoral theology, missiology, and evangelism develop. These theories provide guidance but are nuanced—or sometimes over-turned—when they shape a ministry response to real people. If the relationships among people and theories become too distant from one another, love and justice may be torn asunder. These ministries may lose their way.

Changing Understandings: Pastoral Care, Evangelism, and Mission

Why are pastoral care, evangelism, and mission usually distinguished? The practical theological subdisciplines[3] of pastoral theology, missiology, and evangelism[4] reflect critically on the ministry practices of pastoral care, mission, and evangelism. These subdisciplines create a lens that views a particular aspect of ministry practice; practical theology provides a way to think about the whole. Critical reflection evaluates the practice, leading to thoughtful discussions about standards and norms. Too often, critical reflection fails to reconnect the various practices of min-istry with one another in an integrated practical theology. This chapter will locate the reconnection of pastoral care, mission, and evangelism in christology, our thought about the life, ministry, death, and resurrection of Jesus Christ. The reason for this is that, at their best, pastoral care, mission, and evangelism seek in different but overlapping ways to imitate the life and actions of Jesus Christ. We will begin with definitions—the narrow and broad definitions of these academic subdisciplines.

Pastoral Care

William A. Clebsch and Charles Jaeckle defined pastoral care in 1964: "The ministry of the cure of souls, or pastoral care, consists of helping acts, done by representative Christian persons, directed toward the healing, sustaining, guiding, and reconciling of troubled persons whose troubles arise in the context of ultimate meanings and concerns."[5] This definition has been both heralded and criticized. The definition helpfully focused thinking about pastoral care as reflection on the actions of a specific group of people, the clergy, in one of their historic functions, counseling. It distinguished their work in the context of "ultimate concerns" from that of the secular psychiatrists, counselors, and social workers who are the twentieth-century helpers of "troubled persons" in the context of "penultimate" concerns. The definition failed, however, to include the ongoing caring functions of the congregation. It disallowed the activities of advocacy and befriending that are often a central act of respect and care for children and persons who are poor. It assumed that care would be marked by hierarchical relationships rather than being grounded in relationships of friendship and mutuality. It dismissed most of the contributions of women who have always been engaged in caring relationships but have historically been denied the "set apart" status of ordination. It decentered the theological foundation for care that guides it. The assumptions embedded in this definition may have "weakened the bonds of care between ordinary people"[6] and contributed to the decline of social solidarity so often noted in the United States today. Furthermore, in the version of pastoral care and counseling that arose in the twentieth century in the United States, pastoral care had been criticized as losing its biblical and theological foundations and becoming almost exclusively grounded in psychological disciplines.

In recent decades "pastoral theology" has emerged as critical theological reflection on the activities of pastoral care and counseling. Pastoral theology affirms the congregational ministries of care and advocacy. Stephen Pattison offers a more theological definition. For Pattison, "Pastoral care is that activity, undertaken especially by representative Christian persons, directed towards the elimination and relief of sin and sorrow and the presentation of all people perfect in Christ to God."[7] This definition intends to communicate that pastoral care is an activity, not just a set of ideas or propositions. It is carried out on behalf of the Christian church by clergy *and* laity with individual persons and in community. It finds the roots of sin and suffering in social conditions, especially "poverty, inequality, and injustice." Pastoral care follows "the example of Jesus who set out to serve the needy of the world... paying close attention to the people, the human situation, and the world in which we live," and interpreting that situation theologically and with reference to "that which transcends," in a way different from "secular 'sources.'"[8] Pastoral theology is christological, artistic, and metaphorical, offering images that guide the activities of care.

How do love and justice intersect with pastoral care? Though various authors offer many answers to that question, one interpretation is provided by Pattison, who quotes Alastair Campbell: "Pastoral care is, in essence, surprisingly simple. It has one fundamental aim: to help people to know love, both as something to be received and as something to give."[9] Pattison makes the further point that focusing pastoral care on love in this way "links pastoral care with ministry as a whole."[10] While affirming the importance of love, Pattison also notes that the pastoral care movement of the later twentieth century emphasized love almost to the exclusion of justice.[11] These trends have changed in the last two decades, as pastoral theology has redefined the subdiscipline. The literature on pastoral care now addresses changing understandings of gender, race, sexuality, economics, family, and international relationships.[12] People concerned with pastoral care have more clarity on the range of contexts and concerns that they confront.

Mission

European and North American Christianity was spread hand-in-hand with European and North American political dominance. In their introductory text on mission, A. Damps, L.A. Hoedemaker, and M.R. Spindler implicate the mission movement in colonialism, white supremacy, and cultural insensitivity.[13] At the same time, the mission movement built institutions, provided medical care and education, and engaged in direct relief efforts. My experience in Tanzania reflects this mixed history. At a Roman Catholic school the topic written on the blackboard was "Christianity as political oppression." Later I asked an African priest what Christianity had brought to Africa. "The people are no longer afraid," he replied, referring to the way that Christianity at times dispels the historic belief in witchcraft.

Missiology as a subdiscipline reflects critically on the unhappy convergence of politics, culture, and religion and also records the achievements of the successes of the mission movement. It studies the "multiplicity of processes" in mission, including the development of institutions, the problems of cross-cultural communication of the Christian faith, the implications of North Atlantic political and religious hegemony, and the social issues that emerge in intercultural relationships.[14] It draws upon a variety of social sciences, including sociology and anthropology, to interpret these processes. Though the field of missiology arose with the rise of anthropology and sociology, Donald Senior demonstrates that the activities of mission are grounded throughout the Bible.[15] Steven B. Bevans and Roger P. Schroeder trace the theological grounding of mission throughout the history of Christianity and attribute expansive understandings of mission to the theological commitments of different Christian groups.[16]

Bevans and Schroeder distinguish the operative theologies of mission as related to three distinct historical theological "types" (labeled A, B, and C) identified by Justo L. Gonzáles.[17] In mission, each of these theological types is related to a theological doctrine: christology, ecclesiology, eschatology, salvation, theological anthropology, and culture.[18] For our purposes it is important to note that the three types (A, B, and C) tend to rely on different theological formulations related to christology. Type A is more likely to understand Christ's work as developed by Anselm, a "satisfaction" or payment due to God for humanity's sins, and to focus on mission as the proclamation of Jesus as the universal savior of the world. Type B understands Christ's work as developed by Irenaeus, as "ransom," or costly suffering that God in Christ undergoes with humanity and so focuses on mission as the *Missio Dei*, the mission of God and Jesus' role within the relationship of the Triune God. Type C is more likely to understand Christ's work according to the "moral example" that Jesus sets by being willing to be put to death to sustain the integrity of his relationship with God the Father and to focus on Jesus as the one who proclaims the kingdom or reign of God.

Bevans and Schroeder propose an idea of mission for the twenty-first century that combines the great commandment, the commandment to "love God and neighbor," with the great commission, the commandment to "make disciples." Drawing largely from the theologies of Types B and C, they propose that mission should be based on "prophetic dialogue" that includes witness and proclamation; liturgy, prayer, and contemplation; justice, peace, and the integrity of creation; interreligious dialogue; inculturation; and reconciliation. Within this construction of the goals of mission, love and justice have a close and interdependent relationship. Love is dependent upon the Christian's being able to live a life that with integrity bears witness to the life of Christ, whether through prayer or compassion. Such a life is an integral witness to justice and the reign of God, especially in situations of violence and exploitation that are pressing in the twenty-first century.

Within this understanding of mission that is written by Roman Catholics who analyze the range of Christian tradition, God has a mission in the world; and that mission has a church. Evangelism includes introducing and forming disciples for God's overall mission. Some Protestant writers in recent decades, however, have attempted to differentiate mission and evangelism, establishing evangelism as a separate academic subdiscipline.

Evangelism

Evangelism, also called evangelization, involves Christians' sharing their faith and initiating new believers in Christ. In recent decades authors on evangelism have sought to overcome negative associations with evangelism. To do so they have distanced themselves from approaches that demean the faith of others, that proselytize persons of other faiths, or that seek church growth as "members at all cost" as a method of institutional survival without concern for the depth or content of faith. Recent authors promote "relational" evangelism. They are concerned that congregations communicate "the good news," or the *evangel,* of Jesus Christ through a genuine and confident communication of who God is within an ongoing personal relationship between two human beings. They teach pastors to invite persons to respond to God rather than to overpower people's belief systems. As with pastoral care, however, authors differ in their starting points, their theological emphases, and their definitions.

Ben Campbell Johnson seeks to overcome the widely held stereotype of evangelism by grounding evangelism in human need rather than in the doctrine of God. He conceives of human need largely as a series of questions about the ultimate meaning of life that the gospel can answer. Understood in this way evangelism is "that particular task of the church to communicate the good news of God's love to persons so that they may understand the message, place their trust in Christ, become loyal members of his church, and fulfill his will as obedient disciples."[19] Campbell, a Presbyterian, explicitly argues against models of evangelism that are centered on church growth. He also disallows a relationship between evangelism and the social ministries of the church. He seeks through this narrowing of the definition of evangelism to focus the church's attention on the importance of Christian initiation and commitment, charging that mainline denominations in the United States failed to take Christian initiation seriously. He argues that conflating evangelism into mission, understood as the social ministry of the church, contributed to this decline.

In contrast, Methodist authors combine initiation, social ministry, and discipleship. Mortimer Arias, a Bolivian Methodist writing in the context of social turmoil, understands evangelism and social ministry as fully integrated with one another.[20] William Abraham, writing in the United States, continues Arias' emphasis on evangelism as initiation of a person into the reign of God but insists that initiation means engagement in a series of activities and experiences that form a new believer in Christian discipleship.[21] Building on Abraham's work, Scott J. Jones continues the theme that evangelism initiates disciples, though Jones argues that evangelism begins by sharing the love of God. God's love expresses God's reign.[22] Love and justice are integrated in Arias's work, though they are also related to one another in the work of Abraham and Jones.

Practical Theological Subdisciplines and Children and Poverty

Traditionally, these three academic subdisciplines—pastoral care, evangelism, and mission—have not focused attention on children, leaving such attention to religious education. Until practical theology emerged as an integrating discipline, theological education focused on the relationship between theory or theology and practice, ignoring dialogue among the practical subdisciplines that focus on discrete practices of ministry. Without such dialogue, those who once studied these subdisciplines and now have become teachers have had little opportunity to learn how other subdisciplines evolved. Pastoral theologians may assume that people who teach evangelism primarily focus on imposing a particular set of beliefs on others and that missiologists participate uncritically in building political empires. Professors of evangelism may still think that pastoral care has no theology and that mission emphasizes social ministry, ignoring Christian initiation. Missiologists may consider both pastoral care and evangelism to be too individualistic in their respective responses to suffering and Christian witness.

Yet the critical disciplines of pastoral theology, missiology, and evangelism that build our understanding of the practices of pastoral care, mission, and evangelism have responded to these criticisms. A potentially creative dialogue among them revolves around the way each of them seeks to develop a contemporary understanding of what it means to follow the example of the Jesus they find in scripture.[23] The activities of pastoral care that include guiding, healing, sustaining, reconciling, advocating, and resisting are specifically rooted in imitating Jesus' ministry in the world. Christian initiation that is based on helping new believers follow Jesus' example of love to bring about the reign of God provides another lens through which to view our ministry as patterned after the ministry of Jesus. Prophetic dialogue that grounds the practice of mission—mission that incorporates the practices of witness and proclamation, liturgy and prayer, peacemaking, justice, and the integrity of creation—allows Jesus to reveal God[24] who suffers with us and helps us resist evil.[25] A christological focus illumines both who the agent of ministry is and the activity that that person engages in.

When each subdiscipline seeks to communicate what it means to follow in the ways of Jesus, then they offer coherence as we study the ministries of Jamaa Letu or the congregation in Pennsylvania.

Metaphors of Jesus That Guide Our Practices of Pastoral Care, Evangelism, and Mission

Three metaphors that are often used for Jesus help us raise issues that are common to the practices of pastoral care, evangelism, and mission. Three scriptural metaphors are chosen from many possible others to help us identify three issues that are important for ministries with children in the midst of poverty. The metaphor of Jesus as the Good Shepherd refers us to the question of power; the metaphor of Jesus as Lamb raises the question of vulnerability; the metaphor of Jesus as Friend illumines our understanding of mutuality in ministry. These metaphors have limits. Some believe the metaphors of shepherd/ess and sheep communicate a clericalism that promotes the power of the clergy and the passivity of the "flock" or congregations. Some think the metaphor of lamb promotes inordinate self-sacrifice. Others suspect the metaphor of friend communicates an inappropriate and potentially dangerous intimacy in ministry that ignores power relationships. Metaphors, however, open up and point toward meaning in ministry. Each of these metaphors has a fuller meaning than the criticism allows.[26] Multiple metaphors also interact with one another, providing checks and balances against misinterpretation of any one metaphor alone.

The Metaphor of Shepherd/ess and the Use and Misuse of Power

The metaphor of shepherd in scripture addresses the use and misuse of power among leaders. In Ezekiel 34:2—6, the shepherds of Israel abuse the privilege of their position by neglecting, exploiting, and isolating those who are vulnerable. Ezekiel considers God to be the Good Shepherd, who replaced those who abused power with David, a good king, who was charged to fulfill God's vision of nourishment, justice, and peace. In the gospels, Jesus becomes this Good Shepherd who loves by seeking the lost and by providing food, mercy, and care and who brings justice by holding accountable those who use the power to care for others to enhance their own decadence. The shepherds of Israel, the rich and powerful ones who have ignored God, need evangelism, mission, and pastoral care because they are in need of God's moral compass as they use their power. The shepherd/esses who follow in Jesus' way have found this moral compass.[27]

All three subdisciplines must think about the use of power, especially when they consider children. In the practice of pastoral care, the right use of power prevents childhood abuse and neglect and enhances relationships between children and their families, congregations, communities, and other natural networks of care. In the practice of evangelism, the right use of power takes children and youth seriously, enhancing the spiritual assets that strengthen children and youth as they grow. Power must be restrained if evangelism disrupts or disregards patterns of faith that are being communicated within the child's family and culture. The question of the misuse of power in mission raises questions of "globalization": how religion becomes the weapon of religious and economic colonizing forces that constrain the self-determination of people in other countries. The proper use of power, however, shows that the church in mission is a vehicle of care that goes where others fear to tread.

The Metaphor of Lamb and Role of Sacrifice and Vulnerability

Just as the metaphor of shepherd depicts a God who guides human action, the metaphor of "lamb" or "sheep" illustrates the way that God took on humanity to renew God's relationship with God's human creation. The idea of Jesus Christ as shepherd *and* lamb provides paradoxical images for the Christian. First, Jesus as lamb, often associated with Jesus' crucifixion, communicates the vulnerability in any genuine relationship, but Jesus as *both* shepherd and lamb is both protective and vulnerable. Second, mutuality develops when the human being engages in role reversals. Just as Jesus Christ acted as both shepherd and lamb, Christians serve as shepherds and lambs with one another at different times in different ways.

Vulnerable and dependent, children need adult protection. In pastoral care, a caregiver stabilizes emotional turmoil and chaos, dignifying a suffering child by finding a word or phrase that offers hope. Caregivers risk becoming entangled in the turmoil so that they cannot guide a child to another place. The lamb, while vulnerable, holds out hope of resurrection even in despair. People doing evangelism risk challenges to their faith. Genuine evangelism brings the "good news of Jesus Christ" to the place of our deepest faith-borne doubts. Children may ask simple, disarming questions that strike the heart of doubts that adults protect with complex answers. Mission enters places left bereft by war, violence, and hunger. Children most in need of food, water, clothing, shelter, and medical care receive these things only if adults risk their physical safety to provide them.

The Metaphor of Friend and the Question of Mutuality

"Friends" in the literature of theological ethics are not "buddies" but companions who enter a reciprocal relationship of joy, help, and accountability.[28] In pastoral care, writers who communicate a relationship of mutuality and reciprocity use the metaphor of friendship, based on John 15:12–15, "This is my commandment, that you love one another as I have loved you. No one has greater love than this, to lay down one's life for one's friends. You are my friends if you do what I command you... I have called you friends, because I have made known to you everything that I have heard from my Father."[29] Such mutuality incorporates power and vulnerability. As a friend Jesus ate with sinners, comforted human pain, provided safety from harm, and offered himself to all who came to him.

Friendship makes ministry immediate and present. When friends appear hungry at the door, we do not turn them away.

When they need water or clothing, we offer what we have. We may tolerate with grace the foibles of our friends simply because we enjoy their presence. Friendship in our care for children enhances our ability to respect children as full human beings who have agency and independence. Friendship in our evangelism presents faith to children without either being reductionistic or overwhelming. Friendship in mission means that we don't allow our friends to die of hunger, thirst, or violence.

Pastoral care, evangelism, and mission aim toward the *telos* of ministry, the eschatological hope of Christian life that is described in Matthew 25:31–40. The acts of care, evangelism, and mission imitate the just, righteous, loving, and vulnerable God on behalf of those who suffer. In this passage the righteous have followed the teachings not because they fear the king's judgment or the shepherd's exclusion. Rather, they are transformed into "the righteous" as they go about their work of loving God and loving their neighbor. They have followed the example of the Jesus in molding their spirits, their relationship with God, and care for "the least of these," as the commandments and the Hebraic law taught them.

Shepherd/esses, Lambs, and Friends in Pennsylvania and the Congo

In the stories of the Jamaa Letu orphanage and the Pennsylvania congregation, the church seeks to respond to those who suffer, to "the least of these." In so doing, they committed their power, vulnerability, and friendship in new ways.

As caregivers, the Pennsylvania congregation imitated the gospel example of the Christ of compassion. Unfortunately, many Christian congregations would have supported the ministry of the pastor's wife as long as she ministered elsewhere; they would have balked at the idea of bringing the ministry into *their* church building. In so doing, they might have become like the shepherds of Israel in Ezekiel who used their power only on their own behalf. Instead, this congregation sought to imitate the Good Shepherd, to "let the children come." The congregation welcomed the community into its church home, providing not only space but social support for the fullness of a ritual intended to communicate pastoral care. Rather than remaining aloof to the sacrifice already made by a child, and discovering the vulnerability of the children with whom the congregation was connected through the pastor's wife, the congregation made itself vulnerable in mission. After a tragic act *in* the community, the congregation was able to cross cultural barriers, so frequently required in the practice of mission, in order to offer a witness of their faith *to* the community. The evangelistic witness of the congregation extended not only to the community but to the congregation itself and to the pastor's wife. The community *may* have heard words of Christian comfort in a new way. But we know for certain that the pastor's wife experienced the response of the congregation in such a way that her faith was deepened. It allowed her to glimpse the reign of God, if only for a moment.

In the account of the orphanage at Jamaa Letu, those who were once the "objects" of mission have themselves become the "agents" of care, mission, and evangelism. The Congolese of Jamaa Letu live in one of the poorest countries of the world. They are overwhelmed by a refugee crisis in the midst of political instability. Certainly, they of all Christians might identify with the sacrificial experience of Jesus Christ, the lamb. Yet they have turned their vulnerability into the power to act on Christ's behalf. As lambs, they have become shepherd/esses. They have grasped a power in Christ to act as missionaries who can be caregivers and can bear witness as evangelists. As the friends of children, they bind children's war wounds and provide for their basic needs. As evangelists they offer Christ to new believers, to the children who are the "Church of Tomorrow." As friends to the children and to the global church, they share the meaning of their experiences with others.

The metaphors for Christ and the different arts of ministry illumine different aspects of these ministries. Yet the actions of these ultimately are not about a specific practice of ministry but reflect the way Christians seek to imitate Christ in his life, teachings, death, and resurrection, or to proclaim Christ, crucified and risen.

We now turn to the larger world contexts in which children and poverty, spirituality and ministry are shaped, and to which those who seek to resist involuntary poverty for poor children, all children, and all who are poor may want to respond.

Interlude Between Section One
and Section Two

In the first section of this book, "Culture, Ethics, and Ministry with Children and Poverty," I have described the way we use language to construct our understanding of poverty and have argued for an integrative understanding of Christian love and justice for children who live in the midst of poverty. This integrative understanding suggests that direct relationships with poor children and activism against systems that create poverty are equally necessary. The vulnerability of children who live in poverty calls those who want to care for children to reconsider several interconnections. Love and justice, which understand children as private and public beings, points caregivers toward forming a spirituality of engagement, dignity, and hope. Such spirituality, which is formed through practices of mercy *and* piety, grounds ministries for children and poverty that do faithful work but are ill-defined. These loving and just ministries seek to follow Jesus' example. Having developed the idea that love and justice are important in building complex understandings of lives and contexts, spirituality, and ministry, I turn now to evaluate the social contexts in which children live, and their effect on children's flourishing.

In Section II, "The Unnamed Children's Issues," I discuss ideas and social systems that shape children's lives. It is difficult enough to focus the church's attention on children in relationship to United States' domestic policy on health, welfare, and education—although churches frequently complement social policy in that area. Only a few local congregations consider the implications specifically for children of international law, the direction of the global economy, the development of environmental policy, and the mentality that governs war and peace. For those reasons the next section of this book analyzes larger public systems as the context for children's lives.

The Unnamed Children's Issues

CHAPTER 5

Can Families with Children Survive Our Social Policies?

The Church's Role

The church most easily understands children, poverty, and ministry in the context of larger systems that shape children's lives in relation to social welfare systems. Ministries of the church most commonly encounter the United States social welfare system through mentoring programs for women and some men moving "from welfare to work," or from public assistance to employment under the new Temporary Assistance for Needy Families (TANF) restrictions. Such women and men and their children often constitute "fragile families"—families with few resources or back-up systems. Such programs bring church ministries into contact with secular not-for-profit organizations and the state.

The church's primary role in work in such programs consists of promoting self-determination for poor persons and anchoring the connection of fragile families in networks of support in their local communities. In the course of such work the church seeks to offer compassionate caregiving *as if* the families are approaching Jesus Christ. The church gives witness *through* our actions to the Christ we seek to imitate, whether or not religious words are spoken. At appropriate times and places—in ministries that are specifically advertised as such—mainline Christians may offer verbal interpretations of their faith.

Creating Bonds, Not Self-Sufficiency

Wanda Holcombe of southwest Texas described one church's response: "Sometimes Texas prides itself in being #1 in the least amount of social services," she explains, and "this is not something to be proud of... It's not like other major cities, other places where you have all of these community services... It has been the role of the church and the not-for-profits to help..."[1] She is proud, however, of the collaboration between the state, not-for-profits, and congregations in finding and training mentors for families who are moving from welfare support to employment:

> The Family Pathfinders Program is a team mentoring program in the congregation that works with a family that the Texas Human Services Department selects... There is a covenant relationship between...the families who participate and the team... Sometimes teams stay longer and work with a family if they need continuous help, but at least it's a one-year commitment, and so that part is dealing with how to help people move beyond the poverty level...[2]

Mentors are trained in the dynamics of poverty and in knowledge of the services that are available in a particular city. People are also trained in the mentoring process so that they know that

> They are not there to tell people what they should do but to help people create a plan for what they want to do with their life and then help them figure out how they can actualize that plan. Many teams go beyond the first year to continue with the mentoring. There is an 80 percent rate of success of the people who have participated in the program who are now off of welfare.[3]

Such programs draw families whose relationships to society may be tenuous into a web of family and friend conversation, job networking, and social contact that so-called "self-sufficient" middle-class families take for granted.

Try for a moment to imagine a nuclear family that never interacts with any other group in the process of raising its children. It does not attend church but prays only in its own family circle. It raises all its own food so the children never enter a grocery store. It uses no technology of any form. It does not send children to school but teaches them at home, using books and materials written only by the nuclear parents themselves. It never sends the children to doctors or nurses but attends to all its health care itself, drawing only on the parents' medical sense. Such families do exist within the context of closed communities or tight kinship systems, and the rest of our society may consider them a bit odd. But this hypothetical family does not live in a closed community—it simply chooses never to visit grandparents, extended families members, or friends; nor does it attend any community functions but keeps entirely to itself. Our society would deem such a nuclear family neglectful of its children, especially if a medical crisis occurs that jeopardizes children's health.

My point is that strong families are interdependent with society in a variety of ways that they take for granted. They are self-determined; they are *not* "self-sufficient."[4] Fragile families, such as those moving from public assistance to employment, should not be expected to become self-sufficient; rather they need strong, interdependent bonds that anchor them to society. The church can assist to create these bonds, but it cannot do that job alone.

Anchoring Fragile Families in Society

The research of the Annie E. Casey Foundation has demonstrated that "children do better when their families are strong, and families do better when they live in communities that help them to succeed..."[5] Wealthy parents in almost any country interact with far-flung communities that extend beyond the borders of countries; they have access to high quality food, clothing, transportation, housing, education, and job networks. Middle-class parents in the United States choose from a variety of foods in supermarkets. Many own their homes through mortgage programs. They take their children to free public libraries at a young age, and they educate their children in preschools, public schools, and pay-as-you-go colleges that provide scholarship help. They expand their children's education and meet their children's social needs through associations and institutions, including sports teams, scouts, music and art lessons, and religious organizations.

Poor families often live in communities where institutions and associations are fragile; access to fresh produce, successful schools, medical care, and recreation may be severely limited. Though other community assets may strengthen the community's network, poor families often suffer from "the poverty of tenuous connections."[6] The church is often the last community institution left in poor communities. Many of the church's efforts in pastoral care and mission, such as participation in the Family Pathfinders program, are specifically aimed at enhancing community supports for families and children.

Who Is Equipped to Stand by Families with Children?

Who is best equipped to stand by families and children who are poor and low income? This we debate. Once, governments were understood to be formed largely for military defense. After the Civil War in the United States a new philosophy of government emerged, one that gave government a role in economic and social policy.[7] The "private sector"—especially women—tried through religious and charitable organizations to assist veterans, widows, immigrants, and destitute others and found the task overwhelming and needing centralization. They pushed government to get involved. Though the United States never developed an expansive European social welfare state, it did create government agencies to assist poor mothers. It created legislation to protect children, following the lead of animal anti-cruelty organizations. For a few years it coordinated care for children under the auspices of the federal government's Children's Bureau that operated under the hugely popular Sheppard-Towner Act.[8] For the last century-and-a-half government and the private sector have engaged in a push-and-pull over who has responsibility and is best equipped to assist poor families and children.

Currently, the United States government is pushing faith communities and the private sector closer to the center of responsibility by pulling funds for government programs for poor persons. Reducing poverty has not been a governmental priority in the United States since the early 1980s; instead, the United States government has emphasized reducing welfare subsidies for those who are poor.[9] A change in the United States tax code did reduce child poverty in the late 1990s, but child poverty in the United States has begun to rise again.[10] Indicators of child well-being, other than poverty rates, have shown that child welfare has worsened since the year 2000. The Annie E. Casey Foundation reported that in 2003 the number of children living in low income families increased by a half million, and "in addition to the rise in child poverty, there was an increase in the percentage of low birth weight babies between 2000–2002, an increase in infant mortality for the first time in forty years, and a rise in the teen death rate."[11]

In recent years, the potential of partnerships between government and the private sector, including businesses, foundations, and faith-based agencies has been widely touted and publicized in national and international venues. This potential has come to the fore particularly since "devolution." Devolution, or dismantling federal public programs that support children and families, and placing the funds for those programs in the states and in local communities, intends to overcome the criticism that people far from a local situation cannot make adequate judgments—rather the resources should be in the hands of local people who know what is going on. That sounds like a good idea, one that people of all political persuasions should be able to agree on. However, when devolution became reality with the first TANF funding, the downside appeared. Devolution did not reduce bureaucracy. Agencies had to scramble to develop proposals to the federal government to receive funds, and funds went unused. Diverse social policies in the fifty states were created. And now, a family with a child who needs to tap into the social service system and moves from one state to another state faces an array of names, policies, and procedures that are as complicated as the United States tax code.

What about faith-based organizations that have received so much encouragement in recent years? In a report titled "Community Ministries and Government Funding," United Methodist agencies remind the church that its involvement in anti-poverty programs is nothing new. Analyzing six cases of congregations involved in government-funded ministries, the document notes that the partnerships between government funding agencies and congregations have been successful when the congregation has adequate seed money, has trained personnel, and has known how to document and report results. In some cases, however, the resources of the congregation were stretched too thin when the government paid for services slowly, when volunteers had good will but insufficient training, when the necessary paperwork was overwhelming, or when the results of the project could not be adequately evaluated and documented.[12]

Partnerships That Stand by Children

The partnerships between foundations, social service organizations, and educational organizations have been part of the anti-poverty landscape in the United States for a long time. Again, results and philosophies differ. People who research and befriend low-income and poor communities, families, and children approach these communities with different perspectives. One approach argues that it is a social priority to identify the neediest individuals and groups and to target services to them. It assumes that children and families in poor communities need assistance from outside the community to edify community networks. This approach points to the history of change in neighborhoods that once were home to people with diverse economic means. For one reason or another, wealthy and middle-class people and businesses left the community, taking their leadership, their jobs, and their money elsewhere. When these assets were not replaced, the communities became needy. This approach assumes that government, foundations, faith-based agencies, and others from outside the community must bring assets into needy communities for these communities to succeed. The other approach assumes that poor communities are rich in initiative, energy, and self-determination. Though they may be poor in material assets, they may have unidentified associational and institutional assets in place on which to build. This approach looks to the leaders within poor communities to set the direction for change in those communities. It primarily seeks to mobilize assets within the community, rather than to seek resources from outside the community.[13]

Each side represents an element of truth: society is morally obligated to assist the neediest persons, and low-income communities do have assets that can be strengthened to promote self-determination and participation. Each approach can build its partnership with communities on the values of accountable shepherding, mutual friendship, and sacrificial service.[14] In the end, these approaches are not necessarily exclusive; rather, they represent two sides of a community coin. The community change in the United States represented by the needs-based view has been well demonstrated; the problem arises when that historical view gives rise to the conclusion that because significant assets left the community, the *only* help for poor communities comes from outside. The needs-based approach may fail to look at the assets remaining in communities or moving into communities and may create attitudes within communities of "us, the providers" against "them, the needy ones." The asset-based approach promotes a positive attitude toward poor and low-income communities. It "maps" the networks, associations, and institutions within the community that are already doing a good job. It suggests that organizers in such communities "mobilize" community leaders to determine the direction of intervention and change within the neighborhood. But it may give short shrift to equipping community leaders to draw assets from outside communities into their local neighborhoods. In other words, as community leaders identify directions for communities, they may well advocate for the support of government, foundations, and other groups who can help from beyond the neighborhood itself. Yet some entities, notably government, are increasingly unwilling to assist.

Both the asset-based and needs-based approaches represent persons committed to reducing poverty. Yet their conflict potentially plays into the hands of larger economic forces at work in the global economy. In the United States today, as in the world in general, two political currents, a rushing torrent from the right and a stream from the left, are converging toward a common river.

The Threatening Torrent from the Right

The torrent from the right rushes to erode the banks of the welfare state safety net of government-sponsored Social Security, Medicare, Medicaid, food, and other public support programs. This torrent threatens the social benefits that created the so-called middle-class and provide support for low-income and poverty-stricken people. This torrent places the future of local economies far away from local decision making in the power of "capital"—it seeks to free up as much money as possible for private investment.

This torrent represents the "market fundamentalism" described by John Williamson as "no anti-poverty program."[15] By design or by ignorance, it lumps all persons who are poor into the "undeserving" category. Our local communities, especially the ones that are struggling, are left to fend for themselves as best they can.

The Stream from the Left

The stream from the left wishes to enhance poor communities, whether in the United States or elsewhere, internally, from the inside out, depending solely upon the assets of local people. It seeks to free them from any dependence on government, foundations, or corporations. This stream intends to place the power of local communities—and economies—only in small, locally owned businesses and projects, away from the overweening power of governments, corporations, and foundations. It assumes that the power of large corporations will always seek to justify itself and can never be used toward positive ends.

In the name of the self-determination of local communities, this stream at its extreme would dismantle government and foundation support for social services and discourage corporate investment in communities where it exists. Any support for low-income or poor families and children would have to arise from within low-income neighborhoods themselves, rather than being provided by government or other entities from outside neighborhoods. In other words, children and families must wait until low-income neighborhoods get their act together.

Local communities and economies must be strengthened by nourishing the assets within them, but I am concerned about the way that, in practical effect, isolationist attitudes from the stream on the left will converge with socially exclusive attitudes in the torrent from the right, drowning our most vulnerable families and children in the rapids created by the convergence.[16]

Utilizing Local Community Assets

The direction of culture, government, the economy, the environment, and the military impinges directly on local communities, changing the conditions in which local communities support families and children. For this reason, low-income local communities must participate in directing the course of government, foundations, and corporations, as well as building the assets of their local communities. The kinds of assets and energies present in local communities make a difference in the ways that the church's pastoral care, mission, or evangelism needs to be developed.

To Stand by Whom: All Families or Poor Families?

This chapter presumes that every family, regardless of income level, needs and gets help raising children from a wide range of community friends, associations, and institutions. The problem arises when—in the presence of exceptionally high needs, inadequate income, and fragile community networks—this assistance is hard to find or slow in coming. The question is: How does society respond to the needs of children and families?

The European welfare state solves this problem by universalizing assistance to children as Social Security, so that all people, even those who don't technically "need" assistance, get some help. Universalized assistance reduces the stigma and eliminates much of the onus of having to demonstrate need. Universalized assistance in the form of Social Security dramatically reduced poverty among the elderly; even so, the United States sustained its social programs for families and children as needs-based programs. Needs-based programs require measurements. In 1963 the federal government established a way to test for poverty, identifying that a family spent roughly one-third of its income on food and two-thirds on everything else. The poverty "line" was established as three times the cost of food. In the intervening years, the structure of budgets of families has changed—food has become less expensive, housing and medical care have become a larger portion of the family budget. [17] Still, the United States calculates "poverty" on the same basis as it did in 1963. The poverty guideline provides a baseline measure for government aid; it does not suggest that once a family's income rises above the poverty line, the family has enough money to provide for children's needs. To compensate for this problem, state measurements refer to families at 130%, 150%, or 200% of the poverty line. Increasingly, research groups such as the National Center for Children in Poverty at Columbia University, the Annie E. Casey Foundation, the Children's Defense Fund, and others are referring to "low-income" families and children as those whose income is below 200 percent of the poverty guideline.[18]

What Has "Welfare Reform" Achieved?

In 1995–1996 the United States Congress confirmed the most significant social policy changes since the 1930s. In 1995 Congress significantly increased the Earned Income Tax Credit—the change was supported by both parties, created no controversy, and went unnoticed by the general public. Of all the changes in welfare distribution from 1995–1997, this change in the tax code drove the reduction in the young child poverty rate from a high of 26 percent in 1993 to a low of 17 percent in 2003. Then, in 2004—2005, the child poverty rate climbed to 18 percent.[19] The controversial Personal Responsibility and Work Opportunity Reconciliation Act of 1996 (PRWORA) represents a change in the cultural attitude toward mothering. In direct contradiction to the intent of Aid for Dependent Children (ADC) in the 1930s and subsequent legislation that supported mothers of infants and toddlers at home with their children, PRWORA required single-parent mothers of young children to be employed rather than receive welfare benefits. Other provisions of the act allowed mothers to keep more of their cash assistance while earning wages and imposed time limits on that assistance. Since 1996 poverty researchers at universities and foundations have followed the effects of this requirement, with the following conclusions.[20]

The employment requirement has in some cases increased income for families who are poor, largely because the employment requirement was accompanied with legislation from 1995–1997 that increased the minimum wage, increased the benefits a working mother could keep as her income rose, and enacted State Child Health Insurance benefits.Full-time employment of a parent, however, does not mean that a previously poverty-stricken family has moved from poverty to low-income. At the time that PRWORA was enacted, most people who worked with poverty-stricken persons knew that many mothers needed time and patience from support persons to develop the skills to negotiate the multiple demands of child care, transportation, and employment. The employment of single mothers after PRWORA rose from 70 percent to 85 percent, prior to the 2001 recession.[21]

Some unintended effects of the push toward poor mothers' employment have been documented. In one of the most successful and best-evaluated projects, the Minnesota Family Investment Plan, researchers found that single mothers increased employment but married mothers decreased their employment. They found little effect on marriage and divorce of recipients, despite the emphasis on family formation in the legislation.[22] Furthermore, breastfeeding among mothers of infants decreased.[23] Other reports indicate that children have benefited from a rise in their mothers' self-esteem and from enrichment in accredited child care centers. Many mothers are newly successfully employed, even if they and their children are still impoverished. Other mothers cannot sustain employability. Researchers have identified the variables that reduce mothers' employability. These data set an agenda for the church's ministries of pastoral care, evangelism, and mission with families and children in impoverished areas.

Some mothers have high levels of health and mental health problems, such that they need assistance with becoming qualified for unemployment benefits as persons with disabilities. Others have erratic employment records because of four conditions, emphasized by the Annie E. Casey Foundation: depression, substance abuse, domestic violence,[24] or prior incarceration.[25] Research on children whose parents have been incarcerated is particularly sparse.[26] Ministries with individuals and families that assist with reducing depression, ending drug and alcohol abuse, escaping or dealing with domestic violence, and transitioning from prison provide critical support for these parents and their children. Often, persons trying to change their lives seek spiritual support.

The direction of U.S. social policy also shapes the lives of immigrant children. Immigrants who arrived in the U.S. after 1996 cannot access most "safety net" programs, though access to Supplemental Social Security insurance and food stamps was restored. Immigrant children suffer economic insecurity and language barriers. Most often, their parents are married and employed, so the policy emphases in PRWORA do not apply; but their parents are often lacking high school education and employment with health insurance. They would be most helped by increasing the minimum wage, the EITC, child care subsidies, and programs of English as a Second Language.[27]

Ministries that support families and children, however, do not exist in a vacuum—rather, the community and governmental supports are constantly in flux, and, in today's climate, under duress. The state and federal government and private sectors do not guarantee continued support for accredited child care centers that serve low-income employed parents. Some legislators have pressed to reduce support for early childhood education programs, such as Head Start, and for child and maternal health, including the popular SCHIP program. Furthermore, legislators and researchers often assume that beneficial effects of "welfare reform" will trickle down to children, but the effects on "welfare reform" specifically on children are not necessarily evaluated.[28] If partnerships between the government and the private sector are paving the way for the community supports for the future, the church will need to build its capacities for tracking, evaluating, and influencing social policy, as well as offering direct social service.

Do Other Countries Necessarily Follow Trends in United States Policy?

Even in the late nineteenth century, the debate over national support for mothering crossed international borders; now technology and international travel allows even more cross-fertilization of ideas. In recent decades Canada has given the provinces more discretion in their benefits distribution. Some communities in Germany began imposing time limits on eligibility for public assistance. Great Britain enacted a working families' tax credit, similar to the EITC, though it benefited families with higher wages than in the United States.[29] In contrast to the United States, Tony Blair declared child poverty a national priority in the United Kingdom in 1999 and set out to eradicate it in a generation. He increased cash welfare benefits and tax benefits, Sure Start early education programs, child care subsidy funds, and tax-free child savings accounts. Spending on children increased 75 percent, 1 percent of the GDP, between 1997 and 2004.[30] All of the countries mentioned above, however, already have substantially more benefits in place for children and families—most notably, national health insurance plans.

The Partial Component in International Social Policy: Health and Welfare?

Danziger and Danziger identified ways in which the experience of the United States and the United Kingdom might inform the development of social policy in Mexico. From the experience of the United States they cited stable economic growth, an emphasis on education that raises the skills of people who are poor, an emphasis on work, and income security for the elderly and for families with children. The gaping hole in their analysis is health policy: they fail to point out that the United States, unlike other industrialized nations, has continually struggled to bring health care to all of its people.

For most countries, health and welfare concerns intersect directly with economic stability and child welfare. The HIV-AIDS pandemic, for example, will change the economy of some countries as HIV-AIDS wipes out those countries' wage-earning generation between ages twenty and fifty: those breadwinners most likely to support both children and the elderly. Other health concerns determine whether adults will be economically productive and able to care for dependents. Health and welfare concerns dominated the report of Kofi Anan, written in preparation for the United Nations General Assembly Special Session on Children in September 2001.[31]

His report, "We the Children: End-decade review of the follow up to the World Summit for Children," reviewed the progress on the international goals for child welfare that were established in 1990 at the World Summit, after the *Convention on the Rights of the Child* was adopted.[32] The report reflects the health and welfare emphases of the international community. Its first three, largest sections review the progress and regress in (1) health, nutrition, water, and environmental sanitation; (2) in education and literacy; and (3) in special protection measures, including child labor, children affected by armed conflict, refugee children, sexual abuse and exploitation, and juvenile justice. The section on "Freedom from Violence" concerns the exploitation of children, especially girls, physically, psychologically, sexually, and economically. These kinds of exploitation, including domestic abuse, emotional manipulations, sexual abuse, coerced prostitution, and labor abuse, put children into unhealthy environments. His report signals enormous health and welfare challenges for children and youth. No one entity—government, civil society, or faith communities—can effectively meet all of these challenges.

"The Church Will Do It...?"

Clergy were aghast in the 1980s when President Reagan announced that, as the government cut back on social services for poor persons, the churches would step in to fill the gap. Churches have long maintained family, health, and welfare ministries.

Churches have supported mental health for many decades. While parents are employed, faith communities often do provide educational programs and support the mental, physical, and spiritual health of children.

Reagan and his successors, however, are presidents, not popes. If they had been leaders of faith communities, they would have realized that faith communities and the Wanda Holcombes of the nation have been augmenting government social services for a long time. Although many committed people are involved in such ministries, many children and their families remain unserved or underserved because such ministries and programs are not extensive enough to meet the need. Other populations have specialized needs that require particular expertise. The need to expand these ministries intensifies as government pulls out of the anti-poverty business. Government, church, non-profits, communities—who will rise to the occasion?

CHAPTER 6

Do We Believe in the Human Rights of the Child?

Shasha and Wendy[1]

Before October 2000, Shasha was a criminal. Some time before that, a man had come to her small, poor town in Eastern Europe. He had smiled and wore good clothes. He had promised her parents he would treat her to a good life. She would travel, drive a car, get an education. They had said, "Go! You are young, but what can we do for you?" Away from her town he had said, "Make some money for me. And don't try to contact your parents."

That's how Shasha came to America. Still her parents' child, she had become an illegal immigrant and prostitute: a criminal.

On October 28, 2000, she became a victim. The United States Congress passed "The Victims of Trafficking and Violence and Protection Act of 2000." This Act criminalized the international traffickers in girls, rather than the women themselves.

Compare a similar scenario: A young-looking man came to Wendy's town in upstate New York and visited the teenage club. He found Wendy and danced with her all night. He found out that she wasn't getting on with her parents. The city is great, he told her. Come with me. Once they were in New York City, he said to her, "Make some money for me. And don't try to contact your parents." They crossed no state or international borders. Still her parents' child and a legal U.S. citizen, now she is a criminal.

On July 22, 2005, National Public Radio reported that New York State could become the first state to declare that child prostitutes need crisis intervention, rather than criminal prosecution.[2] Wendy would become a victim like her international sister if New York passed the legislation "Safe Harbor for Exploited Youth." She would have the same rights as a child who becomes a victim of an international sex trafficking ring. As of May 2007, the bill had not become law, having passed in the New York General Assembly in 2006, but not the Senate.[3]

UNICEF estimates that 1.2 million children are trafficked for a variety of exploited purposes each year.[4] Did international trafficking of women and girls reach the Congressional agenda because the international community was discussing the *Convention on the Rights of the Child (CRC) Optional Protocol on the Sale of Children, Child Prostitution, and Child Pornography,*[5] which the U.S. signed on July 5, 2000, and ratified on December 23, 2002? Is the United States, the only country never to ratify the *CRC*, slow to protect its own children because opponents never allowed the *CRC* to provoke widespread discussion on the human rights of the child in the United States?[6]

Local congregations and ministries can be very good at building skills in their congregants and, at the same, time be unaware of the larger legal frameworks that support the rights of children. These frameworks seem remote from children's lives, until a specific case demonstrates the way that these legal systems protect children. One such system is the web of international law that has emerged from the Universal Declaration of Human Rights. Mainline denominations have largely supported human rights as part of their social advocacy; child advocates in denominational offices and congregations have sought justice for children, in part, by promoting the discussion of the *Convention on the Rights of the Child (CRC).* In so doing, they have tried to bring to light the serious ways that children can be exploited.

The Convention on the Rights of the Child

Many international treaties since the *Universal Declaration of Human Rights* in 1948 have defined the rights of populations who need special attention. The *CRC* addresses the unique human rights issues that apply to children. The *CRC* affirms the child and his or her family as the basic social unit in need of protection. The Preamble connects the international community's "faith in fundamental human rights and in the dignity and worth of the human person" with "the family, as the fundamental group of society and the natural environment for the growth and well-being of all its members, particularly children." The Preamble affirms that "the child, for the full and harmonious development of his or her personality, should grow up in a family environment, in an atmosphere of happiness, love and understanding" and recognizes "the importance of the traditions and cultural values of each people for the protection and harmonious development of the child." It affirms the child's freedom to live within the social ecology that makes the child unique—his or her distinct family, nation, and culture. Within this social ecology, the *Convention* affirms that a child has a right

- to free expression of his or her views;
- to free association and peaceable assembly;
- to "the highest attainable standard of health";
- to "a standard of living adequate for the child's physical mental, spiritual, moral and social development,"
- to "education";
- to play;
- to diversity of sources of information, especially those which are aimed at the promotion of his or her social, spiritual, and moral well-being and physical and mental health;
- to protection and humanitarian assistance when seeking refugee status, with and without his or her parents;
- to full rights for children with disabilities;
- to preparation for a responsible life in a free society, in the spirit of understanding, peace, tolerance, equality of the sexes, and friendship among all peoples, ethnic, national and religious groups and persons of indigenous origin.[7]

Through these kinds of provisions for the positive rights of the child, the *Convention* presents a vision for every child's flourishing.

Although the vision of the CRC considers childhood in the family to be normative, the CRC also recognizes situations in which children cannot flourish because their rights are being violated. Individual adults, families, and nation-states at times need to be constrained from violating the human rights of the child. The most public restraint against adults allows governments, following proper procedures, to separate children from parents when parents are abusive or neglectful. Governments must also prevent the violation of the human rights of the children from forces outside the family. Governments agree:

- to prevent discrimination of any kind, irrespective of the child's or his or her parent's or legal guardian's race, colour [sic], sex, language, religion, political or other opinion, national, social or ethnic origin, property, disability, birth or other status;
- to prevent children from being separated from parents against their will, particularly across national borders;
- to prevent the illicit transfer of children across borders;
- to prevent arbitrary interference with a child's privacy, family, home or correspondence, or to unlawful attacks on his or her honour [sic] or reputation;
- to prevent traditional practices that harm children's health.
- to prevent children from being used as combatants in war.[8]

These rights and restraints offer a vision of the variety of ways in which, at best, children's flourishing is supported, and at worst, children are exploited.

The *CRC* has been ratified by all countries belonging to the United Nations, except the United States and Somalia.[9] Each country that has ratified the treaty is allowed to register "reservations" when the language of the treaty conflicts with a country's practices or culture, so that the country clearly states how it will implement the treaty. Even so, "children's rights" creates controversy.

The Difficulty of Talking about Human Rights of the Child

The rhetoric of human rights attempts to develop a common language in the midst of international diversity. It provides a way of expressing our beliefs about who individual persons are and how they should relate to one another. It expresses the duties, responsibilities, and claims people have on one another. Talk of human rights allows people in different countries, or with different viewpoints within one country, to struggle toward common values about which they can be mutually supportive. It is finally about the power of the international community to persuade the governments of countries to act in accord with agreed-upon values. So, it represents the persuasive power of the international community against local power, and it raises suspicions.

Talk of human rights is difficult in part because the epistemological foundations for the discourse are constantly shifting. It has legal, moral, religious, and practical sources.[10] With these varied sources the international discourse of human rights might be considered a version of what some scholars call "civil religion." Civil religion may be unifying; it also leads to culture wars.

In the United States, civil religion refers to the values transmitted through religion *and* the "sacred" documents in political life—the Declaration of Independence, the Constitution, the Gettysburg Address, etc. Civil religion in the international arena, then, reflects mixtures of values and traditions that are handed down from political documents held in international esteem, such as the Magna Carta, the Bill of Rights, the Universal Declaration of Human Rights, the Uniform Civil Code in India, and 1996 South African constitution, and explicitly sacred documents, such as the Bible or the Koran. Human rights' discourse records our debates concerning our deep-seated secular and interfaith beliefs about who we are and the social reality in which we live.

The discourse of human rights of the child adds further difficulties. When the Enlightenment philosophers developed the language of rights, they had in mind the idea that property-owning men in different classes with power in society ought to respect each other as human beings. The documents that originally laid the legal groundwork for rights challenged the power of the King of England on behalf of property-owning men, rights that were built upon and claimed anew by the gentry of the American colonies (still the property-owning men). Rights-talk did not originally apply to intimate relationships between husband and wife, master and slave, or parent and child. In the nineteenth century, the discussion of rights began to apply to adults in domestic settings. The early twentieth century brought with it the inevitable discussion about the rights of children. Here lies the problem: as the intimate circle narrows, the language of rights becomes more difficult. Rights-talk about intimate relationships acknowledges that something may go drastically wrong, not only between the king and his subject, but between the mother and her daughter.

Christian religious narratives lend superficial support to the idea that tension occurs in public but not intimate relationships.

In the Hebrew Scriptures, just and wise kings are expected, but they are few and far between. Prophets and petitioners who seek to modify the king's judgments and bring nations to account reflect the tensions between the ideals of leadership and real life. The New Testament offers no such resolution for tense intimate relationships but assumes that the human parent and child, who relate to each other through tenderness, mercy, and compassion, can be the metaphor for the Godly parent and child. In many of our cultural-religious stories the wise king is the exception, but the tender parent is the norm. These stories suggest that confusing family relationships with power-laden talk of human rights grates against our deepest desires and most heartfelt expectations. In other words, talk of the human rights of the child lands us squarely in the bifurcation of private and public, love and justice described in chapter 2.

The Fear of the Human Rights of the Child: Families Know Best[11]

People around the world with very different political and social agendas have debated whether the discourse of human rights is helpful in the domain of family life, including childhood. These arguments lie on the intersection of law and culture and underline the concern of many that rights-talk has the power to change culture and even religion.

For some, rights-talk is liberalizing: it has the power to break down traditional cultures, specifically their family practices. Thandabantu Nhlapo argues that in the minds of many Africans, rights-talk reflects the values of Western culture. After summarizing the arguments against human rights-talk, he admits his fear that the human rights-talk in the 1996 South African constitution has the power to influence the culture and family customs of African communities.[12]

For others, rights-talk is conserving: it has the power to eliminate gains that vulnerable populations have already won. Nivedita Menon, an Indian feminist, claims that the equality of women has not always been served by the documents produced by the legal human rights tradition. In India, the human rights-inspired Indian Constitution produced legislation regulating Hindu marriage in 1955–1956 that actually reduced women's rights in some local areas. Feminists in India have backed away from believing that a Uniform Civil Code would protect women's rights. Individual communities, in her opinion, might advance women's rights further than communities informed by the kind of uniform consensus sought by human rights discussion.[13]

These concerns deposit us, in a very practical way, squarely in the middle of the debate over modernity and postmodernity. Modernity codified the idea of human rights into constitutional and legal documents that made the language of human rights a common, international conceptual tool. This conceptual tool is dependent upon the idea that people across cultures can affirm a set of values they hold in common. Postmodernity heralds the demise of what are often called "grand narratives" and questions whether any consensus can be achieved around universal values. It argues in favor of recognizing the importance of local knowledge, traditions, customs, and differences. Many people sense that each position holds some truth: some universal values that the international community ought to fight for must exist, such as the value that restrains adults from exploiting children; but we must preserve some way to respect the local traditions, customs, cultures, and practices of the diverse peoples who populate the globe.

In the United States, the *CRC* has never been ratified, in part, because the United States' constitution anticipated this portion of the modernity/postmodernity debate. Early on the United States gave the states jurisdiction over family issues. It generally gives smaller units, the family, the community, or the state more authority over children's behavior than the federal government. Take, for example, encouraging children to participate in society. While the state must establish procedures and policies, such as the age at which children can drive a car, the adults responsible for children often prohibit or enable whether a child *will* drive a car. Does a state law that allows children to drive a car override parents' veto power when parents believe a child is not ready to drive? Not usually. Yet, at times, federal courts do override decisions of states and communities, as the Supreme Court did in *Brown vs. the Board of Education*, the decision that forced public school desegregation.

Such differences loom large in debates over the *CRC* because people differ about the party that has the authority to make decisions about children. Opponents to the *CRC* fear that international law that promotes particular rights for children will remove exactly such authority from parents and local communities. They claim that the *CRC* invades family life on "hot button" issues: it potentially turns children against their parents and promotes abortion and family planning that contravenes various religious practices.[14]

The language of the human rights of the child carefully negotiates this dilemma by stating that children participate "according to their developmental ability." But what party—the child, the parent, or the state—finally determines what children's "developmental ability" allows?

The Hope for the Human Rights of the Child: Human Cruelty Can Be Restrained

If the discourse of human rights is so contested, what makes the dialogue on the human rights of the child compelling to so many? As people encounter humanity's ongoing capacity for cruelty, especially when it is unleashed in the violence of corruption and war, they turn to human rights discourse. The destruction of two World Wars crystallized the international conversation on human rights in the *Universal Declaration of Human Rights,* the charter document of the United Nations.[15] Human rights-talk defends adults against the effects of war and corruption; human rights of the child are promoted for the same reason. Children are often the victims of war and corruption—directly, as they are conscripted into militias, killed, maimed, or raped by an army seeking to demoralize a culture; and indirectly, as in the aftermath of war they are left with poor nutrition, disease, destroyed schools and hospitals, and hot munitions and land mines. Much of the *CRC* and the conversation it has provoked seeks to create agreement around proper treatment of children by states—for example, states will provide children with proper birth registration and all of the rights that come with citizenship. It prevents children's abduction from their families across international borders. The *CRC* protects families against the invasion of the state in matters that are usually transmitted through family life—religion, culture, and identity.

Just as it is horrifying to think of children subjected to the violence of war, it repulses most people to think of children being subjected to violence in the family. The *CRC* addresses not only public violence but violence in intimate family territory. It recognizes that the state has a duty to protect children in those cases where families neglect and abuse children.

The conflict comes when international culture defines "harm" at odds with local cultures. The most contested cases state the point: is it harmful to allow female circumcision? Is it harmful to stone women who have had sex, consensual or forced, with men other than their husbands? Is it harmful to allow older men to engage in sex with premenstrual girls? Is it harmful to provide girls with less education or protein than boys? Is it harmful to conscript young girls and boys in military service? Is it harmful to allow medically safe abortions, even under certain extenuating circumstances, including a threat to the health of the mother? Should child prostitutes be charged as criminals, or should they be considered victims of abuse and neglect? Each of these questions represents a historically accepted practice that local communities have considered just but international dialogue has contested.

Even when people generally agree over what constitutes harm to children, they are confused over positive and negative rights of the child. Marshall and Parvis use the language of "human rights of the child" to signify that the child is a particular case within the general discussion of human rights.[16] In general, the human rights of the child include participation in the community, the family, and the culture into which a child is born. When these positive rights cannot be sustained because of neglect or abuse, the negative rights of the child to protection from the community, the family, and the culture come into play. People hear "children's rights" and think this confers upon a child the right to contend against community, family, or culture even when no situation exists that society defines as harmful. That, however, is neither the principle nor the text of the *CRC*.

For these reasons, in the United States most mainline denominations, especially their women's and child advocacy units, have considered the discourse of human rights to be generally consistent with love and justice in their religious traditions. They have worked hard to keep the importance of the *CRC* in their denominational discussion. They have referred to the *CRC* and other human rights declarations when they have discussed the treatment of juvenile offenders, the recruitment of child soldiers, the protection of children from violence, and other children's concerns.

Children's Flourishing: Health, Welfare, and Capabilities

The idea of the human rights of the child emerged from the United Nations' health and welfare emphases that have defined harm, protected against it, and promoted conditions for flourishing. These emphases are outlined in the General Secretary's report for the United Nations General Assembly Special Summit on Children, held in May 2002. When we talk of human development, we are often talking about the way that we measure, qualitatively and quantitatively, human health and welfare. These measures describe the condition of the human community, assess the social conditions that help human beings fulfill the freedom given to them by their human rights, determine the effect of policy choices on those conditions, and chart the changes in conditions that promote or deny the exercise of human rights. Health and welfare language depends on science, rationality, and common sense—by itself it does not adjudicate the meaning of "harm," "neglect" and "abuse."

The language of human capabilities, developed by Amartya Sen and Martha Nussbaum and used in the United Nations' *Human Development Report,* attempts to bridge the distance between rights-talk and health and welfare. Human capabilities are defined as "what human beings are able to be and to do."[17] This concept suggests that nation-states, through law and supportive institutions, are responsible for creating the conditions that allow people to choose the direction for their lives. It contends that societies can agree on some universal values. In *Women and Human Development: The Capabilities Approach* Martha Nussbaum develops philosophical justification for the idea of capabilities and refutes three arguments against universal values: "the argument from culture," "the argument from the good of diversity," and "the argument from paternalism."[18]

1. *"In our culture women want men to head households."* Echoing the sentiments of Thandabantu Nhlapo (above), some contend that universal values that support the equality of women represent a Western imperialism toward Eastern cultures. Against this claim Nussbaum argues that the traditions of women's defiance and

struggle for equality can be found within the ancient strands of tradition of every culture. Every culture has narratives that assert male dominance and narratives that assert women's rejection of that dominance. Analogously, we could say that every culture has narratives that assume that children are the property of their parents and their communities and may be exploited accordingly, and every culture offers alternative traditions that uphold the dignity and value of children. The value of human dignity and freedom is communicated from *within* local traditions and narratives and seeks more public expression, rather than being a value that is being imposed from some Western grand narrative.

2. *"We need to protect the diversity and uniqueness of cultures."* This argument suggests that when universal values such as equality are promoted, they reduce the richness of a culture by flattening out various unique strands within that culture. Nussbaum argues back that oppressive norms are the least rich and stultify human expression. Those that support human freedom and choice create diversity of expression in human community. In other words, the universal values suggested by the capabilities approach help the human community grow in its particularity and its diversity. These values would support justice and love in a child's life by promoting the conditions for maturation that help children develop in the ways that most fit their own gifts and personalities, rather than in ways proscribed by others.

3. *"People don't want other people making decisions for them."* Echoing the sentiments of Nivedita Menon (above), proponents of this view believe that more freedom is possible when people negotiate with local communities for that freedom, rather than with larger governing entities. Nussbaum argues that the universally held values promoted by the capabilities approach specifically support the political conditions that are needed for genuine freedom of choice. A woman can genuinely choose a traditional life if she has the choice for other life paths. In the case of children, the capabilities approach supports universal values that allow a child to grow and develop in a way consistent with his or her sense of self and exercise of freedom, in connection with his or her family and immediate social ecology.

Nussbaum proposes a list of basic capabilities that government should support to support conditions of justice in India at this time. To develop this list she interviewed poor Indian women about the capabilities they would not want to give up, once they were achieved. These capabilities include: (1) Life: being able to live and not die prematurely or have life so reduced that it is not worth living; (2) Bodily Health: being able to have good health, including nutrition, reproductive health, and shelter; (3) Bodily Integrity: being able to move place to place and to be free from bodily assault; (4) Senses, Imagination, and Thought: being able to use one's senses, imagination, thinking, and reasoning processes; (5) Emotions: being able to love and to give care to persons outside ourselves, and to form a conception of the good life and to plan one's life accordingly; (6) Practical Reason: being able to form a concept of the good, to reflect on it, and to plan one's life in accordance with it; (7) Affiliation: being able to relate to others, showing them concern, justice, and friendship; (8) Other Species: being able to live with concern for the world of plants, animals, and nature; (9) Play: being able to laugh, play, and enjoy forms of recreation; (10) Political and Material Control over One's Environment: being able to participate in political processes and to hold property on an equal basis with others.[19]

When political societies support such capabilities for women's growth, they in turn contribute to children's growth. The affiliate needs of love flourish best when they are supported by the conditions of justice, and the conditions of justice bring a fullness of life because they make possible the flourishing of love. The conditions of justice and the possibilities of love are essential for the most vulnerable of human beings among us.

Though Sen and Nussbaum's work is grounded in modern ethical and philosophical perspectives, it provides rooms for the "postmodern" personality that is not bound by "a" tradition but understands itself to evaluate critically and be shaped by many traditions in international conversation.

Love, Justice, and the Human Rights of the Child

Christian theological tradition suggests that the care of children resides at the center of God's mission. It affirms that children are made in the image and likeness of God. It affirms likewise that as we care for or discard children, we care for or discard God. Such doctrines have led Christian denominations to affirm human rights as a part of their narrative and tradition.[20]

Methodist Bishop Aldo Etchegoyen, human rights activist of Argentina, suggests a simple definition of what we mean by love, justice, and the human rights of the child. "Justice," he says, "is bread on the table."[21] If a child has no bread on the table, the child's capabilities have been diminished. Bread may be absent because war caused the child to flee from his home, because the toxicity of the soil has blighted the grain crop, because systems of production have not allowed bread to reach his family at a price they can pay, because his parents are sick and unable to buy the bread. Bread may be present on the table but may be absent from her plate because her rights are being violated. Her parents may think it is more important to give the largest of a meager portion to the father, to the educated child, to the older child, or to the boy child. In all of these situations she needs conditions that bring justice—social conditions of peace that allow the adults of her family to harvest their gardens, to maintain their businesses, and to seek employment, in order that adequate bread is available. Once enough bread is available, social and cultural conditions must allow her access to her portion of bread—she must be deemed human and worthy of being fed what her body needs. Clearly, she needs justice to survive, to have "bread on the table." However, even if an entire loaf of bread is before her day after day, if she has no one with whom to eat the bread, she will still die. She requires love to survive. For we know that children must have human contact, the physical contact of human warmth, the mutual gaze of human eyes, relaxation and delight in the expression of the human face. The point of religious support for the *CRC* is that conditions that support love and justice—that allow affection, protection, and flourishing to be present—are protected under the *CRC*.

If justice is bread on the table, as Bishop Etchegoyen says, families must be able to grow or buy the ingredients to bake the bread. The legal and civil rights of this chapter point us toward social and economic rights for communities, families, and children and toward a system much discussed today: the global economy.

CHAPTER 7

How Do Children Fare in the Current Global Economy?

Economic Globalization: Can We Live with It? Can We Live without It?

As national and international organizations constructed the system of human rights, the system focused mostly on legal and civil rights—those rights guaranteed under law or argued to be self-evident to people in civil societies. As the voice of the countries of the Southern Hemisphere emerged, Southern voices argued for the importance of social and economic rights. The international community has discussed social and economic rights but has gained little consensus on what those rights might be and how they might be guaranteed. In the meantime, the conversation about economic rights has been largely overwhelmed by discussion of the effect of economic globalization. *This chapter argues that the current form of economic globalization on children has negative and positive effects for children.*

Kids and Computers

A blast of cold air, jumbled footsteps, and shuffled chairs, and the rural, South Dakota pastor knows the Kingdom Kids have arrived. He pokes his head into the church basement that is lined with computers. For the next hour the kids will study the Bible, research religious subjects, do homework, and discuss topics important to kids.

The "Kingdom Kids" have signed a contract with the senior pastor and their parents agreeing to pass all their subjects in school, to attend school 95 percent of the time, to do all of their homework, to do community service work, and not to be involved in fights or use any mind-altering substances during the term that they are with the lab. At the end of the school year, if the child lives up to the terms of the contract, they receive the computer they have been working on all year and a brand new printer as a gift of the ministry.[1]

Access to computer technology—or lack of it—sets children apart as "haves" or "have nots." Those who find information on the Internet and have easy access to computers at home, in school, or in public libraries have a ready source of up-to-date information. They have educational programs available to them that are presented in formats that are imagistic and fitting to children's memories. They can communicate with other children all over the world.

Consider the alternative. In Kamina, the Democratic Republic of Congo, an occasional satellite telephone linked Kamina to the outside world. The one doctor could not research a child's medical problem. Business people could not negotiate global trade or maintain contact with others on a regular basis. In July, 2003, businessmen and women gathered to share their hopes for small business ventures. They eagerly desired an Internet café that would connect them to the outside world. In spring of 2005, a nongovernment organization established Internet access and e-mail for Kamina.

Even children in highly affluent countries do not always benefit from easy access to information technology. The computer so programs entertainment for affluent children that they may not develop the logical, analytical, creative, and imaginative abilities they will eventually need. But the total absence of access to information technology harms children. Information technology enhances a child's life in education, health, and even the ability to bring food to the table.

Information technology symbolizes the intimate presence of economic globalization. Normal human interchanges have been altered: during the last day as I worked in Kansas City I asked a question of a person in Africa, received the bibliographic details of writing projects in Germany, and inquired about flight details from friends who live in Connecticut, though their response came from an Internet café in Finland. All of these exchanges are connected to the global economy: most directly, to education, writing and publishing, airline, and recreational industries. But each of those industries depends upon other global technology-based businesses that may not be benign for children. For example, war in the northeast Congo that has killed at least 3.8 to 4 million people, whole villages and children, was fueled at least in part by the technology industries' need for access to coltan, a mineral used in cell phones and lap top computers.[2] In this war, as in so many others, warring forces have conscripted young children to fight. As Kristin Herzog so bluntly states, "Should it be any business of academics—especially in the field of religion—that countless children around the globe are laboring instead of going to school and learning to kill before they can even read and write?"[3] Economic globalization and the systems and industries upon which it depends have the potential to save, enhance, detract from, and destroy children's lives.

What Is Economic Globalization?

Economic globalization occurs when many countries' economies become interdependent through trade, banking systems, and human migration. Economic globalization happens any time people who live in different political systems cross their borders to exchange goods, to develop systems for barter or for the transfer of money or to employ, enslave, or voluntarily seek work in another political system.

The current era of economic globalization began in the sixteenth century when Europe colonized much of the rest of the world. In the period before the Great Depression the large countries' economies were even more economically interdependent than in 2000, according to Harold James, an economic historian.[4] Each era has aroused challenges to globalization that echo the reactions against the current version.

In the sixteenth century, new discoveries of land and products increased Europe's wealth. New European political centers rose in power, and older ones declined. New diseases spread between Europe and colonized lands. Inflation and pricing destabilized Europe's economy, justifying larger armies. New religious language, developed through the Reformation, interpreted these changes. This language changed people's sensibilities about poverty. Rather than assuming that rank, wealth, and poverty were legitimate orderings of the world, some people began to believe that their own wealth and the wealth of others was illegitimate, as was their own poverty or the poverty of others. While Renaissance humanists imagined a world needing to be "tamed," Lutherans and other Christians confessed that poverty and wealth revealed human sin.[5]

In the nineteenth century, globalization was nourished by changes in mobility and communication: the transatlantic cable, railroad, steamship, and refrigeration instigated a new kind of globalization. Standardized items as diverse as the gauge of railway track and the brand of the desired sewing machine enamored the world. New meanings of economic globalization surfaced. Politicians hoped that economic interdependence would deter warfare, and philosophers imagined that the modern nation-state should be concerned not only with military defense, but with social welfare. Economists argued that long-term capital investments helped and short-term investments destabilized society;[6] the gold standard, central banks, and a public lender of last resort would secure the international economy. Again, these changes wrought new beliefs. Ideas about the institutions needed for a global economy emerged, and so did the fears: the common person scrutinized both immigrants and robber barons for foul play. James claims that psychological fears that launched a search for security, an increased welfare state, and a defense against predatory capital also set the stage for the Great Depression.[7]

Whether religious or psychological rhetoric frames the debate, economic globalization upends our values. It disrupts the way we understand our humanity and, at times, what it means to relate to God. Is this crisis warranted by the effects of economic globalization, or are human beings simply too unsophisticated to cope with global economic life? Let us ponder this question as we consider the relationship between economic globalization and the welfare of children in the post–World War II era.

Child Welfare in Industrialized Countries after World War II

After World War II, new relationships and institutions heralded the current form of economic globalization. In the industrialized countries, child welfare improved enormously. Compare the infant mortality rates in three countries that represent different strategies for economic development. The United States developed as a capitalist country with a limited welfare state; Sweden continued as a capitalist country with an expansive welfare state; Yugoslavia emerged with a communist economic strategy. In those countries the five-year averages of infant mortality rates fell:

Deaths per thousand live births[8]			
	1950–1955	1970–1975	1985–1990
United States	28	18	10
Sweden	20	10	6
Yugoslavia	128	45	25

Giovanni Andreas Cornia and Sheldon Danziger conclude that, in the period from 1945 through the early 1970s, in all forms of industrialized countries, child welfare improved, though unevenly. Cornia and Danziger attribute increased child welfare to better nutrition, the beneficial effect of antibiotics, improved preventive and curative health services, increased school enrollment, rapid growth in household incomes, policies that created more equality of income, and nuclear family stability. In capitalist countries the welfare state expanded, increasing pensions, health benefits, unemployment benefits, family allowances, and public assistance. In communist countries subsidies increased for basic foods, children's goods, energy, transportation, and housing. In this "golden age" child welfare blossomed.[9]

Conditions were already developing, however, that slowed the gains in child welfare. Even in the 1945–1970 era, children fell behind who lived in pockets of "traditional poverty."[10] New forms of poverty developed as a result of urbanization. Community solidarity decreased. Public space was reduced. Interaction between adults and children became less frequent. Children were socialized differently, and migration increased.[11] Nuclear families separated from extended families. Among some populations, specifically African American families in the United States, the single-parent family developed as an important family form after World War II.[12]

From the early 1970s through 1989 child welfare continued to improve in some countries, but leveled or declined in others. Child poverty rose globally from 1967–1991, as noted below:

Changes in poverty rates in selected market economies, 1967–1991, in percent of child poverty in the child population[13]			
	Before 1971	1972–1975	After 1990
USA	13.2	17.9	21.5
Canada	15.2	13.1	13.5
UK	5.2	6.7	9.9 (1986-88)
Sweden	5.7	1.9	2.7

Cornia and Danziger attribute unevenness to slower economic growth, rising unemployment, worsening income distribution, and increasing family instability. Countries neglected social policies that enhance the well-being of children and adolescents, including maternity and paternity leave, child care leave, child care benefits, child support payments, and free or highly subsidized education. Poverty decreased among the elderly but increased among the unemployed, those employed in precarious jobs, migrants, and single parents. A rise in poverty overall contributed to a general rise in child poverty in Western and Southern Europe, the U.S.A., Hungary, Poland, and Yugoslavia. Overall poverty decreased in Japan, Sweden, and Belgium. In general, Cornia and Danziger conclude that child welfare varied depending on region, country, community, and locale.[14]

During this time, African countries won their independence from Europe, beginning with Ghana in 1957 and concluding with the former Portuguese colonies in 1975. Many of these countries showed a general improvement in child welfare from 1960 through 1995, as judged by under-5 mortality rates. Still, their child welfare indicators fell far below industrialized countries at their worst.

Deaths under age 5 per 1000 live children[15]		
	1960	1995
Angola	345	292
Congo	220	180
Kenya	122	75
Madagascar	219	95

In 1979 the United Nations recognized the decline in child welfare and declared the International Year of the Child. Through this means it sought to begin a serious focus on child development. Then, in 1989 nearly all the countries of the United Nations signed the *Convention on the Rights of the Child (CRC)*. (We have already discussed the United States' abstinence from signing.) In September 1990, the UN convened the World Summit for Children. For the first time, heads of state established international goals to improve child welfare.[16] Optimism was high.

Even so, from 1989 through the 1990s child welfare declined. Child poverty increased in formerly communist countries after 1989. These countries privatized their economies rapidly, benefiting their already elite segment of the population. Child poverty peaked in the United States at 23 percent in the mid-1990s, as social entitlements for children lost popular support. After the 1995 increase in the Earned Income Tax Credit, child poverty in the United States decreased to about 17 percent, still the highest child poverty rate among industrialized nations. However, homeless and hungry children, especially among two-parent working families, increased after the 1996 "Personal Responsibility and Work Opportunity Reconciliation Act (PRWORA)," popularly known as "welfare reform." When the United Nations General Assembly Special Session on Children convened in 2002, most of the goals established in 1990 had not been met.

Child Welfare and the Recent Era of Economic Globalization

The stages of the most recent phase of economic globalization parallel Cornia and Danziger's three eras of child welfare: from roughly 1945 or the end of World War II through the early 1970s, from the early 1970s through 1989 and the rapid disintegration of the Soviet Union, and from 1989 through the late 1990s.

The end of World War II brought about a rebalancing of economic and military power between the United States, Great Britain, and other parts of Europe. The post–WW II agreement established the Bretton Woods organizations—the World Bank, the International Monetary Fund, and the International Trade Organization, predecessor to the General Agreement on Trade and Tariffs and the World Trade Organization. These organizations were charged with stabilizing the economy, regulating trade, and fighting poverty. At Bretton Woods the world currency exchange system fixed exchange rates, backed by gold and the U.S. dollar.

In part, this shifting balance of power provided the opportunity for former colonies of Great Britain and other European countries to bid for national independence. Ghana achieved independence in 1957, and the decolonization of Portuguese colonies in 1975 completed the process. Many former colonies entered the world market with only one export product. Their raw materials had to be bought internationally; their struggling economies were quickly controlled by international cartels that sold necessary products, including food.[17] During the Cold War, the United States and the Soviet Union created allies in smaller countries, particularly in Africa, through enticements of aid. Often, U.S. aid was supplied to dictators who favored the U.S. The dictators enriched themselves rather than building the infrastructure of their countries.

During 1971–1973 the original Bretton Woods system broke down. Deficits accumulated because of the Vietnam War, and increased inflation stressed the U.S. dollar. Until then the U.S. dollar was "as good as gold," meaning that U.S. dollars served as the equivalent of IOU's for the U.S. gold reserves. The ratio of dollars circulating around the world to gold in the U.S. gold reserves became dangerously high, should a large country decide to exchange dollars for gold. President Nixon abandoned both the gold standard and fixed currency exchange rates. The U.S. and Europe could not prevent the OPEC countries from raising oil rates. "Oil shocks" followed. OPEC countries became wealthy and patronized Western banks.

Like the rich countries, countries that did not produce oil, especially those in Sub-Saharan Africa, needed to buy oil at the higher rates. They suffered devalued currency and high inflation. Some countries in Africa also experienced civil wars fed by a series of factors after independence: by internal political instability, by the bids by the U.S. and Soviet Union for allies during the Cold War, and by an escalating arms trade.

In 1979 inflation was rampant in the United States. The Federal Reserve raised interest rates. Poor countries could not repay debts at the new interest rates. In the 1980s these debts grew. International aid, from the Bretton Woods institutions but also from other major banks, depended on a country's willingness to decrease social expenditures and develop a market economy. In theory a market economy would create enough wealth for the poor countries to pay back their loans. But it didn't happen. Meanwhile, new technology increased the money to be made in stock markets and currency exchange for those with means.

In 1989 the Soviet Union's centrally planned economy fell. Instead of distributing a share in the ownership of former state enterprises among many people, people in positions of power in the former economy became the new economic elite as they bought the formerly publicly held companies.[18]

Responses to Economic Globalization

Professional economists have disagreed about the advantages or disadvantages of significant economic interventions; so have lay observers. Terms such as "The Washington Consensus" or "Casino Capitalism" represent viewpoints on the global economy that have meaning in popular culture and among professional economists. The Washington Consensus, in its popular version, suggests that by raising the standard of the rich, the living standard of the majority of people will improve. Otherwise known as neoliberal economics, the popular version of The Washington Consensus promotes free trade, deregulation, privatization, monetary discipline, structural adjustment programs, minimal government, and minimal economic intervention that relies on "the invisible hand" of market self-regulation.[19] Casino Capitalism, in its popular rendition, charges that, under neoliberal economics, the global economy has become a casino where betting on outcomes is more important than the actual production of goods and services.[20] The casino atmosphere has been promoted by deregulation in banking and trade, advances in technology, and the dismantling of social supports.

In their original professional versions these viewpoints were significantly more nuanced. "The Washington Consensus" was originally coined by John Williamson, Senior Fellow at the Institute for International Economics, and was specifically designed as a plan to promote economic growth and reduce poverty in Central America.[21] Williamson argues that those who by "the Washington Consensus" mean "free market fundamentalism," a term he attributes to George Soros, have no program for fighting poverty.[22] Williamson used the term "The Washington Consensus" to identify ten economic strategies around which he thought there was general agreement in Washington in 1990 after the initial glow of "Reaganomics" had faded. He included six strategies for fighting poverty that are challenged by those concerned about Casino Capitalism:

1. Fiscal discipline in spending to avoid inflation that hurts the poor the most.
2. Tax reform that lowers the highest tax rates and broadens the tax base. Lowering the highest tax rates is assumed to be a stimulus to economic growth, which in turn increases the tax base, social service provision, and income redistribution.
3. Flexible, rather than set, interest rates. (He gives no explanation for flexible rates as an anti-poverty program.)
4. Trade liberalization. Free trade increases the demand for unskilled labor in low-income, resource-poor countries.
5. Deregulation of trade. Deregulation dismantles barriers that protect the privileged classes.
6. Secure property rights. The poor are the first to suffer when property rights are ill defined.

He also proposed four strategies with which those concerned about Casino Capitalism would probably agree but those promoting "free market fundamentalism" would not:

1. Public expenditure for social services. Public expenditure would be "redirected towards fields offering both high economic returns and the potential to improve income distribution, such as primary health care, primary education, and infrastructure."[23]
2. Stabilized exchange rates. Currency exchange rates would have limited flexibility rather than the widely floating rates that exacerbate currency speculation.
3. Long-term international investment. In particular, long-term investment that raises growth and spreads technology without excessive import protection.
4. Privatization that is conducted *with care.* Privatization must include competitive bidding and protect against plundering state assets for the benefit of the elite.

A crisis of values among professional economists becomes obvious when we compare these proposals to those forwarded by Susan Strange, formerly an economist at the London School of Economics. She coined the term "Casino Capitalism" in 1986 to expose the increasingly speculative basis of the global economy.[24] Strange claimed that globally integrated markets and accelerated technological change increased the volatility of the economy. She analyzed decisions and nondecisions that led to the turning-point crises of the early 1970s,[25] and, for our purposes, the end of the "golden age of child welfare."

In her view, when the gold standard was abandoned in 1973, another authority needed to be created to stabilize the foreign exchange currency market. When the 1973 oil crisis developed, the United States and Europe needed to negotiate with, rather than oppose, Arab oil-producing states (OPEC), and buffer oil prices for the whole world. When in 1974 banks failed, a "lender of last resort" needed to be established that could intervene, avert, or redirect potential disasters, such as those that eventually developed in Mexico, Asia, and Argentina.

At the same time as these historic controls were lifted from the economy, technology integrated markets, allowing banking and finance to develop their own systems without governmental or geographical boundaries. Businesses other than banks extended credit. Furthermore, Strange argued, the United States made domestic decisions that changed the course of the rest of the world. The U.S. decided to allow the borrower, rather than the lender, to assume the risk for loans, so that when interest rates increased, the borrower bore the brunt. The U.S. lifted regulations on short-term credit and on banking across state and country boundaries. These decisions increased economic volatility.[26]

Market Intrusions in Children's Lives

As the power of global markets accelerated through new means, market logic and values increasingly impinged on children's lives. Shortly after Susan Strange offered the metaphor "Casino Capitalism" for the emerging economy, Alan Wolfe described the ways that the market was encroaching on areas of society that heretofore had been protected from it. The United States, he claimed, increasingly relied on the market to communicate moral values and philosophies to the whole of society. Milton Friedman and the Chicago School of economics prophesied that a market philosophy holding rational choice as its highest value could guide all of life's decisions. The Chicago School provided philosophical grounding for new market practices in such areas as housing and education that formerly were mediated by civil society.[27] Wolfe specifically warned that the distance between the market and the family was narrowing, with some positive effects for women's freedom in job markets but largely destabilizing effects for communities, families, and children.

In Cornia and Danziger's analysis, the Scandinavian welfare states provide the consistently best outcomes for children. Wolfe also analyzed the effects of Scandinavian welfare states on communities, families, and children. He calls the Scandinavian welfare state "the great success story of modern of liberal democracy,"[28] pointing out that "at the same time as other states have been used primarily to wage wars or exterminate whole races, the Scandinavians use it to instill a sense of moral obligation."[29] By "moral obligation" Wolfe means that state benefits have communicated a concern for family and for strangers in the national mindset. The willingness of Scandinavian welfare philosophy to emphasize that societies should provide the minimum of what all people need contrasts the market philosophy that emphasizes that individuals should maximize their self-interest.

Wolfe is not sanguine, however, that all is entirely well in Scandinavia. After World War I the welfare state primarily served as a transfer of wealth from one segment of society to another. In the 1970s it took on the new character as a builder of institutions that helped the family function, providing day care and after-school programs for children. As it became more involved in these areas, it also became more interventionist, moving children out of home environments that exhibited poverty, alcohol or drug abuse, violence or maternal stress. Wolfe speculates that a transition from transferring income to setting up institutions that replace the functions of families will ultimately undermine the welfare state's ability to communicate its underlying philosophy of care for all.[30]

Even as Wolfe analyzed the potential effects of the tentacles of the markets and states on civil society, others in the market world actively sought to shape childhood with markets. Joyce Mercer has summarized the wide-ranging effects of market influence on children's lives. Quoting James McNeal, an early architect of advertising aimed directly at children, Mercer describes three ways in which children themselves *are* markets. The spending power of children constitutes one market: advertisers profit on shaping the immediate desires of children in a way that parents can't resist. The influence of children on the spending power of others, whether peers or parents, creates a second market: advertisers seek to persuade children to advocate to parents and peers on behalf of a particular solution to parents' and peers' needs. The future spending power of children creates a third market: advertisers hope that establishing brand loyalty in children now creates an income for the future.[31] Mercer notes that consumer society applauds middle- and upper-class children as they respond to market influence, but denigrates poor children for succumbing to such pressure. According to author Elizabeth Chin, journalists overreport "a minority child's willingness to kill to obtain a status brand of athletic shoes, or unmarried black teen mothers buying CD's and potato chips when their babies need milk."[32]

In the last twenty years the United States has depended more heavily on market economy, dismantling its rudimentary welfare society, as we saw in chapter 5. The majority of middle-class American parents do not seem to resist this change. Markets provide young American parents the benefit of economic freedom—they may, truly, achieve the American dream of big economic success. They may quickly develop lifestyles that match or exceed their parents—or they may fall and find little safety net in place to catch them. In return for that opportunity, American parents seem to want low taxes, freedom of choice in child care, education, health care, and housing. For those freedoms they pay a huge financial price—high costs in day care, college, health care premiums, and homes. They may be distressed by social indicators such as poor health outcomes and high child poverty rates, but so far, the freedoms parents think they enjoy seem to make the trade-offs worthwhile. Ironically, even as American parents seem to value these choices, they seem troubled by the influence of markets on their children, as their children become consummate consumers. Meanwhile, the effect of markets on children must give pause, especially in the virtual village—do American parents have the freedom to choose everything but the influences that shape their children's lives?

Resisting the Global Economy

Though their fingers are very aware of children as potential markets, the invisible hands of powerbrokers in politics, banking, and trade guide the global economy, far away from local communities, families, and children. The imbalance in power between the economic systems of the world and local communities and families has led to what Rebecca Todd Peters calls "resistance theories of globalization."[33] One resistance theory calls global companies to account for their effects on nature and world ecology (see chapter 8 of this book); the other resistance theory claims that economic globalization perpetuates neocolonial relationships between Europe, the United States, and the Southern Hemisphere that were established in the sixteenth century.

The postcolonial theorists argue that economic globalization perpetuates colonial dynamics in that the United States and Europe still control the economies of former political colonies. Though political independence may exist formally, economic dependence continues. Grass roots groups in these countries argue that the economies of their countries should develop from the ground up. They prefer systems of business, currency, and barter that represent indigenous patterns of subsistence to strategies of economic growth that perpetuate economic dependence upon the United States and Europe. International trade, banking, and labor patterns must be challenged in favor of local economic systems.[34] Grass roots groups and professional think-tanks in North America promote strategies for their own local communities that "grow the economy from beneath," including government-sponsored small business entrepreneurship, farmers' markets, and ecologically sustainable community projects.

Even before we fully consider resistance strategies, however, we can identify a crisis of values among those who are trying to shape the direction of the global economy. For some people, poverty is an individual problem to be largely resolved only secondarily by international agreement and policies; for others, distinct global strategies are necessary to combat poverty. All of these concerns have consequences for children. How might the concerns for theology, spirituality, and practical theology speak to this crisis?[35]

The Crisis of Values

The metaphor of the "shepherd/ess" developed in chapter 4—the shepherd/ess as one who is accountable for the power and leadership that he or she is given—invites powerbrokers who are shaping the global economy to consider the ways they use their power. The shepherd/ess must look for the effect of general policies and theories on families and individuals—whether a policy or theory supports the engagement, dignity, and hope of individuals and the peacemaking of society. A shepherd/ess has a critical eye on economic globalization, attempting to discern norms by which to evaluate the kind of global economy that is developing.

The metaphor of "friend" reminds us to listen to those whose children are vulnerable to the worst effects of economic globalization. How do our friends in extremely poor countries think about economic globalization? Our friends are not unanimous. Jim Poling, author of *Render Unto God: Economic Vulnerability, Family Violence and Pastoral Theology,* reports that the Nicaraguan conversation partners listed in that book have no sympathies toward any economic globalization.[36] For them, the colonizing dynamics of economic globalization override any possible good that can come from international economic relationships. My conversation partners in the Democratic Republic of Congo have a different perspective, one that I find more typical of Africans in general. They are very aware that economic globalization forces have, in the past, enriched African dictators rather than the populace, but they believe that some of the forces shaping the global economy will also restrain the power of corruption in African countries. Since such corruption has created political instability and has destroyed the trade and banking, these friends welcome globalizing forces that have the power to create constructive economic "transparency." Emmanuel Lartey attributes the difference between Latin and South American and African perceptions to the fact that Latin and South Americans have lived under direct U.S. economic control and the African–U.S. economic relations are once removed from direct colonialism by the United States. He also attributes the difference to the "practical" African personality that tries to identify the opportunity present in any circumstance.[37]

As we have seen, however, critical thought and norms help to shape our practices in relationship to economic globalization. The strategies of the nuanced versions of The Washington Consensus and Casino Capitalism point us toward a crisis of values but also toward policies that will make a difference in children's welfare.

Children in all countries, especially those who live with poverty, need public expenditures for social services in the areas of proper nutrition, health, education, and child care. Children's programs *that are proven to work,* including public programs for nutrition, education, and child care, are threatened year after year. While the world is awash in capital from speculative gains that amount to market gambling, we are told that governments can't afford social programs.[38] This unchallenged crisis in values—the value of speculation vs. the value of child support—continues to shape child welfare. We need to evaluate the global economy by the extent to which policies reduce speculation and support adequate public programs for children's flourishing. Stable institutions support children's welfare. Whether in the United States or Africa, they require long-term investment that can be sustained through times of contingency. When investors are only interested in short-term investments and profits, they are unlikely to reinvest in particular communities and their institutions. We need to evaluate the global economy by the stability of a network of community institutions. We need to scrutinize the relationship of public and private holdings from the vantage point of child welfare. For example, in the United States the disadvantage of a private medical insurance system that left large numbers of poor and middle-class children uninsured was largely overcome in the last decade by public state insurance programs. Now, those programs are being reduced and eliminated. In Africa the private, religiously based educational institutions have educated children where public education systems are almost nonexistent. To eliminate illiteracy in the general population, however, these private systems need to be augmented by free public systems.

The Global Economy, Love, and Justice

Human beings are intertwined with the global economy in both its presence and its absence. Ordinary human beings in the United States usually have easy access through technology to many aspects of the global economy—whether we use it for communication, information, research, or financial participation. Ordinary human beings in Africa have little access to the global economy whether to communicate with friends, to find information they are seeking, or to participate in a secure banking system. Ordinary human beings on both continents with access to technology have been drawn into the risky speculation in the global economy that access to technology allows. Is it possible to think of love and justice when we are so entangled in a network that for good and for ill inevitably entraps us in its tentacles? How might we sort through a way to live in the midst of its tenacity?

John Wesley, Dorothy Day, and Martin Luther King Jr., by their emphasis on living the Beatitudes after the imitation of Christ, remind us that our first concern is the treatment of the neighbor with whom we are face to face. It is the tangible, physical practice of neighbor love with those who are immediately around us that claims our immediate time. They also remind us to establish direct relationships with neighbors around the world, those who are affected by our actions but whose faces we cannot physically see. They urge us toward a spirituality of engagement, one that participates in long-term commitments, whether in friendship, church, or our financial commitments. They remind us to keep the concerns for dignity foremost. Economic relations that promote participation and self-determination preserve dignity and reduce infantilization. They remind us that the future bends toward justice, promoting the hope that the good can meet questionable circumstances.

The growth of the global economy accelerates the toxicity of the earth with the by-products of industrialization. We are grossly aware that most of our economic growth is dependent on depleting and polluting the planet Earth. This growing toxicity has direct and indirect effects on children's lives. We turn now to Mother Earth and her children.

CHAPTER 8

Do Children Graze in Good Pastures?

Ah, you shepherds of Israel who have been feeding yourselves!
Should not shepherds feed the sheep? You eat the fat, you clothe
yourselves with the wool, you slaughter the fatlings; but you
do not feed the sheep... For thus says the Lord God: I myself
will search out my sheep... I will feed them on the mountains of
Israel, by the watercourses, and in all the inhabited parts of the
land. I will feed them with good pasture. (Ezek. 34:2b–3, 11b,
13b—14a)

George and Dawn; Mutombo

In 2002, George, a United Methodist pastor of an inner-city congregation in the United States, and his wife, Dawn, took their two-year-old child to his pediatrician for a routine check up. The pediatrician discovered elevated lead levels in the child's blood, indicating lead poisoning. The source of the poison was likely hid in their stately, hundred-year-old parsonage, so they immediately moved into a hotel. Inspectors tested the parsonage and found lead around the windows, in wall paint, and particularly on a painted radiator. The congregation replaced the windows and radiator and repainted the walls, but still the child's blood lead level climbed. Dust wipe testing showed lead in excess of the Environmental Protection Agency (EPA) standard on the attic and basement floor where the child played. Moreover, the lead on the front porch floor was in excess of the EPA standard for interior floors. Paint was peeling on the houses in the neighborhood. The church hired a contractor to rectify these issues. The interior of the parsonage was now safe, but deteriorated houses around the parsonage contaminated the soil. Neighbors painted their homes, and the church laid a new layer of topsoil in the yard. The child's blood lead levels came down. Now, the church regularly tests the house to maintain a safe environment for the child.

Childhood lead poisoning causes a loss of intelligence and an increase in emotional and behavioral problems. Most houses built before the late 1960s contain lead-based paint unless it has been abated. Lead accumulates in the dust in window wells that are opened and shut frequently and on the floors of surfaces painted with lead-based paint, such as porch floors and stairs. Also, deteriorated lead-based paint from walls, ceilings, windows, and trim may contaminate the floors. Small amounts of lead in paint cannot be seen by the eye but will poison a child.

Human use of power in the development of our economy has directly contributed to the destruction of an environment in which children can thrive. Our economic growth has produced toxic by-products that poison children. One of these toxins, lead, disproportionately shapes the lives of poor children, but is a potential danger to all children.[1]

Young children play in their homes, get their hands dirty, put their fingers in their mouths, and absorb lead into their bodies. The amount of lead necessary to poison a child is miniscule and, unfortunately, is not generally noticed, or even seen or felt. Because the lead sticks to surfaces such as wood floors, it must be cleaned with soap and water to be removed. In some inner-city communities, more than one-third of the children in the community have elevated lead levels in their blood. In these communities, one wonders how many of the behavioral problems of children in school are actually the direct result of the unsustainable communities in which they live. National and local actions have brought significant improvements to some homes. Can we broaden those improvements to include all God's children? Mother Earth and her children are "in distress" from environmental toxins such as lead.

Still, we should not ignore the real environmental improvements in some areas. They offer hope that even more change is possible.

Between 1978 and 2002, the Environmental Protection Agency (EPA) estimates that the number of American children with elevated blood lead levels has fallen from 3 to 4 million to about 310,000, as lead was phased out of gasoline and reduced in drinking water, air emissions, and residential paint.[2] This represents real progress for all children. Even so, the danger of this debilitating disease disproportionately affects poor children, who often live in older rental housing that is not maintained adequately. Nor is the 310,000 necessarily a stable number if communities are not vigilant. Lead is usually contained rather than abated, and as children are born and move in and out of older, deteriorating housing, significant numbers of children in one neighborhood can become poisoned. This pattern parallels the one identified in 1987 by the United Church of Christ in which they discovered that poor and ethnic minority communities were being disproportionately chosen to become the site of toxic waste dumps.[3]

In 2002 a Congolese United Methodist pastor, Mutombo, his wife, and children heard the rebels were coming. They gathered some food and left for the bush. They walked south till they joined other United Methodist pastors in Kamina in the southern DRC. There, they would appeal through their bishop to the larger church for help. They built mud huts at the edge of this isolated, pristine town of 100,000 people. Even before the war the food system was strained; the church had operated a center for malnourished children in the community since 1986. The diet of the people of Kamina was very limited—beans, rice, termites, sweet potatoes, and kasava. Occasionally a chicken or a goat could be raised and killed. The church grew additional beans and rice to feed the newcomers. When I visited Kamina in 2003, the lack of diversity in the diet was striking. The church had introduced Chinese cabbage, one of the few green vegetables, and no dairy products were part of the local diet.

Kamina may seem remote and romantic, but it is as deficient an environment for children's growth as an inner city in the United States that is filled with lead paint. It was made unsustainable not by the presence of toxins from a growing economy but by patterns of a Belgian colonial economy that destroyed the natural environment. When the inhabitants were required by Belgium to work in the mines, the society lost the knowledge of the land and how to farm it for food. Instead, natives hunted large game for food until the game was gone. Kamina does not face problems with removing chemicals, or even garbage, except in the main street where people discard the packaging from a few imported products. Rather, the sustainability of Kamina depends on building the agricultural knowledge and skills of the people so that they can feed themselves a balanced diet. *The sustainability and flourishing of natural creation directly supports the sustainabilty and flourishing of children's lives.*

What Is Sustainable Community?

We, the people of planet Earth, live with an enormous amount of deferred maintenance. In our homes we defer maintenance when we postpone repairs. Sometimes, we prioritize quality family time, education, or hard work: we spend our time and energy on other good endeavors besides home maintenance. In some places, we can barely afford to purchase our homes at any price because the deferred maintenance is too expensive. We are no longer like my grandfathers who knew mechanical and electrical systems intimately and repaired their homes themselves: we may not know how to maintain a home. We, like the Congolese who lost their agricultural knowledge, in two generations are as bereft as they are of the local knowledge of our homes. When we get around to it, we hire the service of others. We have justifiable reasons, but so what? Eventually, the effects of deferred maintenance ignore our excuses; like rain, the effects fall on the just and the unjust alike. Eventually, we need to change our ways or the house will fall down around us.

Creating sustainable community is like moving into a home with unique, lovely features and regularly maintaining that home. The home has certain features that attracted us. Rather than allowing those features to deteriorate, we polish them. We prevent them from getting damaged. We repair our home on a regular maintenance schedule. Our home, though, is our town, our nation, or the planet Earth.

The idea of sustainable community is most closely associated with humanity's need to live *in and as nature* in a careful way. Our current carelessness may do irreversible damage to the earth and to ourselves and may destroy our children's and grandchildren's planetary home. Sustainable community suggests that we create our towns, lifestyles, and relationships in such a way as to protect the earth for future generations. By protecting the earth, we protect ourselves and our children.

Sustainable community is healthful community—not one where toxins pollute our homes or the earth around us, causing disease for which we need to seek cures, but one where toxins and their diseases are prevented or contained. Sustainable community is politically stable community—not one where the human organization of power leaves behind the devastation of war, but one where human power is used for peaceful purposes. Sustainable community is economically sound community—not one where the economy promotes the idol of wealth, but one where the economy supports the needs of people. Sustainable community bequeaths to our children a world that can support them. The problem is, there are few, if any, sustainable communities.

We learn how far we are from sustainable community when we examine the limits of communities whose goal is sustainability. Wilderness areas in the United States have particularly stringent rules that support natural ecology. In the Boundary Waters Canoe Area Wilderness of Minnesota, the wilderness is sustained by a set of rules designed to support human participation within nature's ecosystem. Under the title of "Leave No Trace," the park system requires that campers camp in small groups, use the latrine that is provided, burn no garbage, bring no food in bottles or cans, use soap away from the water so that the earth can filter it before it enters the water system, and leave the wildlife—including plants, animals, and earth—undisturbed. The wilderness practice of "low impact camping" teaches the rules for "low impact living." Families, youth groups, and other groups of campers discover that group dynamics frequently change in the wilderness: with reasonable expectations for physical effort, people often become more considerate and respectful, more free to try new things and less likely to posture, more able to rebound from distress and less brittle. Campers seem more attuned to living in relation to the benefits of wind, bright sky, and water; clouds and storms; sunlight and darkness. They learn to be respectful guests in a place where the moose, bear, deer, squirrels, and fish comprise the permanent population. Wilderness camping calls forth imagination and creativity, as campers try new ways of blending daily support and entertainment; it also calls for ritual and order, as experienced happy campers put away their tools—their knife, whistle, cooking kit, flashlight—in the same place after each use. Children usually thrive on wilderness camping experiences.

Wilderness camping shows us how little we know about taking care of ourselves. Even though we may live in ecologically sound ways, few campers would know how to live for long if they lost their packs of gear or dried food. Few of us have learned from previous generations the ways that nature cares for us as an earth mother. Few of us know what to teach our children about how to feed and clothe themselves from nature's bounty. Wilderness camping does teach us, however, to live without deferred maintenance. When a camper must canoe for several days for equipment repair, a grocery store, or professional medical care, a camper learns to keep one's belongings, food, and health in good shape. That practice, in addition to ecologically sound living, witnesses to the kind of sustainable communities from which humanity benefits.

Sustainable Community and Natural, Social, and Monetary Capital

Sustainability—or living in such a way that we do not defer the natural costs of our lives to future generations—has been widely studied in recent years. Mark Roseland, in *Toward Sustainable Communities—Resources for Citizens and Their Governments*, has outlined a range of urban issues that must be considered. These include the use of green space, provisions for water, sewage, and waste reduction, new ways of thinking about energy efficiency, atmospheric change, transportation, housing and land use, and community economic development. These proposals build on two ideas: natural and social capital. Modifying this term, capital—or wealth that is available for generating value—with the words "natural" and "social," Roseland reminds us that worthwhile human endeavors depend on more than money.

Roseland suggests three categories of natural capital: non-renewable resources, renewable resources, and carrying capacity. *Nonrenewable resources*, such as minerals and fossil fuels, cannot be used a second time. *Renewable resources*, such as crops, forestry products, and water supplies—or, in Kamina's case, large game—are reproduced in nature if they are not overused and exploited. Systems also have a *carrying capacity*, a limit to the amount of emissions and pollutants they can absorb. Roseland suggests, "Each generation should leave the next a stock of assets at least as great as that which they inherited themselves."[4] In other words, we would live in our natural home, earth, as we live in a wilderness campsite: leave it as clean or cleaner than we found it.

In some areas, the Unites States may be achieving this goal. Since major environmental legislation of the 1970s, pollutant emissions, including toxins, have declined significantly. The United States has gained ground even while both population and the gross domestic product have increased.[5] However, the legacy of many decades of uncontrolled pollution haunts our environmental progress. For example, when we read headlines such as "Debate on Climate Shifts to Issue of Irreparable Change" in *The Washington Post*, we are reading about natural cycles of climate change combined with the legacy left to us of human degradation of the environment.[6] Even though the current generation pollutes less than the previous generation, our environmental bank account remains dangerously overdrawn.

How we use our natural capital depends upon our social capital—our way of relating to one another. Social capital is "shared knowledge, understandings, and patterns of interaction that a group of people bring to any particular activity."[7] Our human interrelating becomes valuable when we build trust, encourage participation in decision-making, and share responsibility for the development of our communities. Communities can reduce toxins or malnutrition when these problems are treated as communal problems that can be resolved when people trust one another and are able to work well together—when they share a spirituality of engagement, dignity, and hope.

If we value social capital, our relationships will help to instruct us about the effects of our exploitation of natural capital. Likewise, if we value social and natural capital, we will use financial capital differently. If we believe that we should maximize our financial capital, regardless of the implications for natural and social capital, we will invest financial capital as if it were the primary consideration. If we believe that natural, social, and financial capital should work together to create a flourishing environment for all people, we will invest all three forms of capital in ways that consider the good of the whole.[8]

Belgian colonialism exemplified the unbalanced relationship between natural, social, and financial capital. As an economic system, colonialism extracts riches from colonies into the colonizing

Richard Louv demonstrates how insidious our separation from nature has become and how this separation is truncating children's lives.[15] Louv contrasts the time of his childhood and children today. He and the parents of today's children recall times spent exploring fields, woods, and vacant lots. Today, a series of forces have alienated children from direct experience with nature—forces that range from fears parents have for their children's safety to covenants that restrict exploration in planned communities. At the same time, as children's direct experience with nature has become more restricted, children are increasingly diagnosed with depression, obesity, and attention deficit disorder. Interest in subjects such as natural history is declining, so that even culture is being reshaped by these changes; at the same time, children's play is increasingly organized, reducing the opportunities for children to develop imagination and creativity. The phrase "the integrity of creation" captures an alternative way of thinking about nature, ourselves, and the world in which we live. Living as if we are part of nature and nature is part of us challenges the direction in which culture is currently developing. Therefore, the idea of "the integrity of creation," for Steven Bevans and Roger P. Schroeder, contributes to the prophetic dialogue of mission.[16] This phrase, attributed to the World Council of Churches, refers to "the value of all creatures in themselves, for one another, and for God, and their interconnectedness in a diverse whole that has unique value for God."[17] "The integrity of creation" highlights the idea that earth is a one-time gift to humanity that is jeopardized by three great instabilities: "injustice, unpeace, and creation's disintegration."[18] That gift is supported by an endless number of natural transactions and an ability to self-organize—a wonderful interdependence and self-regulation. Most importantly for those who think in religious terms, creation has integrity because it comes from a "divine source" and consists of "independent expressions of divine love."[19]

If we think of humanity *as* and *in* nature, and nature—earth and even the universe—as having integrity as God's creation, then children are also part of God's good creation. The children of God's good creation include destitute children dying of malnutrition in Kamina and healthy, energetic children who are the Congo's next leaders; they include lead-poisoned children in the inner cities of the United States who struggle with neurological country. In the Congolese case, King Leopold and his successor mined the natural capital of Congo and disrupted existing social relationships. Belgian colonialism was particularly noted for its inattention to rebuilding social capital through training, education, and participatory decision-making with native Congolese. Unlike other African colonies, Zaire (the former name of the Democratic Republic of Congo) at independence had fewer than thirty university-trained Congolese and no army officers, engineers, agronomists, or physicians.[9] Belgium did not reinvest natural, social, or financial capital in its former colony. Bereft of adequate leadership, the "failed state" of the Democratic Republic of Congo resulted.[10] As we invest our social, financial, and natural capital, Larry Rasmussen suggests that we consider three principles of "earth's economy." First, "waste equals food." Waste material from some forms becomes food for others. Second, "nature runs off of current solar income." Earth is a closed system with the exception of sunlight—sunlight is the only source of energy that is added to earth's system. Third, "nature depends on diversity, thrives on difference, and dies in uniformity." Supporting rather than reducing diverse life forms keeps our interdependent ecosystem healthy. These evolutionary principles help us think about ways to live *in* and *as* nature, rather than in opposition to it.[11]

Mother Earth, Wild Wilderness, Apartheid Thinking, or the Integrity of Creation?

How we treat natural capital depends in part on how we think about nature. Prior to the modern era, Nancy Howell notes, earth was "mother earth," suggesting that the earth cared for humanity, provided for it, and was generally benevolent toward it.[12] In the era of wilderness exploration that led to modern colonialism this female metaphor for earth changed—earth became "a wild and uncontrollable woman who needed to be tamed." Explorers understood themselves as conquering nature, rather than being nurtured by it. Rasmussen notes that humankind got in the habit of "apartheid thinking" that separates humanity from the rest of nature. However, he says that instead we need to think of ourselves as *in and of, or in and as* nature.[13] Howell reminds us that the lines between humanity and other primates are not as distinct as once thought.[14] When we destroy nature we also destroy parts of ourselves. We also risk destroying our children.

damage and children free from the effects of lead. Bevan and Schroeder's "prophetic dialogue" of mission includes not only care for all children but care for the conditions that prevent disease and violence against God's good creation and promote their flourishing.

Integrity of Creation and the Global Economy

Books that promote "strong sustainability," or a goal of living within our natural means, frequently argue against any form of economic globalization. For some, any economic globalization will overpower the will of small communities to determine their own economic future. For example, Rebecca Todd Peters describes "people's resistance movements" that protest all economic globalization and its institutions, for fear that they will not be able to sustain their current livelihoods, lifestyles, and traditions under its pressure.[20]

The World Social Forum brings together people and ideas for economic projects and systems that function separately from the global economy. These entrepreneurial activities are not dependent on the global economy, nor are they calculated in the nation's GDP. But they contribute significantly to people's self-determination and ability to support themselves. Many such projects and small businesses need protection from their destruction and absorption into multinational corporations. Many people in the United States support such enterprises in their own local communities and through fair trade organizations and organizations such as 10,000 Villages. For some people, these local, entrepreneurial economic enterprises will exist apart from the global economy; for others, they represent an aspect of shaping a global economy that has existed for centuries into a kind of economic globalization. *They can be judged by the criteria of community participation and ecological sustainability.*

Leaders in Kamina, for example, believe that some forms of global economy's power are necessary to stabilize the political system. After 1996 and fall of the dictator Mobutu Sese' Seko, war engulfed the northeast Congo. The vacuum of political and economic power allowed neighboring countries, military, and corporations to scramble for profits from Congo's natural resources. Local companies and military groups raced to supply such goods to the world market. After several interactions in the global economic network, the origin of diamonds and minerals such as coltan, needed for cell phones and computers, was hard to trace.[21] The United Nations has intervened in the war in Congo, not only with a peacekeeping force, but by intervening with corporations whose interests were seen as perpetuating the war. Two-thirds of the corporations that were identified as perpetuating the war have cooperated with the United Nations—one-third, most of which are Congolese corporations, have refused. With a multipronged effort that disrupted the profit from war and supported the social capital needed for peace, the war in Congo subsided. Such intervention shows the range of skills needed for "shepherding" a sustainable global political economy.

A Future for Children: Shepherd, Lamb, Friend, and the Earth's Distress

We are still bequeathing to our children "earth's distress," to use Rasmussen's phrase, distress that children often carry in their own bodies. Children sick from the effects of lead poisoning groan in unison with the earth; children hungry from the disruption of their families' ability to farm "good pastures" cry the earth's tears. Concerned adults, such as Mary Elizabeth Moore, have called us to the "repair of the earth."[22] How do the metaphors of shepherd, lamb, and friend help us think about our relationship with children, earth, and God?

Lead-poisoned children who fight in school and recent violent hurricanes that have been attributed to the warming of the oceans by one degree suggest that children and the earth are not meek and mild lambs but angry victims who hope that someone will listen. If Jesus' death is a once-and-for-all atonement, children and the earth are not meant to atone—to suffer for the sins of the adults, especially those who broker the power to contaminate the earth. Jesus, however, ongoingly atones for us by agonizing with children and the earth in their distress. Are we living *as if* the earth and children can atone for the sins of humankind? Do the earth and children love us with *agape*, a suffering love that may lead the lover to death? Should we live this way?

The metaphor of "friend" helps us envision an alternative way to live. In mutuality the earth is our friend and we are the earth's. Friendship, Howell reminds us, is often thought of in terms of *eros*, a counterpart to *agape*.[23] *Eros* is passionate love, love that is mutual and engaged. *Eros* is not necessarily sexual. It is committed love, but committed not from duty but from deep attachment and connection. Erotic love knows its lover and seeks the lover's good. It is a love that is sustained.

Though most North Americans do not love the land with erotic passion, others can help us understand that love. Indigenous persons in North America and elsewhere, family farmers, gardeners, and others may know this kind of erotic friendship with the land in different forms.[24] Can we pass this love to our children? When asked, American children today frequently list the environment as one of their major concerns, yet are we teaching them the skills they need to turn that concern into a sustainable world? The last several decades seem to have shown us that—at least in some parts of our society—environmental improvement and economic sustainability can coexist. Let us hope that our children can shepherd that improvement to all corners of our world.

How, then, do we use the power of the shepherd/ess? In under two short centuries the United States and Europe have largely been responsible for significantly altering the ecology of the earth. Since the 1970s we have also significantly curbed our polluting practices. Still, we have not achieved strong sustainability. As China and India, two huge populations, rise in the global economy, the additional potential for permanently altering the earth will grow. The overall direction of the planet seems to be toward large-scale alteration of the earth, but economists are also predicting that "green" companies will be a major force for our economic future.[25] Will people who have the power to ignore the earth's toxicity, whose lives do not seem to be directly changed by the earth's poisons, become better shepherd/esses, return the good pastures to the earth, and feed the children from the good pastures?

As with the global economy, one hope rises from individuals and groups who come in direct contact with ecological destruction, who are able to build relationships with the people most affected, and who stand by those persons in search of direct relief and a voice for change.

The United Methodist Church is rebuilding Kamina's agricultural infrastructure. The church, through the initiative of Bishop Ntambo, the support of many Annual Conferences and congregations in the United States and Europe, and the United Methodist

Committee on Relief, began with a number of agricultural experiments to help diversify the diet of the Congolese. They introduced Chinese cabbage, hogs, and chickens and cows, mainly for dairy products. They identified and cultivated marenga trees for their health effects, and they increased production of rice and vegetables. The church purchased a former Belgian farm and has converted it into an agricultural training center. In 2003 the farm had functioning fields but was largely a renovation project; in 2005 the farm was filled with livestock and had established itself as a production and training center. Simultaneously, the church has been at the center of brokering a peace agreement among factions who threaten the political stability of the area. Diversifying the diet of an entire population is an overwhelming endeavor, especially when civil war constantly threatens. Yet for Bishop Ntambo, the shepherd, lamb, and friend of Kamina, the goal is simple: that the people won't go hungry. The primary act of care, evangelism, and mission of the Christian gospel is to feed the people—and church growth follows.

In Rochester, the Coalition to Prevent Lead Poisoning has achieved a major victory, one that provides a model for primary prevention of lead poisoning for the nation. In 2001 Ralph Spezio, an elementary school principal, discovered that 41 percent of the children in his inner-city elementary school had elevated blood lead levels. Since the 1960s anti-lead efforts in Rochester had proceeded in fits and starts, and he began a campaign to galvanize an effective effort for lead reduction. Meanwhile, New York State had an effective law for secondary prevention of lead poisoning, requiring that children at one and two years of age be tested. Concerned pediatricians, lead inspectors, and community groups worked together under the auspices of Get the Lead Out (GLO), to identify and treat children who were at risk for lead poisoning and to bring the seriousness of the situation to the attention of the medical community.

As is always the case in "prophetic pastoral care,"[26] their attempts to change "the common sense of the community" were not greeted with enthusiasm. They were "friends" to the children and families at risk, assisting them in making their homes into safe space, but they were also "lambs" who risked their own income and reputations to dedicate themselves to this work. The power of "shepherding" grew as University of Rochester Medical School and other significant community groups lent leadership and support. Lead was now recognized as dangerous *whenever* and *wherever* lead is present and uncontained in the environment.[27] In 2004 the Coalition to Prevent Lead Poisoning hosted a summit attended by five hundred people, and "community groups, local funders, health care organizations, county government and many others vowed their support" for ending lead poisoning in Rochester by 2010.[28] As Katrina Smith Korfmacher, Community Outreach Coordinator of the Environmental Health Sciences Center at the University of Rochester Medical School reports, however, it was unclear exactly to what the community had pledged its support. Medical researchers, community groups, the realtor association, the county government and the city government had different perspectives on the way to move toward the goal. In the end the city council passed a strong *primary* prevention law that considered the newest knowledge of the medical community about the effect of lead and aimed at preventing lead poisoning from ever occurring.[29] This law requires visual and laboratory testing of public assistance housing in which most lead poisoning of children occurs. The Coalition is now working to find funding that relieves the burden of renovation, which at this time falls solely on individual landlords, making it less likely it will be accomplished.

These two examples show the aggregate power of helpers, educators, and activists in a hopeful journey toward a flourishing future for the world's children.

CHAPTER 9

What Do War and Peace Mean
for Children?

He shall not judge by what his eyes see, or decide by what his
*   ears hear;*
but with righteousness he shall judge the poor,
*   and decide with equity for the meek of the earth...*

The wolf shall live with the lamb,
*   the leopard shall lie down with the kid,*
the calf and the lion and the fatling together,
*   and a little child shall lead them.*
The cow and the bear shall graze,
*   their young shall lie down together;*
*   and the lion shall eat straw like the ox.*
The nursing child shall play over the hole of the asp,
*   and the weaned child shall put its hand on the adder's den.*
They will not hurt or destroy on all my holy mountain;
for the earth will be full of the knowledge of the LORD
*   as the waters cover the sea. (Isa. 11:3b—4a, 6–9)*

We care for children: how does that relate to peace? War destab-
ilizes countries: war assaults the natural environment, disrupts
countries' economies, and creates conditions in which human
rights are violated. *War diminishes children's health and welfare: in*
war children die and are maimed, are sexually assaulted, contract diseases

128

because medical services are disrupted, lose education, are orphaned, and become refugees. I could document all of these claims with stories and statistics that are widely available. Instead, this chapter will take a more autobiographical turn.

In August 1968, as a sixteen-year-old high school senior I blissfully flew across the Atlantic Ocean for the first time. My church sent me to spend a year in Germany through the International Christian Youth Exchange (ICYE), a program begun after World War II to reconcile hostility between Germany and the United States. For me, like most of the teenagers in the program, World War II was a prehistoric event. The original reason for the exchange didn't sink in. In the winter we crossed Checkpoint Charlie into East Berlin to meet with youth who attended a church whose congregation had been divided by the Berlin Wall. Two of the U.S. students coyly exchanged passports to see whether the East German guards would notice. They did. In contrast, a sixteen-year-old East Berliner in the congregation vowed to escape through the wall or die trying before his eighteenth birthday. *He* knew the guards would be watching.

In the spring ICYE organized two trips to Prague. I was permitted to go, but I remember the unspoken misgivings on the face of Rosemary, my exchange mother. I didn't realize then that a month earlier on a similar trip my closest American exchange friend, Judy, saw terror when Soviet tanks rumbled down Prague's main streets. For me, the trip to Prague provided a chance to travel, an opportunity not to be passed by! On this loosely organized trip I first tasted the personal freedom to come and go as I pleased. (As we later discussed this experience in 2006, Judy and I agreed: as American teenagers, even with signs of political turmoil all around us, we expected immunity from entanglement in war.)

Only years later did I realize what it must have meant for my family to send their child to live for a year with a German family, a hated enemy in my own parents' teenage years. Only later did I realize the depth of generosity of the German family of five with whom I lived: a single mother, Rosemary, who received public child support assistance and waited tables on occasion for extra money; her two teenage daughters, Petra and Iris, who badly wanted an American "sister"; and Rosemary's parents, Opi, who had lost a leg in the war, and Omi, who had ridden a coal train to southern Germany to rescue him when he was ailing.

Only later did I realize the courage of the parents of Margaret, my closest German friend, who were still helping East Germans escape through what we would call an "underground railway." I learned of their efforts in 1974 when I planned a trip to Munich but discovered that all the rooms were booked for the World Cup Soccer Match. Margaret's parents arranged for me to stay in a group home for East Germans who, they said quietly, "owed them something." I am no longer oblivious to the fact that a life outside the war zone comes to us both as a gift we have not earned and as a promise that God unceasingly seeks to deliver to all people.

In 1968 we talked about war and peace, in general and in very personal ways. As I struggled with trigonometry at the kitchen table, Omi reminded me that I could study without wartime distractions. "Rosemary did homework with war planes flying overhead." When Rosemary criticized my potato peeling, she reminded me that in the West German "peace" held in place by the Cold War they were not so worried over food security that I needed to leave the potato eyes. "You peel potatoes like that only in wartime," she said. This particular peace brought very personal changes.

In 2007 we argue whether we are for or against "the war." War, such as the United States' current war in Iraq, draws us nearer to a war zone, though our entire population is not reminded daily of its effects. The pilot asks the passengers on the plane to applaud for the military personnel on board; a construction crew ends its work early to attend the funeral of a crane operator's son killed in Iraq; children of military persons worry over their parents' safety. But we say little in public about peace. A pilot who would ask a plane to applaud for a returning peacemaking team would create a stir.

We rarely speak of peace, how we feel about it, and how to teach our children and grandchildren to promote it. We rarely dwell long enough with peace to imagine our lives if peace—not just freedom from war but the deep peace of Isaiah 11 that is brought through living in *shalom* with our neighbors—should prevail. The dream for peace has personal meaning for individuals that we rarely share in public.

Violence, war, and political turmoil disrupt most children's lives, yet God seeks peace—*shalom*—in which, "They will not hurt or destroy on all my holy mountain." Peace is both the precondition of and the aim of the best development of the social contexts of children's lives discussed earlier in this book—basic support services for families, respect for international law, a clean environment, and an accessible and just economy. We depend on relative freedom from political instability for each of these to flourish; and yet, it is unclear whether we seek peace or war through the way these systems develop. *Shalom* offers a way of being that few of us access.

Peace remains a very personal subject for all of us. Therefore, I have chosen to write the bulk of this chapter in the form of a letter to Bob, a fellow student in my writing group at the Iowa Summer Writing Festival.[1]

August 1, 2005

Dear Bob,

"Think about Hitler," you said. I had anticipated your response to my chapter on children, violence, and peace—not the exact words, but certainly the sentiments. The first night of our writing group when you introduced yourself, I thought, "I'm in trouble now." So many of our group work for children: David and Diane are social workers, Carol raises money for a children's non-profit; Donald tutors immigrants; Lorrie is a medical doctor. A great test group for my manuscript! Then you: career Air Force, former rocket scientist, and active member of the United Church of Christ. On the way to Iowa City I had heard the interview with Sally Ride, in which she described how fragile the earth's atmosphere looks from space. I had just drafted the chapter on children, earth, and ecology, and when you mentioned that you ran experiments on Earth's atmosphere, I wanted to hear your perspective on threats to our environment. You seemed to agree with the basic thesis of my sustainability chapter—that we are polluting without restraint or concern for future contamination. In fact, you thought it absurd that companies be allowed to sell to other companies their "rights" to pollute the atmosphere. Still, I'm sure you were in the back of my mind when I told the group about my anxieties—that once I reveal that my christology and the effects of war on children have pushed me to reject war, the reader will put down the book.[2]

I do not believe that my conclusions represent the only thoughtful Christian position on war. I also do not believe that those who risk their lives in war necessarily do so in vain. I believe that other Christians may weigh the evidence and legitimately conclude that Christian tradition justifies violent revolution or war under certain conditions. I believe God is with us in all of our suffering and all of our actions. But I also believe that the tradition of active nonviolent resistance to evil, as an alternative to war, warrants a hearing, especially in this time of war mentality.[3]

In the United States we have blended patriotism and Christianity into a war mentality that seems to eliminate any discussion of that portion of Christian tradition that seeks alternatives to war. I say "seems to" as I hope I am wrong. We promote this war mentality by sanitizing the wars we make. Media coverage of war makes bombs look like fireworks; reports of funerals of our war dead are banned. We reduce the effects of our wars to "collateral damage," even when children die, are maimed, lose their families, and become refugees during war; and when children lose life and limbs to leftover land mines and hot munitions when "peace" comes. Yet we fascinate ourselves with the effect on children of other people's wars—images of child soldiers recruited, girls raped, HIV-AIDS spread, children mutilated, diseased, and unschooled. Some of our best children's organizations are "branded" with these images—marketed with the emotional appeal of children's bodies brutalized by war.

In contrast to the justification for war in Christian tradition,[4] Christian nonviolent resistance to evil uses Jesus' life, particularly the Sermon on the Mount, as a guide for living. Jesus responded to the violence directed toward him with a variety of strategies—all borne of his relationship with God. He negotiates with power. He confuses with word play. He shows compassion for the poor, gains popular support, and risks the suspicion of the Roman and Jewish elite. He dines with persons who have become the tools of Roman oppression. He destroys the property of temple authorities as they extort money from others. Eventually, his relationship with God leads him back to Jerusalem. He goes, knowing his enemies will seize him and he will die.[5]

He sees evil clearly, and he resists it. But he is not one of the party of Zealots who revolt against Roman rule. He demonstrates what he means in the Sermon on the Mount when he says, "Love your enemies, and pray for those who persecute you." He meets sin and evil with moral good, and he depends upon the contrast between evil and good to convert people to increasing good. If he had met evil with violence, he would have played into its hands. Meeting violence with force, as war is designed to do, may overpower violence, may displace violence, may slow violence, but does not end a cycle of violence as Jesus sought to do. Ultimately, violence must be met with its extreme opposite, good, to show the way, not only to reduced or displaced violence, but to peace.

The practice of nonviolence begins long before we begin thinking about going to war.[6] A lasting peace is nourished by extending symbols of respect from nation to nation, by understanding one another's cultures and religions, by engaging in conversations about shared values, by making sure that all people have a way to meet basic needs such as food, shelter, clothing, education, and health. We create systems for resolving conflict when it arises. When hostility within and between nations rises, these practices and values are tested. The practice of nonviolent resistance calls us to sustain relationships with our adversaries even in the bleakest of circumstances.[7]

To answer your question, Bob, I have tried to think about Hitler through the mind of Dietrich Bonhoeffer, a pacifist who, like the other theological voices in this book, considered the Sermon on the Mount and its teaching on peacemaking to be essential to Christian discipleship. Even so, Bonhoeffer conspired with others to assassinate Hitler in a *coup d'etat* that would open a vacuum of power that could be replaced with another government. His biographer, Eberhard Bethge, says readers cannot find in Bonhoeffer's *Ethics* a rationale for his movement from pacifism to conspiracy. Bonhoeffer's *Letters and Papers from Prison* and Bethge's biography of Bonhoeffer, *Dietrich Bonhoeffer,* allow one to read between the lines. Even so, the larger question is whether, in light of these seemingly conflicting positions, he offers us insight that might be useful today as we consider children, war, and peace.[8]

Hitler consolidated his power during Germany's economic roller coaster that gained momentum after the Treaty of Versailles, cascaded through the 1920s, and landed in the worldwide Great Depression of the early 1930s. As a teenager I participated in an exchange student program that began as an effort toward building cultural peace and reconciliation between the United States and Germany. I asked a friend, "Why did Germans follow Hitler?" Though scholars offer complex theories about German culture, economics, religion, and Hitler's personality as contributing factors, I believe my friend's answer explains the enthusiasm of the common person for Hitler: "Fear of poverty." Hitler offered Germans a way out of the Great Depression. Without the Treaty of Versailles and the Great Depression, Hitler might never have gained the power to create the genocide that destroyed the lives of Jewish families and children and a war that devastated Europe. This he did in the name of "healthier" German children.[9]

As he consolidated his power, the blind obedience of the people, borne out of this fear of poverty, allowed him to silence those groups who offered an alternative. The Christians in Germany responded with multiple voices. Some Christians embraced his political ideology. Some Christians challenged his attempt to take over the church and interpret Christianity in his own image. Some Christians spoke a resounding "No!" until they exhausted all legal means to do so and fled. Some Christians remained in Germany and resisted his racism and his war machine with their lives. The circle around Dietrich Bonhoeffer dissented with a series of practices: legal challenges, sermons and statements, "illegal" education such as the seminary at Finkenwalde, and finally, participation in a series of attempts at *coup d'etat*.

Bonhoeffer became a pacifist during his studies at Union Theological Seminary in New York. His German Lutheran forebears had interpreted the Sermon on the Mount as an impossible ideal that convinced people of their guilt and threw them into the arms of God's grace as the only possibility of salvation. In New York he encountered Jean Lasserre, a French Catholic, who convinced Bonhoeffer that Jesus intended the Sermon on the Mount to be a guide for living a Christian life. (The conversation between Bonhoeffer and Lasserre was roughly contemporary to the conversations between Peter Maurin and Dorothy Day—the emphasis on the Sermon on the Mount was also current in ecumenical circles.) Having been convinced by Lasserre,[10] Bonhoeffer had hoped to study with Gandhi in India. Instead, he returned to Germany to direct the seminary of the "Confessing Church"–the movement of Christian ecclesial resistance against Hitler—at Finkenwalde.

Gandhian-style nonviolent resistance, facing governments that could intimidate, torture, and kill, broke the power of apartheid and colonialism in India, the United States, and South Africa. We will never know what additional means Gandhi might have offered to Bonhoeffer had Bonhoeffer gone to India rather than back to Germany at that time. Instead, we know that at Finkenwalde Bonhoeffer engaged his seminarians in an intense "life together" that taught them to witness to the Sermon on the Mount and other Christian practices as a community set apart from politics. Finkenwalde offered that witness of monastic communities today who seek by their community life to demonstrate to the world that Christianity offers an alternative, peaceful way to live. Still, Finkenwalde did not prepare seminarians to resist conscription into Hitler's army. Regardless of their ambivalence over Hitler's aims, half of the seminarians later died in World War II.

During the time that Bonhoeffer taught at Finkenwalde, members of Bonhoeffer's family, who were employed in government and military positions, found sympathetic colleagues with whom they could form the rudiments of political resistance. Under Hitler's increasing threats against Jews, Bonhoeffer's twin sister and her Jewish husband fled to England. The Confessing Movement collapsed under internal conflict. Bonhoeffer, suspected of being a subversive by Hitler's government, traveled to England and then back to New York. There, he wrestled with his conscience and returned to Germany to join his siblings in the political resistance that led to several coup attempts. The question remains: How can we reconcile the Bonhoeffer who often and openly states that Christianity cannot sanctify war with the Bonhoeffer who sees a *coup* attempt as part of his "responsibility for the world?"

Pacifism is sometimes understood as the rejection of any act of force or retaliation for physical violence; it is actually a range of positions, including what Bethge calls "conditional pacifism." Bonhoeffer may have understood any act of violence, including the assassination attempts on Hitler's life, as a situational, necessary sin for which the Christian needed to seek forgiveness. However, the resistance engaged in other activities that give a broader meaning to this particular act of violence in the midst of a generally pacifist mindset.

By the time Bonhoeffer decided to join the political resistance, Hitler had silenced all means of legal, political, religious, or other public dissent. The resistance could no longer use any institutions of the German Reich as a means to change the course of the history they saw unfolding.

Theologically, the Confessing Church, which authored the famous "Barmen Declaration" against Hitler, never became unified. Among other confusions, it could not agree on whether it was called to a witness to the church only or to the German public also. When it sought international support, the ecumenical community wavered. The ecumenical community sought neutral ground between the Christian nationalists who had the power of the Reich behind them and the fledging Confessing Church. Eventually, Bonhoeffer lost the support of the Confessing Church in resisting Hitler, though some individual, powerful ecumenists tried to assist him.

Politically, the resistance tried to reach the British government with a message that differentiated Hitler from Germany. They sought to communicate to Churchill's government, through church leaders and others, that a well-organized resistance movement wanted to overthrow Hitler with the intention of reestablishing peace. They did not seek to replace Hitler with a government that would fight the Allies but with one that would be in a position to negotiate a settlement that would bring a quick end to the hostilities. Neither England nor, eventually, the United States could hear the pleas for support; these countries were by then committed to seeking all military means to bring any form of Germany to "unconditional surrender."

For Bonhoeffer, a pacifist, the situation warranted a particular act of killing. Here lies the difference between Bonhoeffer's action and war mentality, or militarism. Rather than beginning with the assumption that violence was a just action, he pursued active, persuasive means to disempower Hitler and persuade the German people of Hitler's evil. When he joined not only the resistance movement but the conspiracy against Hitler, he may have still believed himself to be in violation of Christian teaching but hoped for forgiveness in the wideness of God's mercy. Regardless, the norm with which he approached life could be found in the beatitude, "Blessed are the peacemakers"; the particular act of violence against Hitler deviated from the norm. He justified this act as one of standing by the Jewish victims of suffering—a stand that he failed to see in the Christian Confessing Church as it sought to resist Hitler at the same time that it protected itself. His mentality reverses the standard in which a culture perceives military might as the norm, and pacifism becomes an irrational and uncomfortable hiccup upsetting the status quo. Bonhoeffer's thinking assumes a norm of promoting peace through civil persuasion, and, for Christians, faithful commitment to the tenets of the Sermon on the Mount. A necessary, pragmatic deviation from that norm becomes a violation to be mourned.

To demonstrate the difference between militarism and active nonviolence as the norm, let's think about the potential for nonviolent intervention that could have prevented or reduced the deaths during the 1995 Rwandan genocide. In this genocide, 300,000 children died, and 90 percent of the children who survived watched the death of someone they loved—an enormous trauma for the childhood of an entire nation. Romeo Dallaire of Canada was the military commander in charge of the United Nations Mission for Rwanda, the international peacekeeping force sent to enforce a peace agreement between the Hutu government and the Tutsi minority. For a variety of reasons, Dallaire had rules of engagement imposed upon him that insisted that his troops use no force, despite the fact that an informant warned him of the impending genocide. After the United Nations pulled out most of the peacekeeping force, he and 250 troops responded to the genocide around them. The International Committee of the Red Cross, under the leadership of Phillipe Guillard, was the only nongovernmental organization (NGO) to remain in Rwanda.

The word on the street is, "The world did nothing to prevent the Rwandan genocide." It is true that just as the British government ignored Bonhoeffer's appeals, the United States and other Western powers ignored the pleas of those who knew what was happening in Rwanda. Dallaire was an obedient military commander left with instructions not to engage militarily. Dallaire and his officers, Guillard and his team, Carl Wilkens, and a few remaining representatives of humanitarian relief organizations improvised techniques that resemble known techniques of nonviolence resistance. They sought to build relationships with the enemy leadership; persuaded them to spare the lives of persons where and when they could; used the symbols of the international community to guard sanctuaries and did so effectively, even without weapons; and established safe houses where threatened Rwandans were hid, at risk to their own lives. Captain Daigne Mbaye of Senegal, in particular, created ways to lead many groups of Rwandans out of the country.[11] The *genocidaires*[12] ambushed

Red Cross ambulances, killing patients. "Those patients did not die in vain," Guillard argued.[13] Guillard sought out the leaders, threatened the *genocidaires* with international public exposure, broke with its tradition of neutrality to make good on the threat, and gained safer passage to travel. Wilkens also saved the lives of children in an orphanage by asking the *genocidaires* to spare the children.

You are probably thinking that in Germany and Rwanda the resistance movements saved peoples lives until an armed force, the Allies or the Rwanda Patriotic Front (RPF), won the day. That is true, but both the Allies and the RPF had larger political and military goals to serve and calculated that innocent people would die for the sake of those goals. You might reply that Martin Luther King Jr. acknowledged that the children integrating schools would have to suffer, and in some cases die, for the larger good of the next generation's equal access to education. The difference is this: a war mentality, and its loyalty to force, seeks to blind us to the social reasons for conflict, to the humanity of "belligerents," and to methods that might reduce or negate the suffering of innocents, especially children.

I wonder how "warfare" would change if we poured as much money, training, and research into teaching people the old methods of nonviolent resistance and new methods of international conflict resolution as we do into teaching them to kill. I wonder how "warfare" would change if the media gave as much attention to those persons who use powerful but nonviolent responses to force as they do covering military intervention.[14] I wonder how "warfare" would change if we tolerated—or even decorated—1800 deaths of our sons and daughters in so-called peacekeeping and humanitarian relief missions, and how ineffective "warfare" would become if we ran from warfare as soon as an American dies, as we do in such missions. I wonder how successful peacekeeping and humanitarian missions would become if they had the training, information, and support that successful military operations rely on. [15]

We will direct our resources toward nonviolence if we adopt a mentality of nonviolence that insists, as do John Wesley, Dorothy Day, and Martin Luther King Jr., that our opponents are human beings, much like us. In our humanness, as Carl Wilkens, the

Seventh Day Adventist who remained in Rwanda, says "We gotta recognize that in each one of us, there's such a potential for good and there's such a potential for evil."[16] Wilkens' insight distinguishes him from Dallaire at the particular moment when Dallaire meets the leadership of the *genocidaires*. When he is being taken to meet with the leadership of the genocide, Dallaire takes the ammunition out of his gun for fear he will be tempted to kill. When he sees blood on their clothes, he recounts in a *Frontline* interview:

> As I was looking at them, and shaking their hands, I noticed some blood spots on them and all of a sudden they disappeared from being human, all of a sudden something happened that turned them into nonhuman things. And I was not talking with humans. I was literally talking with evil. The meeting became a very difficult ethical problem. Do I actually negotiate with the devil to save people, or do I wipe it out? Do I shoot the bastards right there? I haven't answered that question yet.[17]

The title of his autobiography, *Shake Hands with the Devil*, alludes to the way he reports his experience to *Frontline*, though he does not write his account of humanity transformed into evil beings in his autobiography. I extend to Lt. General Romeo Dallaire my greatest respect for his commitment to the Rwandan people and the depth of religious and psychological trauma that he endured on their behalf. His interpretation of that experience is sacred and honorable, as it is. His interpretation points toward theological tenets, however, that offer other nuances.

His account raises the question about how Christian theologians think of the relationship of human beings to evil. Some insist that the image of God always resides in some small way in human beings, even when they are perpetrating evil acts in evil systems. Others contend that evil is *incarnate* in humans, depraving them totally, as God, in the opposite, *incarnates* humanity in Jesus, creating a sinless person. The person who believes that the image of God resides in humanity must always struggle with the god-likeness of the enemy; the person who believes in evil incarnate in humanity might well feel obligated to destroy the other or be plagued with guilt if he or she doesn't. Wesley, for example, struggled with gross inhumanity around him—the violent overthrow of the monarchy that etched the history of sixteenth-, seventeenth-, and eighteenth-century England in blood, the violent revolt of mobs against those who perpetrated their poverty and against economic systems built on slavery. Yet he insisted that the image of God remains in every human being—distorted almost beyond recognition, but not obliterated.

Dallaire's question about whether he should have destroyed the Rwandan *genocidaires* is not quite parallel to Bonhoeffer's question about whether to plot to kill Hitler, as Dallaire was not prepared to fill the vacuum with an alternative government as was Bonhoeffer. But the struggle of both men hangs on what Bonhoeffer distinguishes as "folly." Folly, for Bonhoeffer, causes reasonable people—in Bonhoeffer's case, the British government, in Dallaire's case, the United Nations—to look away from evil. Bonhoeffer offered this understanding of folly:

> Folly is a more dangerous enemy to the good than evil. One can protest against evil; it can be unmasked and, if need be, prevented by force. Evil always carries the seeds of its own destruction... Against folly we have no defence [*sic*]. Neither protests nor force can touch it; reasoning is no use; facts that contradict personal prejudices can simply be disbelieved—indeed, the fool can counter by criticizing them, and if they are undeniable, they can be pushed aside as trivial exceptions. So the fool, as distinct from the scoundrel, is completely self-satisfied; in fact, he can easily become dangerous, as it does not take much to make him aggressive. A fool must therefore be treated more cautiously than a scoundrel; we shall never again try to convince a fool by reason, for it is both useless and dangerous.[18]

It is interesting to compare the emotional responses of Dallaire and Guillard—both remarkable, strong men—after the genocide. They witnessed equally as much blood and death and engaged in similar nonviolent activities saving lives, though from different frames of reference, with different aims, and with different institutional support. Dallaire suffered post-traumatic stress syndrome and became suicidal when he returned; Guillard affirmed life.

Guillard attributes the difference to the fact that Dallaire's institution, the United Nations, abandoned him while Guillard's institution, the International Committee of the Red Cross, supported him. True—what eats at Dallaire is not only the bloodshed he saw but his inability to move the United Nations, in its "folly," to take the genocide seriously. Dallaire, a very admirable, caring, and passionate man, has understood his whole life in military metaphors. He rightly concludes, "I'm a military commander; I didn't keep the peace. 'I did my best' isn't good enough. I failed."[19] Guillard, an equally admirable, caring, and passionate man, works for an organization that exerts active, nonviolent presence in war by tending to the sick and the wounded of both sides. On his return, Guillard reports:

When we came back from Rwanda...it was evident for [my wife], for me, that after this experience, we both wanted to create life. I had never explained to my son that he was a product of the genocide. That's not easy to explain. That's all.[20]

Perhaps Dallaire would be comforted by Bonhoeffer's words from Tegel Prison:

I'm still discovering right up to this moment, that it is only by living completely in this world that one learns to have faith. One must completely abandon any attempt to make something of oneself, whether it be a saint, or a converted sinner, or a churchman (a so-called priestly type!), a righteous man or an unrighteous one, a sick man or a healthy one. By this-worldliness I mean living unreservedly in life's duties, problems, successes and failures, experiences and perplexities. In doing so we throw ourselves completely into the arms of God, taking seriously, not our own sufferings, but those of God in the world—watching with Christ in Gethsemane. That, I think is faith; that is *metanoia*; and that is how one becomes a man and a Christian (cf. Jer. 45!) How can success make us arrogant, or failure lead us astray, when we share in God's sufferings through a life of this kind?[21]

War mentality and concern for children are at odds. War mentality directs all of our energies toward a common enemy and a common goal. War mentality once required that we glorify the killing of the enemy. In World War II and even in the Viet Nam era enemy dead made headlines. Now, instead of counting how many "enemies" we have killed in Afghanistan or Iraq, we avoid acknowledging that anyone has died. Warfare can no longer distinguish between enemies and the innocent civilians. In our folly we avoid public recognition that children are dying in our wars, that they are maimed, that they are hungry, that their education is interrupted. We ignore the effect of war on our own children who are left behind when their parents to go to war, our children whose development is shaped by their fears and losses.

Our media readily report the effect of other peoples' war on their children. A hospital in Congo stitches the vaginas of young girls who have been gang raped in war. A Red Cross unit in Sierra Leone binds the wounds of young children whose fingers and hands have been chopped off by machetes. An orphanage in Rwanda rescues children and posts their pictures in refugee camps in hopes that the parents are still alive. A military faction entices young boys with food, shelter, and power in the form of a gun. Those children who survive civil war in Africa and elsewhere learn to meet violence with violence to protect themselves. The others die. Our media tell us so.

If scenes of war provide the backdrop for children's lives in many countries in Africa and around the world, then the stories of peacemakers such as Bishop Ntambo deserve the stage. As a child, Ntambo was primed for violence by the culture around him. Witchcraft and colonialism perpetuated that violence. In the poor Congolese village where he grew up his grandfather practiced witchcraft. He recalls walking into his grandfather's hut and discovering that his grandfather was eating a human leg. He became a teenager during Congolese independence; he hated the Belgians and could have easily joined the mobs of youth who threatened white residents. He was saved by his desire to meet the girls and get an education—he was told he could do both at the Methodist Church. There he discovered the writings of Martin Luther King Jr. and nonviolent protest. Something inside him identified with this King—this black man—who wrote against violence. The paradigm shift came: a life he had assumed would be conducted through violence now was framed by the range of actions that arise when one assumes that active nonviolent resistance is the only option.

During the Congolese war of 1996–2001, Ntambo improvised means of nonviolent resistance. Irrationally, he continued building churches and parsonages in Kamina, literally transporting building supplies as a sign of stability. According to people in Kamina, as people heard that the fighting was approaching and prepared to flee, they came across building supplies still coming into town. The building projects gave them a reason to remain in Kamina; and the town, still occupied by residents, never became an easy target for the fighters. Unlike Bonhoeffer who decided that he would not have the credibility to rebuild Germany if he did not return, Ntambo and his family fled to Zambia during a portion of the war. They had skills that the fighters wanted to co-opt. Upon his return to Kamina, however, Ntambo created and sustained humanitarian projects and supported refugees, always under the threat of political instability. He has brokered conversations leading to peace agreements between various factions in the continued conflict in Congo.

African leaders such as Ntambo are deeply concerned with the witness for peace to the next generation of African children. Ntambo and other African church leaders fear the chaos that conflict in Africa has brought to their children's lives. They fear the way the culture of violence has shaped the next generation. They present a powerful witness that in no uncertain terms offers a risk-filled but dramatic nonviolent alternative. It imitates Christ's hope and Christ's *atonement*, the word theologians use to describe the way Christ takes on the suffering of the world.

Their witness interrogates those of us in supposedly "secure" countries about our presence in the world and in our local communities. What alternatives do we offer to the children in our midst? Must we surround our children with a war mentality?

We have alternatives. We can promote the wide range of practices that come under the heading of "nonviolent resistance." We can reduce despair and promote hope by making sure that all people have food, shelter, education, and medical care. We can seek intercultural and interfaith understanding. We can teach the traditions, the practical trials and errors, failures and successes of societies such as South Africa where the philosophy of nonviolence has responded to violence with a different kind of force. When necessary, we can demonstrate the honor of risking our health and lives in peaceful resistance by finding the image of humanity in our opponents. Surely it is worth recruiting our children into these stories and traditions, so at the very least they can make informed decisions when they struggle with violence and its alternatives.[22]

Your friend in Christ,
Pam

Interlude from Section Two to Three

In the second section of this book, "The Unnamed Children's Issues," I have explored the larger social contexts that shape children's lives—social support systems for families, human rights, the global economy, the environment, and war and peace. These systems are often not considered when we think about issues related to children or even children and poverty. Even if these systems are not usually the focus of "children's ministries," the church *does* engage in significant endeavors in advocacy and direct service for children. What does the church do for children? And, what are these children doing to renew the church? Do these ministries represent a current version of the accomplishments of John Wesley, Dorothy Day, and Martin Luther King Jr.? Those questions are answered in the concluding three chapters.

How does the church concretely resist poverty? In speaking engagements and public presentations, I have been repeatedly asked for stories that provide ideas and inspiration—signs of hope. The concluding section, "Rhizomatic Ministry: Engaging Disciples and Apostles," demonstrates that a wide range of effective ministries do exist. The next three chapters include interviews with people who are committed to ministry with children and poverty and who mentor others into that ministry. Most of these persons served as area coordinators for the United Methodist Bishops Initiative on Children and Poverty, an emphasis of the United Methodist Council of Bishops from 1996–2004. These interviews show that the church does significantly more in direct ministry with poor children than is commonly known or acknowledged.

Many of these area coordinators are rightly concerned that the church is not adequately involved as a voice for children in larger systems where justice must be sought, such as were described in the last section. Their concerns are justified. The denomination actively advocates for the *Convention on the Rights of the Child*, a clean environment, for a just economy and for international peace, but those involved *in local ministries* do not seem to have engaged these issues as issues for children and people in poverty. The interviews with area coordinators record significant advocacy on behalf of children in family, health and welfare, education, and prison ministries. However, in no case did a respondent report that advocacy efforts for children at the local church level focused on the potential for good and ill in international law, the development of the global economy, environmental policy, and international peacemaking. I do not conclude from this sample that such efforts at the local congregational level do not exist. They must be rare, however, when such a broad sample of leaders fails to report any such efforts.

The resources for such ministries do exist through such legs of the denomination as the United Methodist Women's Campaign for Children. Local ministries that understand larger social and cultural issues as children's issues can be found in the global church. Bishop Ntambo of the Democratic Republic of Congo, whose community has been an example throughout this book, was an active participant in the Task Force for the Initiative on Children and Poverty for its entire existence and often spoke of the devastating effect of political instability in his country on children. Congolese children's future in all areas usually considered children's issues—food, health, education, and family life—is dependent on his and others' success in brokering peace.

My research suggests that the combined efforts of the United Methodist Women's Campaign for Children and United Methodist Bishops Initiative on Children and Poverty created a focus on children and poverty among United Methodists as extensive as in any mainline denomination. Such efforts renew the church, but they are not yet at the center of denominational life. Even as I record the current limits of the mainline Protestant ministry with children and poverty, I celebrate the enormous commitment of a wide network of usually anonymous Christians who have dedicated their lives to ministering in love and justice with children and the poor and sustaining others in these ministries. These ministries are described in the interviewees' own words so that they may serve as a model and inspiration for others who want to find a way to contribute to the well-being of children at this time.

Rhizomatic Ministry: Engaging Disciples and Apostles

CHAPTER 10

Rhizomatic Ministry in a New Century of the Child

Despite their limits, the Christian mainline churches have sustained a concern for children and poverty, even as that concern ebbs and flows in local congregations, and even as those ministries produce new patterns. In this chapter I seek to explore the breadth of that concern across the mainline denominations and the depth of that concern in the United Methodist denomination. *Ministries with children and poverty are arising in new patterns of partnership that resemble rhizomes, the root systems of grass.*

Centuries of the Child

In *The Century of the Child* (1900), Ellen Key, the philosophic architect of the Swedish welfare state, suggested that in the twentieth century the welfare of the child would move from the margins of concern to the center.[1] To an extent, Key characterized important aspects of the twentieth century: the twentieth century produced previously unheard of advances in child welfare in education, health, labor policy, and government support for all families and the recognition of the child in international law. It globalized communications and information on a previously unheard of scale. As a century of the child, however, the twentieth century had its limits: it produced the highest child poverty rates in the industrialized world in its wealthiest country—the

United States—and child destitution in many countries of the Southern Hemisphere. It infected the planet with environmental degradation that some now think is verging on irreversible. It transmitted the assumption in wealthy cultures that children are the lifestyle choice of individual parents and do not deserve general social support. The twentieth century also spread the belief that wealth is an end in itself rather than a means of social support for communities, families, and children.

For the mainline Christian churches, the twentieth century continued to be a century of the child, even as their concern for all children became increasingly countercultural.[2] After social welfare support became decidedly out of favor with the majority of legislators, mainline denominations continued to advocate for support for children and families. Awareness, advocacy, and ministries for children proliferated in the mainline denominations in the 1990s, and, in many cases, these initiatives of the Christian church responded to children in their most vulnerable state: poverty. Searching the Web sites of the denominations that relate to the National Council of Churches in the USA[3] in January, 2006, I found specific initiatives:

- the United Methodist Women's Campaign for Children and the United Methodist Bishops Initiative on Children and Poverty
- the Episcopal Church's "Children's Charter" and advocacy efforts on behalf of the November 2005 "Assistance for Orphans and other Vulnerable Children Act of 2005"
- the United Church of Christ's numerous social policy advocacy papers on topics such as the Child Care Development Block Grant, No Child Left Behind, Child Sponsorship, Excellence in Public Schools, international children's support, talking to children, terrorism, welfare reform, and child soldiers
- the Presbyterian Church (PCUSA)'s Decade of the Child 2001–2011 and "Congregations Covenanting for Children," with issue papers addressing conditions of vulnerability
- the Evangelical Lutheran Church of America's "Safe Haven for Children" that includes a resource guide for congregations and specifically builds from a strategy of reaching women and children living in poverty
- American Baptist curriculum on Race and Poverty in which children are specifically addressed (2005)

- the Church of the Brethren's attention to child exploitation, TANF, and recognition of alarming trends toward hunger, homelessness, and lack of insurance as their first story of 2006
- the Moravian Church's publication of numerous articles on children and poverty
- the Philadelphia Yearly Meeting of Friends' recognition of family challenges such as abandonment, homelessness, poverty, and job stress
- the Reformed Church of America's publication of numerous articles on international ministries related to children and poverty

In addition to these representative examples, the Unitarian Universalist Association has established an emphasis on Children, Youth, and Violence,[4] and the United States Conference of Catholic Bishops continues to educate Catholics about the root causes of poverty and promote empowerment of persons who are poor through the Catholic Campaign for Human Development.[5]

In the twentieth century, advocacy for children and poverty in the political arena, program design for children, and leadership in training for local church ministries was carried out by boards and agencies who served as arms of the denomination. These boards and agencies still serve highly specialized functions, linking congregations and the outside world and providing resources for congregational ministry. The structure of Protestant denominations in the United States is changing, however. It is now commonly accepted by those who study and lead mainline denominations that the late twentieth century brought a significant drift toward congregationalism, even in those denominations that locate denominational power in larger structures. What are the implications of these changes for ministries with children and poverty in mainline Protestantism? If congregations are becoming more important as originators and organizers of ministries with children and poverty, what effect does this have for ministries with poor children and for the renewing of the church?

From 1996–2004 I served as an educational consultant with the United Methodist Bishops Initiative on Children and Poverty. In the United Methodist Church the Council of Bishops (COB) is not a program agency; initiatives from the COB have always limited themselves to teaching efforts. The Initiative on Children and Poverty began as the denomination grappled with its growing congregationalism. As a result, the task force that guided the initiative early on made two decisions: (1) since people learn by doing, not only by studying documents, a teaching initiative had to significantly involve itself in doing ministry; and (2) the Council of Bishops could emphasize the importance of ministries with children and poverty and provide resources for the bishops to use in their areas, but each area and each congregation would have to discern for itself the appropriate ministry for that area. These decisions were difficult to communicate: some agency persons resented the Council of Bishops for treading on the turf of program agencies; some congregations resisted another "top down" initiative. Despite this resistance, in almost every area of the denomination, including its judicatories in Europe, Africa, and the Philippines, existing ministries were strengthened and new ministries developed. What might be learned from this example of how such ministries might renew denominations in the twenty-first century?

A research team and I conducted interviews throughout the United States and in other countries where possible, in part to study the effect of the Initiative, but more importantly, to determine the presence of the United Methodist church in the lives of children and poverty and the effect of children and poverty on church renewal. The stories from area coordinators for the Bishops Initiative, stories that are undoubtedly echoed in the initiatives of other denominations, show that ministries with children and poverty are changing the lives of some of our most vulnerable children and renewing the church.

Rhizomatic Ministry: Using Ecclesial Knowledge to Restructure the Church from the Ground Up

People who study the way knowledge is organized use plant root systems as metaphors for knowledge. In the twentieth century knowledge was organized like a "tap root," with a primary root of knowledge from which specialty knowledge sprouted. It is a vertical root. Much of our organizational life is a concrete form of this organization of knowledge. We assume that different groups will be responsible for a particular kind of knowledge and its subspecialties. Some cultural theorists suggest that, increasingly, knowledge is organized more like a rhizome—the root system of grass, for example—in which a shoot of knowledge seeks other shoots with which to connect. It is a horizontal root. When it gets blocked, it simply sprouts in another direction. Rhizomes are structured by a logic that allows them to survive in different conditions than do tap roots.[6]

Keith Clements, in *Learning to Speak: The Church's Voice in Public Affairs*, writes about what the church knows. He says:

> The Christian community, simply by virtue of what it is and does, knows a great deal of what is happening on the ground... The church is the bus-drivers and home-helps, the doctors and the farmers, the teachers and the bank clerks, the shopkeepers and the nurses, the production-line workers and the computer programmers, the local councilors and the social workers...and all who seek to live by faith within the human scene. Here lies the basic data-gathering of the church in the world, by those who experience most fully the pressures thought of more abstractly in political and economic terms...the church is the most widely distributed network of concern and information in the nation.[7]

This network is growing its own structure through rhizomatic interconnections. In one place there are shoots of connection between agency programs and congregations and the Bishops Initiative; in another, between congregations and social services; in a third, between local congregations and other ministry organizations. The question is not, "Which program or agency on the whole has been most effective in ministry with children and people living in poverty?"—in other words, which tap root should we support and which should we weed out?—but, "How can we discern and support the emerging networks of local knowledge and action—the rhizomes—that do the church's ministry and are strengthening the church below the obvious displays of new growth?"

A Ministry Rhizome: Supporting Family Relationships

One set of rhizomatic ministries center around family support, often building relationships among the church, government departments of social services, civic organizations, and educational institutions. Local congregations have long operated an extensive number of child care centers in the nation. These ministries have benefited from the denomination as it supports the preschool by training teachers. The teachers, in turn, support parents who are struggling with contemporary parenting issues. Wanda Holcombe of Southwest Texas trains preschool teachers and staff who work in congregations on issues that help to shape the climate of the preschool. Teachers and staff, in turn, work with parents to make their home environments more educationally effective. Holcombe describes some examples of training:

> They asked us to work with staff people...on violence in the media and how that affects kids all the way down to little ones, even the infants who might be placed in front of a TV set, hours and hours. And [that] can even sometimes happen in centers, educational structures as well. And the next year I did one on cultural accumulation, how you help families and staff begin to look at—there's a great video "I Want That, I Need That, Buy Me That" —and how you help families and children [decide] what are our needs and things. And...how do you help even little children begin to learn the whole process of relationship—well, in high school they call it mediation. So we try to choose things like that, that deal with real core issues ...[for] children in poverty and families...that they can do in the classroom and work with parents.[8]

A similar collaboration between the Baltimore-Washington Annual Conference and the State of Maryland produced some "new shoots" for the child care rhizome. Sandy Ferguson emphasized the connection between congregations' child care centers and Head Start, the program of early education for low-income children. She also suggests that congregations can play an unusual function in stabilizing conflict between unmarried or separated parents:

> We created a wonderful manual that we produced in rela-tionship with Head Start...encouraging local churches...to provide a place for a Head Start program... We created a manual in relationship with the child support arm of the government... It had information...on how local churches could get involved to have a safe sanctuary for the parent,

with two parents not being able to get along, that this could be a place...the money could be dropped off. It would be like a peacekeeper.[9]

Gayle Davis of the Troy Annual Conference describes a rhizome that kept on spreading in collaboration with Vermont social services, Borders Books, the Rotary Club, and Literacy Volunteers. The effort was eventually adopted by Fox Television.

The Bright Red Bookshelf...started off small... We built small bookshelves and painted them red and put them in... WIC offices, they went to Head Start, they went to jails, they went to all kinds of places where children are who are not usually able to afford books and they went to places where children really shouldn't be as well. They were in waiting rooms at Social Services where they were a huge hit because instead of running around, kids now got to sit down and have a positive experience with a parent. The people in the waiting room started calling us, and it was not one of those projects where it was, "Oh, we hope this goes away." They'd call us and have them replenished... We gave up finally trying to number the books, but we think [we gave away] about 100,000 books... Other people have adopted...our project... It's turned into a huge project."[10]

Several conferences report ministries with families transitioning from welfare to employment. Such families need a variety of kinds of assistance, including assistance with transportation. When families live in rural areas, the transportation needs can be acute. Judy Lybeck describes an innovative rural ministry that involves small local congregations, auto mechanics, financial consultants, and a hunger ministry:

In the northwestern part of the state a church started a thing called "Car Care" ministry. Up in small communities there is no bus service, and with "W-2" in Wisconsin, families have to work, and if their car doesn't work, they can't get to work. So, once a month, the church has an event; people can bring their car in, and they've done tune-ups and they do things like brake jobs. It has evolved to a point where people will donate cars and the [church] group will fix them up and donate them to the families...While your car is being fixed, you must attend a budgeting/financial workshop...just talking about ways to spend money... There's an organization from the Twin Cities that once a month will truck, literally, a "semi" full of excess food to that particular town and other towns in upper Wisconsin. So the car care ministry goes on, the budget counseling, and it's also a food distribution. And all that happens once a month.[11]

Joyce DeToni Hill of the Rocky Mountain Annual Conference describes the way that a range of efforts over a period of years, including making small grants to congregations that were involved with children and poverty, led to the rescue of an interfaith preschool in a small, low-income community:

> In November we were at an All-Clergy meeting and dis-
> covered that our committee is getting to be known as a
> resource. Because our state has been hit so hard by fires,
> the state was forced to rechannel money away from child
> care. There was a small church in the southwest corner of
> the conference who operated an interfaith preschool in
> a poor area. It was the only child care and preschool in
> the area, and it would have to close because of the cuts.
> They went to the [District Superintendent] and told him
> that they needed $20,000 to stay open. The D.S. pointed
> to us and said, "Talk to them..." We found out that we
> could use discretionary funds, and we made the executive
> decision to send them $3000. We found out later that the
> pastor was able to get matching grants and found local
> support as a result of that initial gift. It was a witness for
> the community.[12]

A Ministry Rhizome: Health and Welfare

Some ministry rhizomes are well-grounded in ongoing networks supported by Annual Conference structures. These rhizomes demonstrate the ongoing effectiveness of well-established conference-level denominational networks, despite the drift toward congregationalism. John F. Lacaria of West Virginia used his denominational network to support children and fragile families. When children must be removed from their parents' home, social service agencies usually try to stabilize the family so it can be reunited. At the very least, case workers attempt to strengthen relationships and establish homes for children within their extended family networks. A dearth of foster families and group homes within West Virginia meant that foster children were relocated in residences out-of-state, dislocating them and reducing the potential for reunion with their parents *or* extended families. Building on a long history of child advocacy, he comments on the effectiveness of the networking between the church, social services, and health and welfare agencies to respond to the need for families for foster children:

> Our child advocacy network was quite effective and it was instituted in part out of Health and Welfare ministries of the Conference for two purposes: to try to create neighborhoods and communities where kids would not fall through the cracks, and also to enable the Conference to participate in kind of a restoration of families and children's lives...The state was sending most of these children to out-of-state families, and [this] was going to give us enough support to try to use our Health and Welfare agencies...[to] meet that need so we wouldn't have to send kids out of state.[13]

Sandy Ferguson also describes the range of partnerships that her Annual Conference office has promoted in comprehensive efforts on behalf of children's health and welfare. Encompassing Washington, D.C., the Annual Conference has particular geographical immediacy that enables it to promote political advocacy with the federal government. Through her office Sandy Ferguson addresses a series of social issues, including disabilities, mental illness, drugs and violence, HIV-AIDS, racism, multicultural issues, and ecumenism and interreligious affairs. Most often these issues are addressed without direct attention toward their effect on the lives of children. A new partnership between the Annual Conference and the American Cancer Society, however, yielded a local church program on health and wellness that included a children's component. This program, "Body and Soul," provides, as Ferguson explains,

> a wonderful model on educating the congregation on how to have a healthier lifestyle. It has components for

children and youth. We have churches that conducted the model during the summer, so it was almost like a vacation Bible school kind of experience; and it matched perfectly because we could use all of our religious materials...and have a component on being healthy.[14]

The Missouri Annual Conference developed a multifaceted dental ministry to fill a need in the health and welfare of Missouri's children. Lin Stern served as a dental missionary, educating children about good dental care and building awareness in communities about assistance available from local congregations. She reflected on her wide-ranging experiences distributing health kits with multiple toothbrushes, so that family members do not share one toothbrush, saying, "Now you can share the love of Christ through a smile."[15] But she urged congregations in the program to go beyond the distribution of toothbrushes. She asked them to consider building in a program that combined dental hygiene and religious education in the church after school. She describes the progress in one congregation: "And there is this group that's doing that... The pastor is teaching them Bible stories and teaching them how to brush their teeth and giving them toothbrushes. But she feeds them first because they come out of school hungry."[16]

A Ministry Rhizome: Advocacy

Child advocates need support and ongoing training through ministry rhizomes to stay current with children's issues. Debra Rogosky of Pennsylvania describes advocacy training that involves the church, the state, and a political action group. This rhizome took on the issue of unequal funding of Pennsylvania's schools:

> We have been having regular advocacy trainings for the last two years... One was to help introduce child advocates to the resources they have in their communities. So we met at a central gathering place and had people from the community come in... We had people representing Head Start, Children and Youth Services. We had some political figures, and they came to say that these were the resources we had in our communities to help the child advocates. Last year we had an organization called Good Schools Pennsylvania. Good Schools is a political

action group, in effect. And what they're doing is trying to develop economic and academic parity across the state school system. As you know, most schools are funded with taxes, and they're trying to get sort of a central kitty so that all the money is distributed equally, so that we don't have rich districts will all the computer equipment and impoverished districts, especially our rural districts, with absolutely nothing. And they came and taught people how to write letters and be proactive in the political arena, so those are exciting things for our Conference.[17]

Advocacy for children in poverty may mean that congregations are willing to help persons with secular power identify options and resources that might be at their disposal when they must make decisions about difficult issues they face. Wanda Holcombe spoke of general excitement that the bishop was

going to meet with Methodist judges at a luncheon... We're going to tie the political with congregations, particularly with juvenile justice for alternative sentencing and family abuse issues. We're going to focus on family court judges, Methodist judges in the congregations that can help from the legal side; but, also, the congregation can help them build ministries that deal with some of those root issues of families. Over 50 percent of the juveniles who come before Juvenile Court come from families of violence and abuse. We have a sixty-six percent recidivism rate for returning to prison. Over fifty percent of our students who come out of high school cannot get jobs so where do they go? They go to the streets, they sell drugs, and they're in prison. Over sixty percent of the people in prison are from nonviolent offences.[18]

Holcombe identified a rhizomatic connection with national church efforts through the Women's Division of the General Board of Global Ministries. The mainline Protestant "Century of the Child" developed largely because women's groups have often prodded, pushed, and poked the denomination and government into paying attention to children. This extensive network of women's groups began after the Civil War, establishing homes and services for children. As women entered the workplace in greater numbers in the later twentieth century, voluntary associations of women declined. Though it is now an older group with fewer members, the United Methodist Women (UMW) has not relented in its passion for advocacy for children. It educates its members and the congregations to which they belong through an extensive national, regional, and local network. Wanda Holcombe credits the UMW with motivating congregations to win a fight for children's health insurance in Texas:

> I work very closely with Advocacy for Children's Issues... We worked a lot with our children's health care program. We turn money back in Texas... But the congregations and the UMW, I want to say their advocacy really helped to get that thing going. If it had not been for them, we would not have had a children's health insurance program.[19]

Rhizomatic Ministry: Making Disciples

Rhizomes often reach people in unusual ways. As people connect, rhizomes provide the opportunity for formal and informal exploration of the Christian faith. They simultaneously support the lives of vulnerable children and their families and renew the church with enthusiasm, energy, and purpose. They provide an educational function in what congregations call "discipleship." Disciples test out unusual connections—often between their faith and their everyday lives.

Libba Stinson of Alabama credits a United Methodist college with educating one of its students in a way that led him to connect his faith to his work in journalism. His family was in the newspaper business, and after college he took up the family vocation. He focused his reporting on education. Funding in county schools was desperately lacking, and the journalist toured county schools where the ceilings leaked.

> The superintendent, the articles in the paper, the Annual Conference children's choir—the folks came home and started talking about the Initiative. They asked to be given a tour of the school and ultimately adopted one of the county elementary schools...in one of the poverty pockets of the state. The children had no enrichment activities. The church came up with backpack and school suppl[ies]... Some of the handyman retirees fixed up a classroom.

The church began a music program, tutoring for homework, and a reading program. The journalist and the "good principal who is willing to do more if she can" have documented the progress with stories and pictures.

The journalist found the power of his job in connection with his faith and his concern for children in poverty. In finding his own vocation he was able to help others "have this wonderful convergence of call on their heart and a place to give that call."[20] In so doing, they have found discipleship *and* apostolicity.

As the United Methodist Church has experienced significant denominational change, it has responded with a call to "make disciples," emphasizing the great commission of Matthew 28:19. Though "making disciples" is a particular watchword in the United Methodist denomination at present, the idea is current in all mainline Protestant denominations. Mainline Protestantism does not necessarily come to mind when the public hears the word "Christian." Mainline Protestantism knows that it cannot assume that people will be exposed to our understanding of the Christian faith, learn its values and principles, and find their lay or clergy vocations in its ministries. "Making disciples" must be an intentional educational effort. In chapter 11 we turn to the relationship between "making disciples" and ministries with children and poverty. Are these ministries optional, or are they at the heart of what discipleship means?

CHAPTER 11

Do Ministries with Children and Poverty Have a Role in Christian Discipleship?

Learning about Children and Poverty

Most Christian denominations have promoted awareness, advocacy, and ministry on behalf of children and poverty for decades, even centuries. As these efforts become increasingly countercultural, they seem to some persons to be a last gasp of 1960s-style social action. *Are these efforts by the Christian churches simply an attempt to hold on to a past in which social action seemed important and Christian denominations had the power to influence society, or do these efforts arise from and contribute to the heart of Christian discipleship?* In this chapter, I seek to demonstrate the latter.

Discipleship necessarily involves either building relationships with children across biological lines or clearly understanding why one should not build such relationships. For most disciples of Christ the church provides a variety of means through which people can understand their caring activities with children, including poor children, in light of their Christian faith. These ministries are built on mutuality: for both children and those who are newly learning to be in ministry with children, these ministries provide an opportunity to place one block in the foundation of Christian discipleship. In light of the description of rhizomatic ministry in the last chapter, Christian discipleship might be envisioned as connecting one shoot of a rhizome to another, until the whole of the root system is strengthened in faith.

What Is Christian Discipleship?

Volumes have been written about discipleship in literature on religious education and evangelism in recent years, but for the purposes of this book, a basic definition will do.[1] Ideas about Christian discipleship are taken from the gospel of Matthew, particularly leading to Matthew 28:19, in which the risen Christ charges his eleven earthly disciples to baptize, teach, and lead others in the way of life that exemplified Jesus' teaching: living under the realm of God. The Greek word for *disciples* is from the Greek word *mathetes*, a derivative of the verb *mathano*, "to learn." A disciple is one who learns the way of life that Jesus taught. This way of life commended personal practices that often countered those demanded by the Roman Empire, particularly as the Roman way of life was driven by Rome's economic and political interests.[2] The eleven disciples, having served their earthly apprenticeship with the rabbi Jesus, now apprenticed others to study the way of life he had taught. People who are in a discipling process are either baptized or anticipating baptism; however, baptized or not, they are in the process of learning about the way of life of those whom Jesus calls. Discipleship is particularly characterized by a formative quality. Discussion of discipleship is growing in mainline denominations, especially in relation to concern for denominational decline. Sometimes, ministries that some people consider "1960s-style social action" are blamed for this decline. Therefore, it is crucial to understand why ministries with children and poverty are essential to understanding and expressing the Christian life of faith we call discipleship.

Building Awareness of Children and Poverty

In the Bishops Initiative on Children and Poverty the United Methodist bishops taught that the way of life that Jesus led is directly connected to faith practices and ecclesial ministries related to poor children, all children, and all persons who are poor. How does the church go about "making disciples for Jesus Christ" who are attentive to children and those who are poor? The interviews with the area coordinators for the Bishops Initiative reveal a pervasive theme of "building awareness" about the relationship between children, poverty, and the life of faith. In some cases, congregations assessed their own congregational practices; in others they studied mission and outreach programs, public policies, or international ecclesial and policy issues. While this range was represented in the content of learning activities, this wide-ranging focus involved creating awareness—any kind of awareness—that brought children and poverty onto the church's and individual's radar screen. Interviews revealed three categories of learning/discipling activities that aimed toward teaching the church about the needs of children and those who are poor: (1) learning by doing, (2) learning by study, (3) learning by expressing our practical theology.

Learning by Doing

In the United Methodist Church, congregations are closely connected into an Annual Conference—for other denominations, a parallel language might be presbytery, synod, or association. An Annual Conference covers a very large geographical area and usually connects 400–1200 local congregations. Bishops may preside over one or two Annual Conferences. Annual Conferences frequently focus their teaching efforts on learning by doing.

The United Methodist Church, especially through the guidance of its Women's Division and Health and Welfare agencies, has always been involved in some way in ministries with children and poverty, but many of these ministries are maintained out of the limelight of the denomination. As the bishops began to focus on children and poverty, some Annual Conferences sought knowledge and inspiration by *learning about their existing and developing ministries* in these areas. Some conferences gathered information formally by asking congregations to describe their ministries on yearly report forms, creating what is usually called an "asset inventory."[3] Other Annual Conferences approached the task of "story telling" informally—the Initiative simply stimulated conversation. Maggie Rogers of Northwest Texas found that the language of children and poverty was a "door opener" that allowed her to tell stories in different congregations about a range of ministries—"after school programs, kid's cafes, and those kinds of things."[4]

Most Annual Conferences and local congregations readily involve themselves in *collections* for important causes. They excel in creating and donating items such as medical kits, and many of these donated items are aimed toward children: school kits, shoes, socks, undergarments, school supplies, medical and dental kits, blankets, and even teddy bears. Collecting items that are genuinely needed contributes to various relief efforts. Collecting, however, is also *a spiritual discipline* that reminds the participants of the vulnerable persons who Jesus touched. It serves the spirituality of the people who collect. This common "learning by doing" practice meets a need and reminds those doing the collecting that there are persons who are without. Such collections by Christian communities echo the collections for the widows of the Jerusalem church in the book of Acts.

A *small grants* program was offered by the Council of Bishops. Individual Annual Conferences also made small grants for congregations that began new ministries. Some Annual Conferences received funds from local foundations that supported grants to congregations. Such grants ranged from $300 to $3000 and provided seed money with which congregations began new ministries that served children in their communities, such as tutoring programs, after-school programs, feeding programs, camp programs—ministries that the local congregations had not envisioned themselves engaging in before. Robert Harder of the Kansas East Conference commented, "Local churches in receipt of the mini-grants showed heightened awareness and more sensitivity to issues of children and poverty."[5]

Learning by Study

Both the Annual Conferences and the Council of Bishops promoted learning by study. Learning by study involved different strategies: Annual Conferences usually developed educational events while the Council of Bishops produced documents and study guides.

Educational events frequently brought new information or caused congregations to look at and beyond their existing ministries. The United Methodist Church is a largely middle-class denomination; much knowledge about children and poverty exists in local congregations among people who work with children and people who are poor. In some cases congregations and Annual Conferences were able to draw from their own ranks or include poor persons who could speak for themselves to the church. Other educational efforts offered letter-writing campaigns, provided handouts and videos, or played simulation games, such as one related to receiving welfare that was played at the New Jersey Annual Conference.

Sometimes people get frustrated by a perception that educational events create excitement and energy but little happens after the fact. However, our data shows that, over and over, educational events *do* spur new ideas, new activities, and, most importantly, provide spiritual support for participants.

Sometimes, for educators, the "a-ha" experience of one person makes the event worthwhile. Libba Stinson of Alabama describes a participant at an educational event who "didn't work with children and didn't really have any reason" to participate in Stinson's workshop on children and poverty, except that she wasn't ready to go home. After Stinson passed out a Voices for Children brochure that showed that fifteen of the seventeen most impoverished counties in the state of Alabama were in their Annual Conference, the participant said, "You know, *The Birmingham News* tells us we're a Third World Country out here in West Alabama, and this starts to make me believe it." Stinson took heart, "You know, if I'm putting materials even in a few hands, then it is having an effect."[6]

Sarah Wilke of the North Texas Annual Conference describes the rhizomatic character of such an event in her Annual Conference. The strategy connected education with an inventory of current ministries that then built a rhizome. As a result of educational activity, shoots of a root system spread opportunistically in many different directions:

> We've had sort of two phases of our program. The first was really a learning, growing, education awareness time... We did a huge conference and had a great response to that,... really got people to dig deep into what they were doing and to sort of vision into what they could be doing, and then we took a big turn:... "Let's hunker down and figure out what we already are doing...and then mobilize more people into it...and connect across the Conference the various Initiatives and begin new Initiatives." So I think that conference was a launching point, but we went quickly beyond just conversation and study to action.[7]

Though many educational opportunities were delivered through educational events, the Council of Bishops also provided several documents for formal *study.* These included two biblical and foundational documents, "Children and Poverty: An Episcopal Initiative" and "Community with Children and the Poor: Renewing the Bishops Initiative," with a congregational study guide. These documents culminated in "Our Shared Dream: The Beloved Community"; a study guide for the foundational statements, "Community with Children and the Poor"; and one ministry guide, "A Church for All God's Children"; and one document that emphasized the widespread destitution of children in Africa, "Hope for the Children of Africa."[8] The German Annual Conference produced its own study of children and poverty in Germany, *Kinder und Armut: Eine Initiative der Bischöfe.*[9] The United Methodist Church in the Philippines produced a study for a National Consultation on Children's Ministries. Annual Conferences used these studies in different ways. Frequently, area coordinators reported that raising awareness about children was easier than raising awareness about poverty or the connection between children and poverty. The studies helped to make connections between children and poverty. One congregation used the study guide for "Community with Children and the Poor" in rural ecumenical circles to promote ministries related to poverty. "A Church for All God's Children" provided direction for a wide range of activities for local congregations, from ways to improve the safety of the physical church building to methods of advocacy on behalf of children. A congregation that worked through the process of accomplishing something in each of the categories was given an award by the bishop at Annual Conference. Many congregations, including small rural congregations, developed notebooks that portrayed their efforts to become "A Church for All God's Children." Charlotte Abram of the Nebraska Annual Conference reports on these and other awards given by her bishop to "churches that have made a significant impact in reaching children and adults who live in poverty... We have received all kinds of reports from local churches, they have either started a significant ministry to children or reached out to the homeless."[10]

These activities contributed to initial attempts by Annual Conferences to build their knowledge about children and poverty. These activities contributed to discipleship as they became connected to the church's practical theology.

Learning through Practical Theology

Awareness of children and poverty needs to be expressed in the practical theology of the church if it is to make disciples for the way of life Jesus taught. The term "practical theology" is used in many ways in academics; "practical theology" as I use it here is the primary expression of the faith in practices such as prayer, Bible study, liturgy, etc. Practical theology also joins the stories found in the Bible or in theological history with the stories of contemporary faith expression. In these joined stories, where people find themselves to be living biblical understanding or Christian tradition in contemporary ways, the meaning of discipleship can be glimpsed.

United Methodists believe in the primacy of scripture for understanding faith, so it makes sense that area coordinators reported a variety of ways in which the concern for children and poverty was expressed as a form of *biblical faith*. Many Annual Conferences approached topics related to children and poverty by inviting speakers who conducted Annual Conference Bible Studies. The Holston Annual Conference, which spans Tennessee, southwest Virginia, and northeast Georgia, created its own curriculum for Bible study related to children and poverty. The Bible study was conducted at Annual Conference and then in local congregations, and a survey was sent to local congregations to find out what congregations had done in response to the Bible study. Anita Henderlight reports a range of ministries that began as a result of the Bible study, including

> food pantries to clothing closets, to donating to a children's home, starting interfaith hospitality networks. There was one sweet little church that the children of the church actually planted and canned vegetables for their local homeless shelter...it was so inspiring.[11]

Barbara Ross and Evelyn Althouse of the East Ohio Annual Conference used a biblical allusion to reflect on the vulnerability of the entire enterprise of ministries with children and poverty:

> But "the poor will always be with us." That's scriptural, and so they will always need somebody who speaks on

their behalf and keeps the rest of us aware of our role...
And [it's] sad, but there will always be children who need
someone to speak for them because they're not in a position
to speak for themselves nor have they been blessed by
families who lift them up as important. So I don't see it
ever going away... The question is, how do we keep it ever
before our folks so it doesn't become unimportant?[12]

Aspects of faith related to children and poverty are expressed in
many forms of *corporate worship*. United Methodist congregations
frequently observe the Children's Sabbath and incorporate a
focus on children or participation of children in worship at
Annual Conference. Ronald Messer of the New England Annual
Conference used the themes of children and poverty at the Good
Friday vigil in his congregation:

So for Good Friday, generally we'd have a vigil from 6
[a.m.] to 6 [p.m.], and the theme would be children and
poverty. What I'd do is put out literature, and people
would go in and pray and realize that there are children
in need out there, and also that there are children in need
out there because they are in poverty.[13]

Many area coordinators reported that faith was expressed in
devotionals. Several Annual Conferences published pamphlets
and books of prayers and Bible stories by children. Janet Hitch
of the Western North Carolina Annual Conference reports that
the conference published "Helping a Child Develop Faith" and a
guide to ministering to unchurched children. Another conference
leader wrote a devotional while on an international mission
trip and sold it, with the proceeds returning to the international
children's ministry.[14]

Many area coordinators found ways *to teach the Christian faith*
to children in formal and informal ways. Formal programs may
originate in the local congregation. Angie Williams of Mississippi
reminisces about the Pleasant Hill United Methodist Church as a
story she wants her Annual Conference to remember.

It is a small rural congregation who wanted more kids, both
children and youth, in their church. So they decided to buy
a van. They drew a circle on a map around their church in
a two-mile radius. They drove that van to mobile home

parks and housing divisions to get kids. Every Wednesday night they feed them a nice hot meal, have some playtime, and help them do their school work and a Bible study. They started out with 30 kids, and now they have 70–80 kids every week. It takes 35 to 40 volunteers from the church every Wednesday...and that's pretty remarkable since they only have about 70 members. It's been going on three or four years now.[15]

Participants in such ministries develop the confidence to teach the Christian faith to children in informal ways. They are able to identify the appropriate opportunities to introduce children to faith stories that they might not learn elsewhere. Debra Rogosky of Pennsylvania remembers this kind of sharing of her faith with a child who didn't know the Christmas story:

He was five and didn't talk to adults. And Santa Claus came that day, who happened to be my husband, and it was the first time I ever heard him speak to an adult. He just like was in a rapture with Santa... This little boy's mom was late, and she didn't pick him up; and it was getting really late so I took him up to the sanctuary. I said, "Come on, Shane, I'll take you up, and we'll see what's going on." And I'm showing the Christmas trees and the poinsettias and the nativity, and he asked me a question. He said, "Who's the man in the window?" And I said, "What??!!" like being paranoid...like, "Who's standing there looking at you?" And he said, "No, that man up there." And it was Jesus. I mean, it was precious. And I said, "Shane, don't you know about Jesus?" And he said, "No." So I took him back, and I picked up the baby in the manger and said, "This is Jesus." And I let him hold him. And I said, "Jesus loves you regardless of what you do, who you are." And he said, "I be able to tell my mom about him?"... I don't know what happened to him, though, because we moved from the area; but that story will always stay with me, and it's almost like my job to say, "This is Jesus, and you can hold him."[16]

Evelyn Althouse and Barbara Ross of Pennsylvania describe the religious education that occurs through a tutoring program:

There was one little boy whose grandmother has custody of the children; but the grandmother is bedfast, and the kids really take care of Grandma, so Maurice's older brother brought him this Sunday evening to read the Scripture... Maurice was asking me about the sanctuary, and I don't think he'd been in the sanctuary except to walk through to the computer lab. He's asking a lot of questions, and I was answering the questions and talking about that this used to be a church that used to have a congregation here, and they have it so we could do things like this now. The older brother was sitting there, and all of a sudden, he reached up and pulled off his stocking cap. It was like there was a sense of awe here...a sense of holy...from tutoring. [17]

Anita Henderlight of Holston Annual Conference summarizes her insight from experiences with children and poverty that characterizes the power of the missions:

Hopefully we've encouraged...churches...not [to] wait for the kids and those families to walk through your church doors, but for people in your church to walk out the doors and figure out how they can help them have a better life.[18]

Area coordinators have studied the *Wesleyan history and theology* around ministry and mission and made connections between United Methodist history and contemporary action. When asked what was the most significant highlight for her Annual Conference in the Initiative, Patricia Magyar of Arizona says:

the fact that we are going back to our roots—John Wesley's ideas and concepts and the movement that he started is being reintroduced, reenergized, moving us in that direction, and that simply is to help "the least of these," which is the call of the Bible.[19]

Similarly, Tina Whitehead, who is doing professional training in spiritual formation, understands that acts of piety and acts of mercy are interrelated means of grace. She says:

I think it's important that we don't just stop [with piety], and Wesley didn't either. He had the acts of piety, and you can't just stop with that. You have to move to the acts of mercy and then just go back and forth between the two, and that makes you a whole Christian, I think.[20]

But many area coordinators are concerned that acts of piety and mercy alone are not enough—these acts need to be extended into acts of justice that deal with the systems that leave people poor in the first place. That, according to Charlotte Abram of Nebraska, is a difficult task.

> [We] are more apt to engage in acts of mercy...before we engage perhaps in acts of justice. It was a little harder for us to get our heads around making systemic changes that would address the worst problems of poverty, especially when they affect children.[21]

Despite the difficulty in creating a course of action that would allow the church to alter the systems that create poverty, the concern for *justice* through advocacy for social policy did come to some general expression. Ed Folkwein of the Yellowstone Annual Conference describes a growing awareness in his Annual Conference that "children in poverty...[are] the ones affected most by cuts in programs, lack of medical care, and the result of abusive behaviors in the home."[22] Many Annual Conferences have conducted children's marches to their state capitals to highlight the fact that whenever legislation is passed, children's lives are affected. Ann Davis describes the Virginia Annual Conference's children's march on the state capital in Richmond:

> Our advocacy program has stayed in touch with the general assembly, trying to...help the local churches know who to respond to on issues and bills and budget requests to empower children at-risk and their families. We've also done a march in Richmond...We would get hundreds of people to go to Richmond on the capital to march for the rights of children. So it was children advocating for other children... We've given prayer calendars and letters to the general assembly spokespeople to let them know that we are caring about children.[23]

Such marches help children learn the relationship between Christian discipleship and advocacy. As Linda Kelly of California-Nevada alludes to the marches in this role:

Last year and coming up again this spring, we did a children's day at the capitol, where we brought out children and we will be bringing them again to converge on the capitol here in Sacramento to have a rally and to empower the children so that *they know that they can make a difference.*[24]

Other Annual Conferences have created marches on their state capitals, provided prayer calendars for their legislators, talked with legislators about specific policies, and generally advocated for attention to the needs of children in any policies that their state legislatures create. These marches frequently take place on the Martin Luther King Jr. federal holiday in January; one particularly memorable march in Bismarck, North Dakota, took place on a sunny day in –13 degree weather![25]

Enthusiasm—and Obstacles!

Though there are many success stories to be told from the Initiative on Children and Poverty, area coordinators also reported many obstacles to a full engagement of the Initiative by their Annual Conferences. The relationship between children and poverty needed repeated interpretation; for many clergy and laity, children and poverty were like apples and oranges. As so often happens, the "same people seemed to be doing everything" in some annual conferences and suffered burnout and depression. Resources were badly needed; time, money, and staff were in particularly short supply. Large geographic areas suffered from communication problems across long distances. Conferences struggled to understand persons with different economic means. Some area coordinators experienced a lack of support and vision from key conference leadership. Some experienced tension between advocates and those desiring hands-on action. For some it was difficult to interpret a vision of senior denominational leaders who encouraged a diversity of responses as Annual Conferences made the Initiative their own—local leaders could only imagine a top-down approach, to be avoided at all costs. Others didn't see the connection of children and poverty with ministry. Some frankly said, off the record, "the problem is the clergy" or "the new bishop didn't continue the support." Given the range of possible resistance to the Initiative, it is rather remarkable that this attempt at a different kind of leadership by the bishops on a complex and difficult subject contributed as much as it did to the denomination's ongoing care for poor children, all children, and all persons who live with poverty.

Disciples or Apostles?

Many mainline denominations have been concerned with a decline in membership, influence, financial support, and a general lack of adequate expression about what the Christian faith means in a time characterized as "postmodern" or "post-Christendom." The United Methodist Church is no exception, and its experience might be a beacon to other mainline denominations. In the midst of these concerns, "making disciples," fulfilling the great commission of Matthew 28:19–20, has become a main theme for the United Methodist Church and for the Council of Bishops. A portion of a reinvigorated discipleship that contributes to mainline church renewal can be found in learning about historical and contemporary practices of care for "the widow, the orphan, and the resident alien."

But discipleship may not be an end in itself. While disciples are called to learn the wholeness of the way that Jesus led, discipleship as "learning," even "learning by doing," has a different meaning from becoming part of an "apostolate," becoming part of a group of apostles who are "called" and "sent out." While more will be said about an apostolate for children and the poor in the next chapter, the story of one whose vocation was reshaped by the Initiative gives us a glimpse of where we might find *apostles* for children and those living in poverty in ordinary places.[26]

Tina Whitehead reports the way her experience with children and people who are poor, filtered through the interpretations offered by the Initiative, changed her understanding of spiritual formation.

> I'm doing a degree...in Spiritual Formation and I'm doing a workshop this weekend [coming up] on spiritual forma-tion, and I asked if I could do the component from Exodus 3...where I've always stopped after about the first seven verses before—where Moses is being at the burning bush and being in the presence of God and that's kind of the formation and the call—and never paid attention to the

scripture below where it says, "I've heard the cry of my oppressed people and I'm sending you." And so last August I said, "Can I do that whole segment as what I want to talk about?" And so I feel like God has called me from a spiritual formation that was kind of a life unto itself, talking about prayer, small groups of faith sharing, and he has called me out of that to hear the cry. But I think it first gave me the foundation to hear God's voice and so that I'm not just doing something good out of my own desire to do... I really feel that God has called me to do this and that the first part was just preparation.[27]

People who consider themselves disciples need to contemplate these questions: Is caring for children and people who are poor one option for Christian ministry among many options? Or is some form of caring for "the widow, the orphan, and the stranger" as necessary to Christian discipleship as prayer, scripture, and sacraments? Is such care essential to Christian practice, or is it one among many options for expressing the Christian life? How do we resolve the conflicts between the multiple demands that the Christian life places upon us? In the last chapter I attempt to answer these questions.

CHAPTER 12

Renewing the Apostolate for Children and Poverty

There are some of them who left a name,
So that (people) declare their praise,
And there are some who have no memorial,
Who have perished as though they had not lived... .
But these were (people) of mercy,
Whose righteous deeds have not been forgotten;
Their prosperity will remain with their descendants,
And their inheritance to their children's children.
Their descendants stand by the covenants;
Their children also, for their sake... .
Their bodies were buried in peace,
And their name lives to all generations.
Peoples will declare their wisdom,
And the congregation proclaims their praise. (Sir. 44:8–15, RSV)

Learning Jesus' way, the task of disciples, is not an end in itself. Through such apprenticeship the awareness of God's concern for children and the poor takes permanent residence in a disciple's heart. A disciple may be further grasped by the reality and importance of God's presence among children and in poverty and redirect his or her life so that it is lived in this awareness. Such disciples have made a transition from apprenticeship to being grasped by God and sent on a mission. They exemplify "apostolic spirituality." John Wesley, Dorothy Day, and Martin Luther King Jr. led famous lives that help us understand apostolic spirituality, but Tina Whitehead and many others named elsewhere in this book are no less a part of its ranks.

Protestants do not usually use the language of "apostolic spirituality"; rather, I take the term from Roman Catholic ecclesiology. Yet the term "apostolic spirituality" can help us identify and explore a phenomenon that deeply frustrates mainline Protestant leadership. When leaders of denominations engage in initiatives on behalf of a particular social change, they often create a curriculum to educate the members of their churches. They hope to help their members broaden their understanding of Christian discipleship and way of life. Leaders get disappointed, however, when those who study are not moved to new practices. Members have "learned"; their minds are broadened; they have a new perspective; but they have not found a spiritual depth that engages them to become "apostles." Perhaps God has not called them, but more likely they do not recognize the call of God to new practice. They have not organized their lives to be "sent out."

Occasionally a person does come forward with a passion for active ministry in care, evangelism, or mission. Either they discover where God has been leading all along, or they are grasped by a new spirit. Leaders are rewarded, even humbled. Leaders open doors so that newly impassioned laity and clergy can find a place to fulfill their vocation. Too often, these persons begin a ministry without adequate supportive community. They join a hard-working few who carry the witness of the Protestant church on their shoulders until they become part of the burned-out many.

This phenomenon repeats itself over and over again with those who are called to ministries with children and poverty. For the sake of poor children, all children, and all persons who live in poverty, such persons need to be recognized and supported as persons who belong to a particular *apostolate* who are engaged in difficult ministries. *This chapter introduces the idea of a Protestant apostolate for children and poverty, and it calls upon Protestant leadership to recognize that such an apostolate already exists in Protestant ranks.* It urges leaders to help the apostolate for children against poverty to identify themselves, to talk about their vocation, and to develop a language and a network that supports their ministries. For change to occur so that children are respected in their cultures, so that children are considered when regional, national, and international policy is made, so that children's care is prioritized by their communities and families, the body of Christ needs disciples and *apostles.*

Disciples and Apostles

The relationship between disciples and apostles differs in the gospels of Matthew and Luke and the letters of Paul. The concept of "discipleship" dominates the gospel of Matthew; and little distinguishes a disciple from an apostle. The writer of Luke/Acts, however, distinguishes disciples from *apostolos*, from the Greek word *apostello* or "to put or place out." Apostles have an active vocation or mission.[1]

In Luke, the "apostles" are those twelve persons who are chosen from the larger group of disciples to be Jesus' inner circle. Commentators have noted that Luke places the choosing of the Twelve in Luke 6:12 in the context of the growth of Jesus' popularity and the conflict and opposition that is beginning to arise. Apostles provide strength: they are a community that helps to build a foundation ministry. We are not told why the Twelve are chosen: they do not seem to be selected because of talent, credentials, availability, or reputation. Instead, Jesus prays and chooses.

The choosing of the Twelve precedes the Sermon on the Plain, or the parallel in Luke to Matthew's Sermon on the Mount. Jesus speaks "on a level place" to disciples, apostles, and people alike—again, these three groups are not distinguished by any particular qualities or qualifications.[2] The Sermon on the Plain, according to John Barton and John Muddiman, focuses on the formation of the people of God, the restored community of Israel.[3] The apostles, though they will not know it until after the resurrection, will become the foundation of this community, the church, the body of Christ.

How might we distinguish between disciples and apostles today? Disciples learn by study; they learn by doing Christian mission; they learn the practices of love of God and love of neighbor—expressed through piety, mercy, and justice—that constitute the wholeness of Christian life. In so doing, disciples participate in the body of Christ and experience what it is like to live in the world "as if" the realm or kingdom of God is truly here. Disciples, as apprentices, can be expected to try out a wide range of Christian practices so that they experience the whole of Christian living. Apostles are never exempt from the demands of Christian discipleship or continued growth in the knowledge of the whole of the Christian life. Apostles differ from disciples, however, as they have been inexplicably gripped by the hand of God for a particular service. They direct the wide range of practices of Christian living toward a particular focus: bringing Christ to the world. They exude a sense of urgency and passion for ministry with children and poverty. They need continued growth and formation as they go about their apostolic journey; they need encouragement and inspiration; they may have doubts about their particular direction. Still, their ethos is formed by their participating in a particular "leg" of the body of Christ.

Apostles and the Apostolate

"Apostles" originally referred to the Twelve; later the term "apostle" referred to other groups of people who were "sent out." Initially, apostles were defined as those who witnessed the pre-ascension resurrection appearances of Christ; later, Paul identified himself as an apostle. In the early church, bishops were considered apostles; "apostolic succession," or a way of establishing recognized ordination, could be officially traced back through the bishop of Rome. By the nineteenth century, the Roman Catholic Church was using the language of "the apostolate" to refer to both clergy and laity. During and after Vatican II the Roman Catholic Church increasingly reflected on the apostolate of the laity as a way to express the active participation of committed laity in the ontological body of Christ through mission and evangelization.[4]

Within the framework of a larger Roman Catholic conversation, Dorothy Day and Peter Maurin frequently talked about the apostolate. Day talked primarily about the lay apostolate, though sometimes also mentioned clergy in this way. Day understood the Catholic Worker movement to be developing an apostolate, though they also talked about lay apostles with different vocations. Day spoke of the married apostolate, the apostolate in the family, the apostolate for interracial relations, the apostles of labor. Many Roman Catholic organizations were considered part of this apostolate. What distinguished the Catholic Worker movement was "pacifism and distributism"—renunciation of violence and interpersonal or corporate form of holding all material goods in common.[5]

As the concept of an apostolate is foreign to many Protestants, let us be clear what an apostolate is not. An apostolate as I am describing it here is not an order of ministry, an organization to which the called belong, an achievement, or a recognition of "spiritual gifts." It transcends the formal designations of persons as "presbyters," "deacons," "deaconesses," or "elders." Likewise, it transcends any particular denominational, ecumenical, or interfaith group. It is not a hierarchical status in relationship to those identified as disciples: an individual may be a disciple, or apprentice, in one part of Christian experience but grasped by consciousness of the apostolate of another part of the body. Unlike ordination, the call may not be necessarily confirmed by others. One may or may not even identify oneself as an apostle! The apostolate is a radical equalizer: people who participate in this apostolate, as a leg of the mystical body of Christ, may include recognized leaders of the church or world *and* homeless or imprisoned men or women. The apostolate confers no worldly status or authority on anybody. But, it is real. When we participate in the mystical body of Christ in an apostolate for children and poverty, we are grasped in such a way that our kindred with others who participate in Christ in that way grows.

Most importantly, apostles need a community—an apostolate—that sustains them on their way. The apostolate verifies the fruits of their labors. The apostolate also shares with one another the commitment, idealism, energy, honesty, and faith that is needed for any apostolic journey. Wesley found such support in the Oxford Holy Club and later in the Methodist classes and bands. Day found such support in the houses of hospitality, farming communes, and roundtables for clarification of thought. King found such support in the Progressive National Baptist Convention and the Southern Christian Leadership Conference.

Together, these qualities of passion contribute to the way the apostolate helps to build and sustain the foundation of the whole body of Christ. The apostolate witnesses to the coherence, wholeness, and peace that comes for persons in community who passionately express the Christian faith through a particular mission at a particular time and place. The apostolate arises from a persistent spirituality that is expressed in worship and stands in the contemporary shoes of particular Christian traditions. It becomes a witness to the interdependence between love and justice in the world. It participates in the fullness of ministry in care, mission, and evangelism. It connects "persons" with "systems and issues." It offers words and actions that shape and mold both individual lives and the communities of which they are a part.

How might the language of the apostolate be helpful to Protestants who need to give expression to their unease with the relationship between those who engage in care, evangelism, and mission as a learning experience and those who are grasped by God and committed to such ministry as an expression of faith in the world? It unites those persons across formal organizational lines who join together in ministries out of different faith expressions for practical action on behalf of children and poverty. It recognizes both the reality and necessity of their kindred spirituality. The apostolate in the twenty-first century is truly rhizomatic—in a horizontal fashion it sends out feelers, connects with others, works around obstacles, including denominational difference and the privilege of particular roles or talents, and generally strengthens the connection of Christ for poor children, all children, and all people who are poor.

Apostolic Spirituality

The apostolate, as I am using the language here, refers to "apostolic spirituality," a participation in the mystical body of Christ, the ontological church. Apostolic spirituality "denotes a conviction that action and involvement in the world constitute a path to holiness and to union with God."[6] Such a conviction is marked by particular qualities—in the seventeenth century, "charity" and "zeal" were considered apostolic qualities par excellence; in contemporary society "discernment, justice, and active patience" characterize apostolic spirituality. In apostolic spirituality prayer "is not a source from which one draws water that will then be dispersed in the world; it is rather a contemplation of the face of Jesus in the world, in the sister or brother who is in need."[7] When people foster the growth of such qualities in themselves, they participate in the mystic communion of the apostolate that forms a "pillar" of the church.

The language of John Wesley, Martin Luther King Jr., and Dorothy Day that we explored in chapter 3 helps us broaden even further the qualities of the apostolate. Wesley talks of "the character of a Methodist" that refers back to such qualities. Martin Luther King Jr. speaks of seeking "brotherhood and understanding" rather than retribution. Dorothy Day reminds us of "hospitality" and "clarification of thought" as practices that communicate Christ's presence in the world. Each of these is grounded in the Beatitudes; the language of each of these three leaders calls to "the apostolate" to form in his or her spirit certain Christlike qualities as the basis for engaging the world.

How is the apostolic spirituality of those who attend to poor children, all children, and all who are poor different from the spirituality of the apprentice? Among apostles for children and poverty I can identify five characteristics: vulnerability, perseverance, integration, mutuality, and connectedness.

Vulnerability

Apostolic spirituality integrates love, justice, and Christian ministry with children and the poor in a way that makes apostles increasingly *vulnerable*. Disciples try out certain Christian practices with children and the poor in specific events or one-time ministries that allow distance to limit the amount of disappointment, despair, or dependence a disciple encounters.[8] Disciples may support mission half a world away or even in neighboring communities as a way trying out new relationships; the level of vulnerability with the poverty in their own communities may be more than they can tolerate. Apostles enter ongoing relationships with children, the poor, and communities *who rely on them* and are aware of the consequences if those relationships are not maintained. Apostolic mentors guide disciples to reflect on ministry beyond their local communities and to reckon with the presence and humanity of people who are poor in their own communities. They are also willing to alter institutional arrangements in the church to create new relationships.

Evelyn Althouse and Barbara Ross of East Ohio exhibited apostolic vulnerability when they took a risk of reshaping institutional life and taking on new demands. They describe their relationship with the revitalization of a congregation that had had significant problems with vandalism from local children and felt threatened by newcomers. Though the original congregation eventually closed, Ross proposed that the congregation house a mission with community outreach during the week, rather than a worshiping congregation whose main activity would be on Sunday morning. The mission supported children of the community, and it became "a very vital, going concern." The vandalism problem was resolved because "kids see it as a safe place and their friends are there." Once the kids see the church as a happening place, however, the community comes to depend upon the adults who run a mission in ways that go beyond usual professional responsibilities.

> We tutor 3rd and 4th graders on Tuesday afternoon and a 2nd grader showed up and she thought that she had registered for an arts program, which was to be on Mondays...Well, it wasn't long till I got a phone number from her...While I was still on the phone I saw a woman there and I said, "Well, I think somebody's here for her," so the grandma said, "I started at the school to look for her but when I saw the church, I knew that's where she was..." There's been a complete change in the community and that's been a really exciting thing because the focus of the mission is specifically children.[9]

Althouse and Ross took the initiative to rearrange usual church schedules. Worship now takes place on Saturday evenings, after which dinner is served. "The mission is closed on Sundays!" Why is this schedule so contrary to the norm? "Well, we had to listen to the community. But I think that's where the Initiative has played a part in making that possible—the listening. And hearing what the need is instead of going in and *saying* this is what the need is..." Listening inevitably increases apostolic vulnerability.

Perseverance

Another of the marks of the apostolic community for children and poverty is *perseverance*. Even when apostles are passionate about their work, they experience many setbacks. Sue Ellen Nicholson of the North Carolina Annual Conference describes high hopes and false starts that are common to many ambitious ministries. She also describes the tenacity of rhizomatic ministry that moves around obstacles to find places of connection. The North Carolina Annual Conference Bishops Initiative committee for the eastern part of the state began their work with a study. Then they encouraged the use of "A Church for All God's Children," the guide for local congregations, and made a report to Annual Conference honoring the congregations that participated. They then got a planning grant with which they

> tried to call together every religious group within the state to try to say, "How can we as people of faith respond to the poor and move outside our four walls?"...Part of that grant went to hire a consultant, and that was just biting-off more than was manageable from the get-go. Not all the faith communities would send a representative. When they did send a representative, it would be a different person every time, every time we met it would be a different group who met with us, the consultant was very lacking in terms of their leadership and ability. They were not even aware of some of the recent research in the area...so we got another planning grant and just sort of punted on that plan. And [we] decided to narrow our focus. Trying to get every denomination in our state was just too big; we needed to start small and go from there. We approached our sister conference in the state;...we approached our children's homes and agencies;...and with a new planning group at the table we were able to discern that the direction we needed to go with this was in the area of partnering churches and school... That became the great vision of our group. And so we created the Hand-in-Hand project...with the partnership of all those groups.[10]

Nicholson continues that the partnership between congregation and public school is different in different areas, but may include prayers of support for educators and staff, volunteers that tutor and mentor children, congregations that provide material needs including clothing, shoes, and school supplies, and after-school programs. The mark of this story in its entirety, however, is the remarkable persistence of the leaders who made false starts, regrouped, prayed, discerned, narrowed their scope, reconsidered local resources, and finally developed a viable ministry.

Integration

Another mark of this apostolic spirituality is the apostle's *integrated grasp of the breadth of the calling to love and justice, without being intimidated by its scope.* Many disciples are simply overwhelmed by the intractable problems of children and poverty. Apostles overcome the sense of deluge by finding ways to focus on the people in their immediate presence at the same time as seeing children and poverty through a wide-angle lens. The broad scope in the wide-angle lens allows apostles to make connections among local and international ministries, direct relationships and advocacy—a rhizome of various contexts and practices. Apostolic spirituality feels the continuum between the organization of ministry internal to the congregation that provides congruence between the local congregation's practice and its message to the world, and the ways that congregations move beyond their own building. This connection involves both local and global communities. Apostles connect these direct relationships to advocacy. Advocacy involves both individuals and social organization. Apostolic spirituality lodges advocacy in direct relationships with those who are suffering, especially when it comes to children, so that advocates hear the voices of these children and know for what to advocate. Apostles recognize that children and people who are poor gain or are prevented from gaining access and resources for support through international, national, and state policies, so advocacy for legislation is important. To promote understanding in a world of the Internet, e-mail, and other forms of global technology, face-to-face virtual and personal international relationships are important. In cyberspace apostles are now able to "Act Global, Act Local." This weblike integration of the scope of children and poverty is more like a road system within which apostles move than a net that impedes their ministry.

Kathleen Stolz of New Jersey describes an example of an integrated framework:

> [It is] what we are calling a "tri-focus." Our one [international] focus has been...[a] partnership...[with] Liberia, with the Annual Conference over there. We had a statewide partnership, which was through Horizon Mercy [an insurance company] and the State of New Jersey. And then we had a local church partnership which was encouraging churches to partner within their own communities with other organizations in the "Shalom Zone"[11] kind of model...I think this has been powerful because everybody felt impassioned to do something in some one of those areas.[12]

Patricia Magyar of the Desert Southwest Conference provides an example of the kind of immediacy that allows an apostle to move along the rhizome. She describes the impact of Sidewalk Sunday Schools, featured in denominational videos, that were begun in her Annual Conference by Billie Fidlin in 2000. Magyar puts the child's face in the kind of apostolic prayer described earlier that is "the contemplation of the face of Jesus in the world, in the [girl] or [boy] who is in need":

> There's a big truck that pulls up and part of the side of the truck plops down...It's like a stage and the Sunday school is put on right there around that truck...One goes to a Sidewalk Sunday School and works with the children and hears their prayer requests,...things like, "I pray that my mother gets out of jail," "I pray that my father won't abuse my mother,"...things that really bring you to your knees and make you realize that the children and the least of these need us so much.[13]

Mutuality

Another mark of apostolic spirituality is its understanding of *mutuality*, a willingness to give and to receive. This willingness to engage in mutual relationships recreates the church itself. A thoroughgoing renewal of congregations uses the local narratives of the people to reshape church life. Rather than asking, "How can we interest others, children and people in poverty, in being part of our life?" the congregation asks, "How can we build a mutual relationship with children and people who live with poverty so that we can create congregational life together?" Wanda Holcombe of Southwest Texas describes the effect of such mutuality on one congregation:

> It was a church going out of existence. And with the change in population,...they began to look around and say, "Who are the people living in our neighborhood?" and began to reach out to the Hispanic people in the neighborhood, whoever was there, and it was a community of medium- and poverty-level people. As they began to build a relationship and invite them to church and again to build the kinds of ministries they needed... They started English classes...because people are going to need to learn English if they are going to have employable skills and jobs...But

they also started a Spanish class at the same time. And then
they had times in which they would have conversation
groups. So the older people would take Spanish, and the
Hispanic people would take English, and they would
have conversation labs in which they shared and taught
each other.[14]

Connectedness

Another element of apostolic spirituality is *connectedness*.
The apostolic community for children and poverty helps people
overcome social isolation. All through the twentieth century, social
critics charged that persons in the United States were losing their
connections to families, community institutions, government,
other countries, and even the church and God. Cultural theorists
suggest that the trend toward social isolation has resulted in
the fragmentation of persons and communities. This isolation is
particularly evident in the way that people of different economic
means are isolated from one another. Alternatively, social isolation
is overcome, and community with children and the poor is
created, when we see the humanity in the faces of those who have
been objectified. How is the renewal of the apostolate reducing
isolation and fragmentation by creating relationships across social
boundaries that are too often breaking down?

One of the most intense boundaries of isolation occurs between
those who are imprisoned and their families and those who are
not. One ministry that has proliferated throughout the United
States has been camps for children of incarcerated mothers and
fathers, which establish relationships between those children, their
families, and members of congregations who serve as mentors for
the children.

Ann Davis of Virginia describes the evolution of "All God's
Children" camp for children of incarcerated mothers.

We determined that children of incarcerated mothers were
indeed the most at-risk group of children that we had.
There's economic poverty, spiritual poverty, violence,
drugs, plus the homelessness that surrounds the child
when their primary care giver is incarcerated. They then
have that extra stress factor of being without a home to
live in. So we determined that those are the children that
we are going to minister to, and to provide overnight

camping settings for these children, and because we have five beautiful United Methodist camps in this conference, we partnered with them and now we have some at all five of the camps. Four week-long summer experiences and a fall weekend in the fifth camp. We are reaching hundreds of children every summer, where we are...taking them out of their situations and surrounding them with lots of adult mentors who commit to staying in touch with them for the whole year. We've actually just expanded that to our year-round mentoring program where we...actually are trying to mentor the children from camp week to camp week.[15]

Judy Lybeck describes the way Wisconsin Annual Conference encourages mutuality with prisoners who help to fund Wisconsin's camps for children of incarcerated parents:

Prisoners...have for the last three years...made different things that we sell at the annual conference as a fundraiser. One year...they folded 10,000 peace doves. Another year, they made bookmark lanyards in the shape of a cross... And we will get donations from prisoners for the camp, and even though it is [only] ten dollars, for them, that is a lot of money.[16]

Global partnerships in the church are an important part of the apostolic community that focuses on children and poverty. Many of these relationships are growing through programs such as "Hope for the Children of Africa," but older partnerships demonstrate the importance of connections that endure over the long term. The focus of "Hope for the Children of Africa" was raising six million dollars to build schools and orphanages in Africa, but a new emphasis has arisen on sustained relationships and partnerships between Annual Conferences in Africa and in the United States and Europe. Area coordinators have reported the excitement over new, ongoing relationships with Nigeria, Congo, Liberia, Zimbabwe, and other African Central Conferences. The effect of such a sustained relationship is reported in the strength of the relationship between Missouri and Mozambique. Peggy Eshelman says:

That's a long-term commitment for us. And the people of Mozambique tell us that they are so pleased with that partnership because we're...not going to come in, build a school, and then be gone. We are people they communicate with, and we have real relationships with them... [The bishop] came face-to-face...with pastors whose children were starving...she rather spontaneously said *we* can support those pastors...just the idea that there were pastors, Methodist pastors, whose children were starving in Mozambique led enough folks to catch that kind of an understanding to where we now partner with every church, every district superintendent in Mozambique and underwrite salary.[17]

Apostolic Living

Apostolic spirituality undergirds church ministry, but, ultimately, it renews and recreates one's way of life. Barbara Garcia demonstrates that building relationships moves beyond a ministry program to become the lifestyle of the apostolate. It becomes part of the apostle's personal identity. The apostolate, or supportive community, helps people make necessary connections where that is possible. She says,

Probably the greatest thing for me happened on a flight home from the General Conference in 2000. We met a young Hispanic man on the plane and became friends. We helped him once we got back [home] to find his brother-in-law. It was the beginning of a magnificent relationship and friendship. He comes to our house often, and it has opened up a network of being able to help people find jobs. His family is still in Mexico City, and they lead a very difficult life... Even our son and his family have become friends with him. I think that's what the Initiative is about:...trying to build friendship and relationships with the poor.[18]

In the Apostolate of Wesley, King, and Day

John Wesley, Dorothy Day, and Martin Luther King Jr. lived very different lives, and their lives show the diverse patterns in the lives of apostles for children and poverty. Voluntary poverty formed the lives of Wesley and Day more so than King. Social critique and activism shaped the actions of King and Day, more so than Wesley. All three were pacifists. They offer a witness of deeply committed Christians—apostles—who found and followed their vocations for children and poverty in their eras. Despite their differences, each one found direct relationships across economic lines to be closely aligned with love, social justice, and righteousness.

Despite different lifestyles, to what are apostles for children and poverty called? The apostles for children and the poor keep children and poverty in their central, rather than peripheral, vision. They understand the dynamics surrounding poor children, and they build practices into their lives that allow persons to resist involuntary poverty. Some of these practices may result in organized programs, but just as often these practices emerge from "traffic patterns" in the apostles' everyday lives that allow them to come into contact with children and poverty. They resist the pressure in our society to segregate groups of people into economic classes, and they work with others—"an apostolate"—to support such practices. They are "apostles for the world" that are deeply rooted in the life of the spirit, and they are fed by their study, their sacramental practice, and other means of grace.

Might God be calling you to become an apostle for children in poverty?

CONCLUSION

Beyond "Cause du Jour"

It's September 2, 2006. I began writing this book shortly after my daughter, Shannon, gave birth to my first grandson, Brenden. As I wrote, grandsons Ethan and Nolan arrived, and as I write these last words, I am flying to the home of my daughter, Meredith, to attend the birth of my fourth grandson, Brady. Once more I am grateful for modern medicine that can handle any emergency. In the intervening two years and two months from Brenden's birth to Brady's, 23.8 million children have died, largely from preventable causes.[1] Of the preventable deaths, many were claimed by "Poverty" and the systems of ignorance, disease, and militarism that clench "Poverty's" grasp.

As I fly to Brady's birth, I assume that I will fly on safe airline transportation that will allow me to leave my home early one morning and arrive at his house 2000 miles away before noon. I believe that Brady's birth will be relatively routine. Modern technology will register every heartbeat. If any emergencies arise, the well-trained hospital staff will be alerted immediately, and they will keep him and my daughter safe. Medically, I am not necessary, but I still hope I will be helpful.

At exactly the same time in Africa and many other places in the world, mothers will give birth alone or attended by a few women of their communities. Mothers who are medically necessary to their daughters' care may not arrive at their sides. A mother's presence may be a daughter's lifeline, but rough roads, illness, war, or

190

death may separate them. Even in the United States, mothers who could function as a nurse's aid or an advocate for an uninsured daughter may not be able to leave work or find transportation to attend her delivery.

Professional economists who seek an end to poverty agree that poor countries must be helped to build social and material infrastructures: secure banking and trade systems, yes, but equally as important are schools, hospitals, transportation routes, and public assistance programs. They have discovered that where there is income inequality, heath declines. Also seeking to end poverty, voices from civil society of social and economic liberation have risen. They remind the political and economic "think tanks" that the people whose lives are to be improved by this infrastructure must create it and sustain it. Those of us who already enjoy the privilege of such infrastructure must aid others to build their world, rather than imposing our version of progress from outside. In our own country we have a responsibility to provide access for all to existing infrastructure. At the same time, we must retain the choices people need to make as they use such infrastructure, especially medical technology. In the interchange between professional economists and civic groups, "Love" and "Justice" invite "Poverty" to dance and relax "Poverty's" grip.

As I fly I to my grandson's birth, I assume the he will be given a birth certificate identifying him as the particular child of particular parents. His birth certificate will establish his right to be raised by his parents (unless they neglect or abuse him), to access the resources of his community, and to claim the privileges of being a citizen of the United States. At my birth the United Nations had just been chartered, and people were concerned to establish an international consensus around human rights that would restrain human cruelty. As my grandson is born, unleashed human cruelty still ravages children as children become enslaved, are conscripted into armies and militias, are sexually exploited, or are left malnourished and uneducated. Boys—but even more so, girls—suffer from the violation of these rights. But legions of the world's children born between my first and fourth grandsons cannot claim such rights because they have no birth registration. In this void, children's advocates can seek love and justice for children under the protection of the Convention on the Rights of the Child. The implementation of any international treaty happens by persuasion rather than force. Justice protects Love through the idea of the human rights of the child. The idea of the human rights of the child seeks to assist even Poverty to offer a protective, rather than exploitive, hand.

As I fly, I assume that my grandson will be raised in a lead-free, baby-proofed home. I am less sanguine that his parents will be able to protect him from global environmental dangers. The summer of 2006 seemed wickedly hot in Kansas City and California. Many people in the general public sat in air-conditioned comfort to view Al Gore's lecture *cum* movie, *An Inconvenient Truth*. The movie demonstrated that current practices, such as increasing our use of air-conditioning, accelerates global warming. Climate change is a great equalizer: no one, rich or poor, will be able to escape its effects forever. However, when climate creates human disaster at specific places, the poor have fewer means of refuge. When they survive, they have much more difficulty rebuilding their lives than do the rich. Like prophets of the Hebrew Scriptures, climate disasters in third world countries have shouted this lesson over and over to deaf ears. The general public in United States may only be recognizing a first word of this prophecy after Hurricanes Katrina and Rita.

I expect that our family, being who we are, will teach my grandson to enjoy and appreciate nature. He will still be a child who wanders in the woods. He will learn the importance of "low impact" camping and translate that to living. Still, our family, spread out across North America as we are, always flying or driving to see one another, will contribute to significant global environmental damage, even as we travel out of love for one another. The flight we take today will likely contribute to the death of a poor child in an environmental disaster a decade from now. Our practices of Love will continue to contribute to climate change until Justice reshapes our society's use of energy and other practices of high impact living. Poverty's hand will have its way until Love and Justice, humans and the earth, find ways to cooperate.

As I fly, I wonder what my grandson's extended families will teach him about violence and conflict resolution, peace and war. At a baptism recently, one grandfather joked with another, "We'll be telling him to go to West Point, while you're talking him into Berkeley!" The comment recognizes differing attitudes toward war and peace. As a symbol, "West Point," for all it may teach about diplomacy, represents a world in which disciplined force sustains United States' power to keep the peace for the United States and its allies. "Berkeley," for all the military research grants it may accept, represents critical thinking and protest against the use of force as the primary means of keeping some people's peace. Both the reliance on force and the protest against it grow from our mentality of militarism.

I am proposing an alternative—that we grow a mentality in which peace, as *shalom*, is the status quo. My grandson will make choices as he develops habits for dealing with his fears and enhancing his sense of security. He will negotiate the way he considers his own needs as well as the needs of others. He will develop this learning first in the family, then on the school playground. Later these experiences will inform the way he plays his part in international relations. Even if he does not have direct influence on economies and governments, he will play a part, as we all do—by voting, by developing viewpoints, and by communicating his mentality toward the needs of others and toward means of conflict resolution. To create a reality in which peace, as *shalom*, is the status quo, we might consider spending as much time, effort, and money—as much of our tax dollars— practicing and teaching our children various means of conflict resolution as we now spend on preparation and practice of war.

In this economy the reign of God draws near, and force is a strange and sad anomaly. It is an economy in which the poor children can flourish.

At my birth the world was still reeling from World War II and the death that results from war. In the search for life and peace the world created an economy increasingly dependent on militarism, rather than on peace. Militarism, the affirmative action employer of the poor, as the United States' primary "full employment" program, seeks the poor to do its most dangerous work. Militarism leaves poor children more vulnerable to its presence. Sometimes it seems that Love and Justice for poor children may only watch from the side, as the military parades its colors, decorating Poverty as Poverty passes the military grandstand.

I am sure that my grandparents, at my birth in 1951, had little sense of the world that has unfolded in my lifetime, and I have little sense of the world in which my new grandson will take his place as an adult. As the world changed significantly in the twentieth century, however, a constant remained: the church provided a place to think and speak about life-threatening issues as they were developing. It brought time-honored stories and values to these discussions. Whatever its imperfections, the church offers a resilient space where life-threatening practices may be reconsidered.

The Church and Its Imperfections

"We live in a *'cause du jour'* culture," says Sarah Wilke of Texas.

And the church is just as much a part of that as anything else. We move from hunger to homelessness to AIDS to abused women to the hungry children. We just kind of float through all these things, and each day one problem is "cured" by the next. We don't know what to do so we just move them around.[2]

The Hebrew Bible and the New Testament indict our tendency to treat life-threatening concerns as if they were fads. The scriptures call us to hold vulnerable groups of people—the orphan, the widow, and the stranger—in our sight at all times. Through primary laws and social organization, through prophetic critique, and through Jesus' example, the scriptures have reminded us that poor children, all children, and all who are poor are welcome in God's community. Their faces reflect the face of Jesus; their bodies and souls offer God's Spirit. The general public can barely see the faces of children in social policy concerning families—in decisions about welfare reform, education, and health. Yet perceptive Christians have found the children in these decisions and led the church in ministries in all of these areas. The church can barely see the faces of children in international law, policies concerning the environment and the economy, and decisions about war and peace. Yet some Christians who have thought about these issues with children and poverty in mind have been grasped by God to make the effects on children and the poor visible. Their and our Christianity has been renewed by their discipleship and their apostleship.

John Wesley, Dorothy Day, and Martin Luther King Jr. are three persons who thought about love, justice, and poverty so organically that children came in their view. Wesley, Day, and

King have in common a deep rooting in scripture, particularly the Beatitudes. They found witnesses in church tradition who helped them figure out how to live their lives with poor and vulnerable persons always at hand. They found it compelling to practice hospitality to those who were cast out of society, though they practiced their hospitality in different ways. They recognized the way that power—social, economic, military—tends to obscure exactly those people. They do not offer us a "program" for living Christian values. Rather, Wesley, Day, and King offer us the opportunity to think about ways of living that may be radically different than the practices of our dominant cultures—in the United States, in Africa, and elsewhere. In so doing, they fan our imagination. They go before us as guides who help us struggle with our own propensities to lose sight of poor children, all children, and those who cope with poverty. They help us learn what it means to include children and poverty in *our* view in *our* time. They help us consider time-honored values and practices for the way those values and practices speak to us now.

A World for Children's Flourishing

In the end, what makes the world better for children in our time? Children and their families—all families—need the support of their communities. Churches have paved the way for such support by supporting early childhood education, support for foster and fragile families, support for family employment, and parenting education. Children without families particularly need the support of international law. Their extreme vulnerability to the worst offences against children—military conscription and economic and sexual slavery—calls the church to stare the perpetrators and laws that protect them in the face, until they must stand down. Decades of data show that children do significantly better in an economy that also supports public social welfare, including general health care and family benefits that provide economic support in vulnerable stages of their life. Children whose bodies are developing have particular vulnerability to toxicity in our environment; they need a clean environment in which to live. Our children bear the effects of an unclean environment now, and we hold our grandchildren's future health in our hands. Children become the victims of war, whether they are killed or raped while wars are fought, or whether they are injured or maimed in war's after-effects. A mentality that holds the biblical image of peace before us—that allows us to believe in peace despite the odds—will lead us to insist that our society will invest in developing skills of domestic, community, national, and international conflict transformation. Such is the nature of resurrection faith: to believe the impossible, to hold out hope for love and justice even when the future seems bleak.

Ministries with children and people who are poor have renewed the church and its ministry throughout history. Sometimes movements such as Roman Catholic religious orders provide ministry that reforms the church from within; other times movements such as the Wesleyan-based Nazarene Church or the Salvation Army have splintered their mother denominations. Regardless of the organizational form, ministries with children and the poor have the power to renew faith and the church. Why should we be surprised? If such ministry bespeaks the heart of Christian faith, if it imitates the example of Jesus Christ, then, of course, it will revitalize the church.

Such ministries have always been rhizomatic—the Methodist movement, the Catholic Worker movement, and the civil rights movement respected none of the traditional ways of organizing institutions in their day. Indeed, they did not seek to be institutions, but movements. Today, as we have seen in the example of the United Methodist Church, such ministries creep and connect in unpredictable ways, growing beneath organizational structures.

Today's rhizomatic ministries grow the faith of new disciples and of disciples who are grasped by God to be apostles. All Christians, as disciples, need some form of apprenticeship in ministry with children and the poor; otherwise, they miss part of the Christian faith. Persons who seek to educate disciples evaluate the impact of their work on disciples who are learning about the church's teachings on children and poverty for the first time. But we rarely stop to consider the impact of such study on persons who are already leaders of the church. A senior staff member of the United Methodist Board of Discipleship, Deb Smith, who wrote the study guide for "Community with Children and the Poor," speaks of such an experience. She writes:

> I had always considered involvement with the poor and children as a response to my faith...I grew to understand

that engagement with the poor and those on the margins was more than just a response. If I want to know the living Christ, I have to go to where Jesus is; and that is among the poor and the children. As I wrote the study guide...I discovered that the increased knowledge compelled me to share that knowledge with others and propelled me to action. I found myself in conversations with everyone from my hairdresser to my plumber to my senator about the realities of children in my community. I have become aware and thankful for the role that the children in the Sunday school class I teach continue to play in my spiritual formation. I have experienced the pushing of the Holy Spirit to go to new places—to expanded job responsibilities, to increased involvement with my congregation's homeless ministry, to educational experiences that increase my awareness of the global nature of our world.[3]

The disciple finds her place in the apostolate for children and poverty in the mystic communion of the body of Christ. For the faithfulness of the unnamed many who are so grasped, and for poor children, all children, and all in poverty with whom they care, I proclaim God's blessing.

Notes

Children and Poverty Timeline

[1]The text of the *Convention on the Rights of the Child (CRC)* and the *Optional Protocols* can be found at www.unicef.org/crc http://www.nccp.org/pub_lic06b.html

Introduction: Seeing and Hearing All Children Despite the Layers That Obscure Them

[1]http://www.unicef.org/specialsession/activities/financing-a-worldfit-for-children-final.doc

[2]"Young Children in Poverty: A Statistical Update," June 1999, The National Center for Children and Poverty, http://www.nccp.org/pub_ycp99.html

[3]"Early Childhood Poverty: A Statistical Profile," The National Center for Children and Poverty, http://www.nccp.org/pub_ecp02.html

[4]"Five Million Children: 1991 Update," The National Center for Children and Poverty, http://www.nccp.org/media/fmc91-text.pdf

[5]Theda Skocpol, *Protecting Soldiers and Mothers: The Political Origins of Social Policy in the United States* (Cambridge: The Belknap Press of Harvard University Press, 1992), 321–40; Pamela Couture, "Public and Private Patriarchy," in *Religion, Feminism, and the Family*, ed. Anne Carr and Mary Stewart van Leewen (Louisville: Westminster John Knox Press, 1996), 249–74.

[6]Richard Sennett, *The Fall of Public Man* (New York: Alfred A. Knopf, 1977), 251–53, identified a similar problem. Sennett argues that, as community disintegrates, as the public and private divide, and as the beliefs and actions of "bourgeois radicals" come under fire, the problematic moves from radical action to radical character, from what the radical does in good tactics with others, to who the "real radical" is. Similarly, when no community is available to unite helpers, activists, and educators, then a potential focus on common goals and strategic actions retreats into a focus on identity—who is the *real* helper, activist, academic?

[7]Charles Wesley, author, John Wesley, ed., "A Collection of Hymns for the use of the People Called Methodist, in *The Works of John Wesley*, V. 1, Hymn 461, Richard Heitzenrater, general editor; Franz Hildebrandt and Oliver A Beckerlegge, editors (Oxford: Oxford University Press, 1983), 643.

[8]See Pamela D. Couture, *Blessed Are the Poor? Women's Poverty, Family Policy, and Practical Theology* (Nashville: Abingdon Press, 1991); Pamela D. Couture, "The Blood the Tells (Knows) the Truth," in *Quarterly Review: Toward a Feminist Wesleyan Theology*, 23:4 (Winter 2003): 347–59.

[9]Bishop James Thomas, "Black Methodism: Legacy of Faith," special session of *Catch the Spirit*, distributed by Ecufilms, 610 Twelfth Ave., Nashville, Tennessee 37203, 1993.

[10]Paul Lendvai, *The Hungarians: A Thousand Years of Victory in Defeat,* trans. Ann Major (Princeton: Princeton University Press, 2003), 21.

[11]Jeanne Boydston, "The Pastoralization of Housework," in *Women's America: Refocusing the Past*, 4th ed., ed. Linda K. Kerber and Janne Sherron DeHart (New York: Oxford University Press, 1995), 148.

[12]Joseph-Edmond Roy, *Guillaume Couture: Premier Colon de la Pointe-Levy* (Montreal: Mercier & Cie., Libraires-Imprimateurs, 1884).

[13]Pamela Couture, *Blessed Are the Poor?,* 27–47.

[14]Pamela Couture, *Seeing Children, Seeing God: A Practical Theology of Children and Poverty* (Nashville: Abingdon Press, 2000).

[15]Emmanuel Lartey, *In Living Colour: An Intercultural Approach to Pastoral Care and Counselling* (London: Wellington House, 1997), 12.

[16]See publications of the Women's Division of the General Board of Global Ministries, http://gbgm-umc.org/umw/; the United Church of Christ, http://www.ucc.org/justice/children.htm; and National Council of Churches, http://ncccusa.org/

Chapter 1: Deserving or Undeserving Children?

[1]Joyce Mercer, *Welcoming Children: A Practical Theology of Childhood* (St. Louis: Chalice Press, 2005), 108–9.

[2]Mimi Abramovitz, *Regulating the Lives of Women* (Boston: South End Press, 1996), 4.

[3]For an example of how "poverty is what we say it is" see a discussion of relative and absolute poverty, George M. Fisher, "Relative or Absolute—New Light on the Behavior of Poverty Lines over Time," http://aspe.hhs.gov/poverty/papers/relabs.htm; for international comparisons, see George M. Fisher, "Enough for a Family to Live On? Questions from Members of the American Public and New Perspectives from British Social Scientists," http://www.census.gov/hhes/poverty/povmeas/papers/ndqppr1c.nnt.pdf; see also the argument for changes in comparison data from poverty level to low-income level (200% of the poverty level) by the National Center for Children and Poverty, www.nccp.org

[4]What do we mean when we say "poor people," "poor children," "children at risk," or "children living in poverty"? According to the *Convention on the Rights of the Child (CRC)*, children are those persons under eighteen years of age. Many argue, however, that it is infantilizing to call teenagers "children"—teenagers are capable of more responsibility and greater social participation than children. Furthermore, some European cultures consider "youth" to be those persons under the age of thirty. Definitions of childhood and youth vary within and between cultures. In this book, "children" will refer to those persons who are under age eighteen, in order to be consistent with the *CRC*, and "youth" will refer to the subcategory of teenagers.

[5]For a fuller biblical interpretation, see Pamela Couture, *Seeing Children: A Practical Theology of Children and Poverty* (Nashville: Abingdon Press, 2000).

[6]William Herzog, private conversation, Rochester, New York, 1997.

[7]A very clear summary of the history of English Poor Law and its relationship to the church and the modern era can be found in William P. Quigley, "Five Hundred Years of English Poor Laws, 1349–1834: Regulating the Working and Nonworking Poor," 30 Akron L. Rev. 73–128 (1996). http://www3.uakron.edu/lawrev/quigley1.html.

[8]Pamela Couture, "Public and Private Patriarchy," in *Religion, Feminism, and the Family*, ed. Anne Carr and Mary Stewart van Leewen (Louisville: Westminster/John Knox Press, 1996), 267. An example of a principled argument can be found in Duncan B. Forrester, "Health, Inequality, and the Decent Society," in *Poverty, Suffering and HIV-AIDS: International Practical Theological Perspectives* (Cardiff: Cardiff Academic Press, 2002), 17–29.

[9]Couture, *Seeing Children*.

[10]George Kenney, "The Bosnian Calculation: How Many Have Died? Not as Many as You Would Think," *The New York Times Magazine*, 23 April 1995. http://www.balkan-archive.org.yu/politics/war_crimes/srebrenica/bosnia_numbers.html

[11]http://globalissues.org/Geopolitics/Africa/DRC.asp

Chapter 2: Love, Justice, and Children in Public and Private

[1]Portions of this chapter were previously published as Pamela Couture, "The Fight for Children: Practical Theology and Children's Rights," *Contact: The Interdisciplinary Journal of Pastoral Studies*, Edinburgh, Scotland. Issue 142 (2003): 28–41. Used by permission.

[2]See chapter 1 for an introduction to these figures.

[3]John Wesley, "Upon Our Lord's Sermon on the Mount: Discourse the Third," in *The Works of John Wesley*, vol. 1, ed. Albert Outler (Nashville: Abingdon Press, 1985), 530. (Hereafter referred to as Wesley, *Works*.)

[4]Patrick Coy, ed., *A Revolution of the Heart: Essays on the Catholic Worker* (Philadelphia: Temple University Press, 1988), 4; Sheila Durkin Dierks and Patricia Powers Ladley, *Catholic Worker Houses: Ordinary Miracles* (Kansas City: Sheed and Ward, 1988), v.

[5]Martin Luther King Jr., *Strength to Love* (Philadelphia: Fortress Press, 1981), 150; idem, "An Experiment in Love" and "Stride Toward Freedom" in *Testament of Hope: The Essential Writings and Speeches of Martin Luther King, Jr.*, ed. James M. Washington (San Francisco: HarperSanFrancisco, 1986), 16 and 447.

[6]Wesley, *Works*, vol. 1, 479.

[7]Richard P. Heitzenrater, "John Wesley and Children," in *The Child in Christian Thought*, ed. Marcia Bunge (Grand Rapids: William Eerdmans, 2001), 279–99.

[8]Wesley, *Works*, vol. 1, 466–697.

[9]Ibid., 478, 481.

[10]Ibid., 483–84.

[11]Ibid., 488–95.

[12]Ibid., 508.

[13]Ibid., 515, 516.

[14]Ibid., 517–20.

[15]Ibid., 525.

[16]Leslie F. Church, *The Early Methodist People* (London: The Epworth Press, 1948), 57. See also Thomas Jackson, *Centenary of Wesleyan Methodism* (London: Mason, 1839), 111.

[17]John Wesley, "Plain Account of the People Called Methodists." Leslie F. Church, a British social historian, insists on the importance of rank and file Methodists who learned and enacted this personal ministry. Leslie F. Church, *More About the Early Methodist People* (London: The Epworth Press, 1949), 177–209.

[18]As Methodist worship emerged in the chapels and while local clergy of the Church of England protested, Methodist worship was potentially illegal unless licensed under the Act of Toleration. The Conventicle Acts of 1664, which were in effect until 1812, prohibited people from attending any exercise of religion other than that of the Church of England. The Conventicle Act of 1670 specified that gatherings in fields, homes, and yards could be prosecuted under the act. When Nonconformist groups continued to defy the Conventicle Acts, the Act of Toleration of 1689 allowed dissenters from the Church of England—in other words, those who renounced their membership in the Church of England—to worship legally if they registered as dissenters.

[19]Church, *Early Methodist People*, 42–52.

[20]Ibid., 180

[21]Ibid., 187.

[22]Ibid., 183.

[23]Dorothy Day, *The Eleventh Virgin* (Kansas City: Sheed and Ward, 1924), 41, 43.

[24]Peter Maurin, *The Catholic Worker*, vol. 1, no. 5, New York City, October, 1933.

[25]Ibid., 1. See also "Christ in His Poor" by Father Elliot Ross, 7, same issue.

[26]Martin Luther King Jr., "An Experiment in Love," in *A Testament of Hope*, 18.

[27]Ibid., 19.

[28]King, "An Address Before the National Press Club," 103, and "Love, Law and Civil Disobedience," 45, in *A Testament of Hope*.

[29]King, "Nonviolence and Racial Justice," 7, and "My Trip to the Land of Gandhi," 25, in *A Testament of Hope*.

[30]King, "Letter From a Birmingham Jail," in *A Testament of Hope*, 290.

[31]King, "The Power of Nonviolence," in *A Testament of Hope*, 14.

[32]King, "Eulogy for the Martyred Children," in *A Testament of Hope*, 221–23.

[33]King, "The Burning Truth in the South," 95, and "Nonviolence: The Only Road to Freedom," 57, in *A Testament of Hope*.

[34]King, "I Have a Dream," in *A Testament of Hope*, 217–20.

[35]King, "A Gift of Love," in *A Testament of Hope*, 63.

[36]King, "A Testament of Hope," in *A Testament of Hope*, 316.

[37]King, "Nonviolence: The Only Road to Freedom," in *A Testament of Hope*, 60.

[38]King, "Nonviolence: The Only Road to Freedom", 59–60, "Behind the Selma March," 126–31, and "Our God Is Marching On," 227–30 in *A Testament of Hope*.

Chapter 3: Love, Justice, and the Spiritual Persistence of the Caregiver

[1]Lisa Belkin, "The Backlash Against Children," *The New York Times Magazine*, 23 July 2000, 30–35, 42, 56, 60–63. See also Herbert Anderson and Susan B. Johnson, *Regarding Children: A New Respect for Children* (Louisville: Westminster/John Knox Press, 1994); Suzanne Johnson, "Women, Children, Poverty and the Church: A Faith-Based Community Revitalization Approach to Addressing Poverty," in *Poverty, Suffering, and HIV-AIDS*, ed. Pamela Couture and Bonnie Miller-McLemore (Cardiff, U.K.: Cardiff Academic Press, 2003); and Bonnie J. Miller-McLemore, *Let the Children Come: Reimagining Childhood from a Christian Perspective* (San Francisco: Jossey-Bass, 2003).

[2]Janet W. Parachin, "Educating for an Engaged Spirituality: Dorothy Day and Thich Nhat Hanh as Spiritual Exemplars," in *Religious Education* 95,no. 3: 250–68.

[3]William D. Miller, *All Is Grace: The Spirituality of Dorothy Day* (Garden City, N.Y.: Doubleday and Company, 1987).

[4]Angie O'Gorman and Patrick G. Coy, "Houses of Hospitality: A Pilgrimage into Nonviolence," in *A Revolution of the Heart: Essay on the Catholic Worker*, ed. Patrick G. Coy. (Philadelphia: Temple University Press, 1988), 239–71.

[5]Wesley, "On Visiting the Sick," as quoted in Pamela Couture, *Seeing Children, Seeing God: A Practical Theology of Children and Poverty* (Nashville: Abingdon Press, 2000), 55.

[6]Ibid., 56.

[7]Theodore Jennings, *Good News to the Poor: John Wesley's Evangelical Economics*, Nashville: Abingdon Press, 1990. See also Richard Heitzenrater, "John Wesley and Children," in *The Child in Christian Thought*.

[8]S.T. Kimbrough Jr., *A Song for the Poor: Hymns by Charles Wesley*. Singer's edition (New York: GBGMusik, The General Board of Global Ministries, 1997).

[9]Martin Luther King Jr., "The Current Crisis in Race Relations," in *A Testament of Hope*, 87.

[10]See Andrew Lester, *Hope in Pastoral Care and Counseling* (Louisville: Westminster John Knox Press, 1995) for the importance of the future in the present.

[11]Martin Luther King Jr., "Love, Law and Civil Disobedience," 44, in *Testament of Hope: The Essential Writings and Speeches of Martin Luther King, Jr.*, ed. James M. Washington (San Francisco: HarperSanFrancisco, 1986).

[12]Ibid., 46.

Chapter 4: Poverty, Love, Justice, and Integrative Understandings of Pastoral Care, Mission, and Evangelism

[1]This letter is part of the response of the Southern Congo Annual Conference of the United Methodist Church to a request for information about the implementation of the United Methodist Bishops Initiative on Children and Poverty.

[2]Interview with Tina Whitehead, Eastern Pennsylvania Annual Conference, The Bishops Initiative on Children and Poverty.

[3]Other subdisciplines include liturgy, preaching, and religious education. In further work these subdisciplines need to be related to the same topic.

[4]The practice and discipline of evangelism are referred to by the same word, just as practical theology and the discipline of pastoral care were referred to by the same word. The reflection on pastoral care is now called "pastoral theology."

[5]William A. Clebsch and Charles R Jaeckle, *Pastoral Care in Historical Perspective: An Essay with Exhibits* (Englewood Cliffs, N.J.: Prentice-Hall, Inc., 1964), 4.

[6]Roy Herndon SteinhoffSmith, *The Mutuality of Care* (St. Louis: Chalice Press, 1999), 15–16.

[7]Stephen Pattison, *A Critique of Pastoral Care* (St. Albans Place: SCM Press, 2000), 13.

[8]Ibid., 13–15.

[9]Alastair Campbell, *Paid to Care?* (London: SPCK, 1985), 1, as quoted in Pattison, Critique, 16.

[10]Pattison, *Critique*, 16.

[11]Ibid., 33.

¹²Pamela D. Couture and Rodney J. Hunter, *Pastoral Care and Social Conflict: Essays in Honor of Charles V. Gerkin* (Nashville: Abingdon Press, 1995). We believed that this volume gave voice to these growing concerns in the Society for Pastoral Theology. Since then the *Journal of Pastoral Theology*, published by the Society, has been replete with articles on pastoral care in the context of social issues.

¹³A. Camps, L.A. Hoedemaker., M.R. Spindler, *Missiology: An Ecumenical Introduction Text and Contexts of Global Christianity* (Grand Rapids, Michigan: William B. Eerdmans), 1995.

¹⁴Ibid., 20.

¹⁵Donald Senior and Carroll Stuhlmuehler, *The Biblical Foundations for Mission* (Maryknoll, N.Y.: Orbis Press, 1983).

¹⁶Stephen B. Bevans and Roger P. Schroeder, *Constants in Context: A Theology for Mission Today, American Society of Missiologists*, Vol. 3, (Maryknoll, N.Y.: Orbis Press, 2004).

¹⁷Justo L. Gonzales, *Christian Thought Revisited: Three Types of Theology*, rev. ed. (Maryknoll, N.Y.: Orbis Books, 1999), as cited in Bevans and Schroeder, *Constants*, 35.

¹⁸Bevans and Schroeder, *Constants in Context*, 37.

¹⁹Ben Campbell Johnson, *Rethinking Evangelism: A Theological Approach* (Philadelphia: The Westminster Press, 1987), 12.

²⁰Mortimer Arias, *Announcing the Reign of God: Evangelism and the Subversive Memory of Jesus* (Philadelphia: Fortress Press, 1984).

²¹William Abraham, *The Logic of Evangelism* (Grand Rapids: William B. Eerdmans, 1989).

²²Scott J. Jones, *The Evangelistic Love of God and Neighbor: A Theology of Witness and Discipleship* (Nashville: Abingdon Press, 2003).

²³Nancy Ramsay, "Metaphors for Ministry: Normative Images for Pastoral Practice," Installation address, Caldwell Chapel, Louisville Seminary, September 13, 1993, 1–2.

²⁴Following the Alexandrian theologians, particularly Origen, and later the nineteenth–century liberal theologians such as Schleiermacher, see Bevans and Schroeder, *Constants in Context*, 51–53.

²⁵Following Irenaeus and twentieth-century liberation theologians, see Bevans and Schroeder, *Constants in Context*, 63–65.

²⁶For an evaluation of the use of metaphors in pastoral care, see Ramsay, "Metaphors for Ministry." For the limitations of the metaphor "shepherd," see Riet Bons-Storm, *The Incredible Woman: Listening to Women's Silence in Pastoral Care and Counseling* (Nashville: Abingdon Press, 1996), 27–29. Feminists and persons concerned to promote the equal worth of the ministry of the laity are concerned about the metaphor of "shepherd" when it promotes the power of the "shepherd" without recognizing that the power of the "shepherd" may also be abused.

²⁷One reason to rethink, from a feminist standpoint, the meaning of "shepherd/ess" is that it is a crosscultural symbol. In a Google image search for "shepherd," I found primarily women as shepherds in many cultural settings.

²⁸Richard McKeon, "Nichomachean Ethics," *Introduction to Aristotle*, Book 7 (Chicago: University of Chicago Press, 1973), 480–509. The theme is carried through in the work of Thomas Aquinas.

²⁹Ramsay, "Metaphors for Ministry," 11–13. See also John Swinton, *Resurrecting the Person: Friendship and Care of People with Mental Health Problems* (Nashville: Abingdon Press, 2000).

Chapter 5: Can Families with Children Survive Our Social Policies?

¹Interview with Wanda Holcombe, Peace with Justice Educator for the General Board of Global Ministries in the Southwest Texas Annual Conference, January 17–18, 2003.

²Ibid.

³Ibid.

⁴This is the main point of my book, Pamela Couture, *Blessed Are the Poor? Women's Poverty, Family Policy and Practical Theology* (Nashville: Abingdon Press, 1991).

[5]Doug Nelson, President of the Annie E. Casey Foundation, writes: "In the next decade, we intend to apply the lessons learned from our work in a set of highly focused demonstrations aimed at restoring the strong connections between vulnerable families and the circumstances we believe are vital to building stronger families and more supportive neighborhoods. These bedrock conditions are ones that most middle-class families have come to expect as a birthright: opportunities to work, earn a decent living, and build assets; social networks that help isolated families link with friends and neighbors as well as social, civic, and faith institutions; and accessible and responsive public services, such as good health care, decent schools, and fair and effective law enforcement." http://www.aecf.org/initiatives/mc

"In even the most bereft and fragmented American communities, we know there are innate strengths and resources of spirit and aspiration that can be tapped and enhanced. We hope that the ideas we bring to this new work will resonate with state and local officials, local residents and leaders, employers, and local philanthropies. If so, we will use these ideas to leverage many different kinds of investments, practical assistance, and empowering activities." www.aecf.org/about

[6]Pamela Couture, *Seeing Children, Seeing God: A Practical Theology of Children and Poverty* (Nashville: Abingdon Press, 2000), 14.

[7]See Theda Skocpol, *Protecting Soldiers and Mothers: The Political Origins of Social Policy in the United States* (Cambridge: The Belknap Press of Harvard University Press, 1992), 7–11.

[8]Ibid., 506–22. The renewal of the Sheppard-Towner Act was passed overwhelming by the House of Representatives but defeated by conservative forces, backed by the American Medical Association (AMA), in the Senate. The AMA considered children's care under the auspices of the public health department "an imported socialistic scheme." Skocpol, *Protecting Soldiers*, 513.

[9]Sandra K Danziger and Sheldon Danziger, "The U.S. Social Safety Net and Poverty: Lessons Learned and Promising Approaches," www.fordschool.umich.edu/research/pdf/Mexico-Danzigers-Jul05.pdf., 6.

[10]http://www.aecf.org/kidscount/sld/profile_results.jsp?r=1&d=1

[11]*Casey Connects* newsletter, Summer 2005, 3.

[12]"Community Ministries and Government Funding," a report jointly written by the United Methodist General Council on Finance and Administration, the General Board of Global Ministries, and the General Board of Church and Society, http://gbgm-umc.org/news/2001/june/faith.htm

[13]This approach is particularly associated with the Asset-Based Community Development Institute, Institute for Policy Research, Northwestern University. See John P. Krentzman and John McKnight, *Building Communities from the Inside Out: A Path Toward Finding and Mobilizing a Community's Assets* (Chicago: ACTA Publications, 1993).

[14]Discussed in chapter 4 of this book.

[15]John Williamson, "What Should the World Bank Think About the Washington Consensus?" *The World Bank Research Observer* 15:2 (August 2002), 7. Available at http://www.worldbank.org/research/journals/wbro/obsaug00/pdf/(6)Williamson.pdf

[16]Concern for social exclusion in Great Britain has not caught on in the U.S. The contrasting language used by social scientists in Great Britain can be found at http://sticerd.lse.ac.uk/case/

[17]Families currently spend an average of 10 percent of disposable income on food, according to Shannon Jung, Professor of Town and Country Ministries at Saint Paul School of Theology. Shannon Jung, "Eating Intentionally," in *Justice in a Global Economy*, ed. Pam Brubaker, Rebecca Todd Peters, and Laura Stivers (Louisville: Westminster/John Knox, 2006), 53.

[18]www.nccp.org.

[19]A 1 percent change represents about a half a million children.

[20]See Greg J. Duncan and P. Lindsay Chase-Lansdale, ed., *For Better and for Worse: Welfare Reform and the Well-Being of Children and Families* (New York: Russell Sage Foundation, 2001); Rebecca M. Blank and Ron Haskins, *The New World of Welfare* (Washington, D.C.: Brookings Institution Press, 2001).

[21]Sandra K Danziger and Sheldon Danziger, "The U.S. Social Safety Net and Poverty: Lessons Learned and Promising Approaches," www.fordschool.umich.edu/research/pdf/Mexico-Danzigers-Jul05.pdf., 7–22.

[22]Lisa A. Gennetian, Cynthia Miller, and Jared Smith, "Minnesota's Family Investment Program Evaluation: Turning Welfare into Work: Six Year Impacts on Parents and Children from MFIP," July 2005. http://www.mdrc.org/publications/411/overview.html; Rebecca Blank, "Evaluating Welfare Reform," 2002, http://www.fordschool.umich.edu/research/papers/PDFfiles/02-003.pdf, 78.

[23]Steven J. Haider, Alison Jacknowitz, Robert F. Schoeni, "Welfare Work Requirements and Child Well-Being: Evidence from the Effects of Breastfeeding," May 2003. http://www.npc.umich.edu/publications/working_papers/paper3/. The authors conclude that breastfeeding among mothers upon whom work requirements were imposed would have been 5.5 percent higher without work requirements.

[24]See also Sharmila Lawrence, Michelle Chau, and Mary Clare Lennon, "Depression, Substance Abuse, and Domestic Violence: Little Is Known About Co-Occurance and Combined Effects in Low Income Families," and related articles, June 2004. http://www.nccp.org/media/dsd04-text.pdf

[25]www.aecf.org/publications/data/connects_summer05.pdf.

[26]One of the few places addressing this issue is the Center for Children of Incarcerated Parents, http://www.e-ccip.org/ and a number of camps for children of incarcerated parents that have developed in response to the United Methodist Bishops Initiative on Children and Poverty.

[27]Ayana Douglas Hall and Heather Koball, "Children of Recent Immigrants: National and Regional Trends," December 2004, www.nccp.org/pub_cri04.html

[28]A particularly comprehensive literature review by Rebecca Blank points out that as of 2002, immigrants and children were unrepresented in the literature. Rebecca Blank, "Evaluating Welfare Reform in the United States," 2002, http://www.fordschool.umich.edu/research/papers/PDFfiles/02-003.pdf

[29]Ibid., 3.

[30]John Hills and Jane Waldfogel, "A 'Third Way' in Welfare Reform? Evidence from the United Kingdom," *Journal of Policy Analysis and Management,* 23/4 (2004): 765–88. Quoted in Danziger and Danziger, "The U.S. Social Safety Net and Poverty," 33–34.

[31]This Summit was delayed until May 2002, due to the World Trade Center bombing.

[32]Report of the General Secretary Kofi Anan, "We the Children: End-decade review of the follow-up to the World Summit for Children," United Nations General Assembly, A/S-27/34, May 2001.

Chapter 6: Do We Believe in the Human Rights of the Child?

[1]These vignettes, in contrast to most of the vignettes opening chapters in this book, do not refer to real people but are constructed as composite examples of children to whom this legislation applied. The example of "Shasha" is informed by the news report listed below by Dina Temple-Raston.

[2]See news report "Analysis: New York could become first state to pass law to protect teen prostitutes," by Dina Temple-Raston, National Public Radio, July 22, 2005.

[3]New York Assembly Bill A 6597, sponsored by William Scarborough of St. Albans, New York. On May 8, 2007 Shawn Chin-chance of Scarborough's offices provided the following information: "The new bill number for the Safe Harbour for Exploited Children is (A5258) in the Assembly, and this year it has a same-as in the Senate (S3175). Last year the bill passed the Assembly but not the Senate."

[4]http://www.unicef.org/protection/index_exploitation.html

[5]The text of the *Convention on the Rights of the Child (CRC)* and the *Optional Protocols* can be found at www.unicef.org/crc

[6]The United States' published rationale for the "Victims of Trafficking and Violence and Protection Act of 2000" cited, with approval, many United Nations treaties for human rights and against international slavery, but not the *CRC.*

[7]Summarized from the *Convention on the Rights of the Child,* www.unicef.org/crc
[8]Ibid.
[9]Kathleen Marshall and Paul Parvis discuss the reasons that the U.S. has not ratified the *CRC.* According to Amnesty International, politically conservative Christian groups believe that "The *Convention* usurps national and state sovereignty...undermines parental authority...allows and encourages children to sue parents, join gangs, and have abortions. The United Nations would dictate how we raise and teach our children." *Honouring Children* (Edinburgh: Saint Andrew Press, 2004), 53–55. Somolia does not have a central government with the authority to ratify.
[10]Marshall and Parvis, *Honouring Children,* 50, 74, outline the historical philosophical, moral, and religious claims for human rights. This volume also has an accompanying congregational study guide. William Schultz, *In Our Own Best Interests: How Defending Human Rights Benefits Us All* (Boston: Beacon Press, 2001), 7, argues for the practical, commonsense reasons for human rights.
[11]For general assessment of the limits of rights talk, see Mary Ann Glendon, *Rights-Talk: The Impoverishment of Political Discourse* (Toronto: Collier Macmillan; New York: The Free Press; New York: Maxwell Macmillan, 1991).
[12]Thandabantu Nhlapo, "The African customary law of marriage and the rights conundrum," in *Beyond Rights Talk and Culture Talk: Comparative Essays on the Politics of Rights and Culture,* ed. Mahmood Mamdani (Capetown: David Philip Publishers, 2000), 137.
[13]Nivedita Menon, "State, community and the debate on the uniform civil code in India," in *Beyond Rights Talk and Culture Talk,* 75–95.
[14]For example, see George Weigel, "Re-reading Cairo: Moral Argument and Universal Human Rights," in *The Challenge of Global Stewardship: Roman Catholic Responses,* ed. Todd David Whitmore and Maura A. Ryan (Notre Dame: University of Notre Dame Press, 1997), 102ff. The argument seems to follow the logic that a contingent of persons seeking to promote worldwide abortion rights also support the CRC, and therefore, the CRC needs to be opposed, because both positions ground themselves in a liberal democratic view of individual rights. This position fails to notice that the text of the CRC never mentions abortion and works hard to uphold the importance of the family for children. The argument is confusing in that Vatican City has ratified the Convention, with registered reservations consistent with its position on abortion (every country ratifies treaties with reservations appropriate to its culture and values).
[15]See Marshall and Parvis, *Honouring Children,* 100, and Martin Chanock, "'Culture' and human rights: orientalizing, occidentalizing, and authenticity," in *Beyond Rights Talk and Culture Talk,* 16–17. For a full legal and ethical analysis of the theory of rights that is beyond the scope of this chapter, including claim-rights and duties, liberty-rights and no-rights, power and liabilities, and immunities and disabilities, see Marshall and Parvis, *Honouring Children,* 100.
[16]Marshall and Parvis, *Honouring Children,* 95ff.
[17]*The Human Development Report 2000,* published for the United Nations Development Programme (New York: Oxford University Press, 2000), 19–20.
[18]Martha C. Nussbaum, *Women and Human Development: The Capabilities Approach* (Cambridge: Cambridge University Press, 2000), 41–59.
[19]Ibid., 78–80.
[20]See, for example, Theodore Runyon, *The New Creation: John Wesley's Theology Today* (Nashville: Abingdon Press, 1998), 170ff.
[21]Bishop Aldo Etchegoyen, personal conversation, at the Oxford Institute of Methodist Theological Studies, Oxford, England, August 2002.

Chapter 7: How Do Children Fare in the Current Global Economy?

[1]Based on interview with Ada and Bob Lower, Dakotas Annual Conference of the United Methodist Church, January 18, 2005.
[2]From www.globalpolicy.org/security/issues/congo/2005/0107volatile/htm. By 2005 the death count had risen to 3.8 and still climbing, and in 2007 the commonly accepted death toll was 3.9 million.

[3]Kristin Herzog, *Children and Our Global Future: Theological and Social Challenges* (Cleveland: The Pilgrim Press, 2005), 72.

[4]Harold James, *The End of Globalization: Lessons from the Great Depression* (Cambridge: Harvard University Press, 2001), 11–12.

[5]Ibid., 7-10.

[6]"We did not really believe that there was going to be a war...people comforted themselves...with the superficial hope that international economic interests with their innumerable interconnections would be sufficient to prevent an armed conflict." Karl Bonhoeffer, father of Dietrich Bonhoeffer, reminiscing about the World War I, quoted in Eberhard Bethge, *Dietrich Bonhoeffer: Man of Vision, Man of Courage* (New York: Harper and Row, 1970), 14.

[7]James, *End of Globalization*, 10–26.

[8]Giovanni Andrea Cornia and Sheldon Danziger, *Child Poverty and Deprivation in the Industrialized Countries, 1945–1995* (Oxford: Clarendon Press, 1997), 26.

[9]Ibid., 27-37.

[10]Ibid., 38.

[11]Ibid., 38-39.

[12]William Julius Wilson, *The Truly Disadvantaged: The Inner City, the Underclass, and Public Policy* (Chicago: University of Chicago Press, 1987), 65–66.

[13]Cornia and Danziger, *Child Poverty and Deprivation*, 56. Based on the percentage of children living in families with disposable cash incomes less than 50 percent of the adjusted median disposable income for all families. Other national comparisons not available.

[14]Ibid., 53–58.

[15]Paul McCleary, president of ForChildren, Inc., provided the historical comparison of under-5 morality rates in African countries, based on UNICEF statistics. From private correspondence, July 25, 2005.

[16]Paul McCleary, private correspondence, July 25, 2005.

[17]Ibid.

[18]A similar summary can be found in Rob van Drimmelen, *Faith in a Global Economy: A Primer for Christians* (Geneva: WCC Publications, 1998), 51–74.

[19]Williamson, "What Should the World Bank Think About the Washington Consensus?" *The World Bank Research Observer* 15:2 (August 2002). Available at http://www.worldbank.org/research/journals/wbro/obsaug00/pdf/(6)Williamson.pdf

[20]A case study of this concern can be found in Bethany McLean and Peter Elkind, *The Smartest Guys in the Room: The Amazing Rise and Scandalous Fall of Enron* (New York: Penguin, 2003).

[21]Williamson, "What Should the Bank Think?" In its original form, the Washington Consensus is closer to Rebecca Todd Peters' category of "development economics" rather than "big business." For these categories, see Rebecca Todd Peters, *In Search of the Good Life: The Ethics of Globalization* (New York: Continuum, 2004), 11.

[22]Williamson, "What Should the World Bank Think?" 257. A good history of the rise of "free market fundamentalism" can be found in Daniel Yergin and Joseph Stanislaw, *The Commanding Heights: The Battle for the World Economy* (New York: Touchstone, 1998).

[23]Williamson, "What Should the World Bank Think," 252.

[24]Susan Strange, *Casino Capitalism* (Oxford, U.K., New York: B. Blackwell, 1986).

[25]Strange documents both decisions and nondecisions that, in light of technological advances and the accompanying accelerated globalization, led to the crises of the 1970s. See chapter 2, "Key Decisions and Their Consequences," in *Casino Capitalism*, 25–59.

[26]Strange died in 1998, but Sarah Anderson, John Cavanaugh, and Thea Lea continued to trace the effects of economic volatility as casino capitalism in: Sarah Anderson and John Cavanaugh, *A Field Guide to the Global Economy* (New York: The New Press, 2000).

[27]Alan Wolfe, *Whose Keeper? Social Science and Moral Obligation* (Berkeley: University of California Press, 1989), 31—41.

[28]Ibid., 133.

[29]Ibid., 132.

[30]Ibid., 136.

[31]James U. McNeal, "An Exploratory Study of the Consumer Behavior of Children," in *Dimensions of Consumer Behavior*, ed. James U. McNeal (New York: Appleton-Century

Corfts 1969), 16, cited in Joyce Mercer, *Welcoming Children: A Practical Theology of Childhood* (St. Louis: Chalice Press, 2005), 71–113.

[32]Elizabeth Chin, *Purchasing Power: Black Kids and American Consumer Culture* (Minneapolis: University of Minnesota Press, 2001), 23, cited in Mercer, *Welcoming Children*, 108.

[33]Peters, *In Search of the Good Life*, 101ff.

[34]Ibid., 139ff.

[35]An enormous literature in theology, ethics, and the church evaluates the global economy. Reviewing this literature is beyond the scope of this book, which is primarily concerned with identifying the economy as a social context that shapes children's lives.

[36]James Newton Poling, with contributions by Brenda Consuelo Ruiz and Linda Crockett, *Render Unto God: Economic Vulnerability, Family Violence, and Pastoral Theology* (St. Louis: Chalice Press, 2002), 65–104.

[37]Emmanuel Lartey, conversation at the Society for Pastoral Theology, Denver, Colorado, June 2005.

[38]Timothy O'Brien, *The Bad Bet: The Inside Story of the Glamour, Glitz and Danger of America's Gaming Industry* (New York: Random House, 1998), 258–281.

Chapter 8: Do Children Graze in Good Pastures?

[1]Bruce Lamphear, Kim Deitrich, Peggy Auginer, Christopher Cox, "Cognitive Deficits Associated with Blood Level Concentrations < Ug/Dl in US Children and Adolescents," *Public Health Reports* 115 (December 2000).

[2]See www.epa.gov/lead

[3]Mary Elizabeth Moore, *Ministering with the Earth* (St. Louis: Chalice Press, 1998), 121.

[4]Mark Roseland, *Toward Sustainable Communities: Resources for Citizens and Their Government* (Gabrioloa Island, British Columbia: New Society Publishers, 1998), 6.

[5]see www.epa.gov/indicators/roe/html/tsd/tsdAir.htm

[6]Juliet Eilperin, "Debate on Climate Shifts to Issue of Irreparable Change," *The Washington Post*, 29 Jan. 2006, A1.

[7]Roseland, *Toward Sustainable Communities*, 8.

[8]Larry Rasmussen, *Earth Community Earth Ethics* (Maryknoll, N.Y.: Orbis Press, 2001), 75; for the disproportionate burden of environmental effects on people and communities of color, see Mary Elizabeth Moore, *Ministering with the Earth* (St. Louis: Chalice Press, 1998), 121, 217–22.

[9]Adam Hochschild, *King Leopold's Ghost: A Story of Greed, Terror, and Heroism in Colonial Africa* (New York: Houghton Mifflin Company, 1998), 301.

[10]Peter Schwab, *Africa: A Continent Self-Destructs* (New York: Palgrave Macmillian, 2001), 54–61.

[11]Rasmussen, *Earth Community*, 113–14.

[12]Nancy R. Howell, *A Feminist Cosmology: Ecology, Solidarity, and Metaphysics* (Amherst: Humanity Books, 2000), 4.

[13]Rasmussen, *Earth Community*, 7, 35.

[14]Nancy R. Howell, "The Importance of Being Chimpanzee," *Theology and Science* 1:2 (October 2003): 179–91.

[15]Richard Louv, *Last Child in the Woods: Saving Our Children from Nature-Deficit Disorder* (Chapel Hill: Algonquin Books of Chapel Hill, 2005).

[16]Stephen B. Bevans and Roger P. Schroeder, *Constants in Context: A Theology for Mission Today*, American Society of Missiologists, vol. 3, (Maryknoll, N.Y.: Orbis Press, 2004) 375.

[17]Rasmussen, *Earth Community*, 99.

[18]Charles Birch, as quoted in Rasmussen, *Earth Community*, 103.

[19]Rasmussen, *Earth Community*, 99.

[20]Rebecca Todd Peters, *In Search of the Good Life: The Ethics of Globalization* (New York: Continuum, 2004), 154–155.

[21]For key documents on the war in Congo and natural resources, including access to the October 23, 2003, United Nations Security Council report, "Letter dated 15 October 2003 from the Chairman of the Panel of Experts on the Illegal Exploitation of Natural

Resources and Other Forms of Wealth of the Democratic Republic of the Congo addressed to the Secretary-General," see http://globalpolicy.org/security/issues/kongidx.htm.

[22]See Moore, *Ministering with the Earth.*

[23]Howell, *Feminist Cosmology,* 121–22.

[24]See Jace Weaver, ed., *Defending Mother Earth: Native American Perspectives on Environmental Justice* (Maryknoll, N.Y.: Orbis Books, 1996). Once, half the population of the United States was employed in agriculture. Now only about 1.1 percent of the population farms. From the Environmental Protection Agency: www.epa.gov/agriculture/ag101/demographics, quoted in Shannon Jung, "Eating Well," in *Justice in a Global Economy,* ed. Pam Brubaker, Rebecca Todd Peters, and Laura Stivers (Knoxville: Westminster/John Knox Press, 2006), 53.

[25]See Eilperin, "Debate on Climate," A1; Thomas Friedman, "A Green Dream in Texas," 18 January 2006; "China's Little Green Book," 2 Nov. 2005; "Green Dreams in Shangri-La," 28 Oct. 2005, each from *The New York Times.*

[26]Charles Gerkin, *Prophetic Pastoral Practice: A Christian Vision of Life Together* (Nashville: Abingdon Press, 1991).

[27]Gardiner Harris, "Low Lead Levels Could Pose Risk," *The Wall Street Journal,* 11 September 2002, D1, D6; Jane E. Brody, "Personal Health: Dally No Longer: Get the Lead Out," *The New York Times,* 17 January 2006, Section F, Page 6, Column 3.

[28]Katrina Smith Korfmacher, "Rochester Moves to Make Lead History," Lead and Environmental Hazard Association, http://www.leadmoldcommunity.com/index.php

[29]www.leadsafeby 2010.org

Chapter 9: What Do War and Peace Mean for Children?

[1]Other authors have used a letter form to mark a particularly personal or intimate interchange in the middle of a story or argument written otherwise. See Erik Erikson, *Gandhi's Truth: On the Origins of Militant Nonviolence* (New York: W.W. Norton and Company, 1969), 229ff.

[2]For another example of responses to common questions put to nonviolence, see John H. Yoder, *If a Violent Person Threatened to Harm a Loved One...What Would You Do?* (Scottdale, Pa.: Herald Press, 1983).

[3]See The United Methodist Council of Bishops, *In Defense of Creation: the Nuclear Crisis and a Just Peace* (Nashville: The Graded Press), 1986, and the response by Paul Ramsay and Stanley Hauerwas, *Speak Up for Just War or Pacifism: A Critique of the United Methodist Bishops' Pastoral Letter "In Defense of Creation,"* (University Park: The Pennsylvania State University Press, 1988). For the range of positions among those who reject war see John H. Yoder, *Nevertheless: The Varieties of Religious Pacifism* (Scottdale,Pa.: Herald Press, 1971).

[4]Just war theory first developed in the fourth century when the Roman Emperor Constantine adopted Christianity. Until then Christianity had no justification for war.

[5]See for example Walter Wink, *Jesus and Nonviolence: A Third Way* (Minneapolis: Fortress Press, 2003); D. Stephen Long, *Living the Discipline: United Methodist Theological Reflections on War, Civilization and Holiness* (Grand Rapids: William B. Eerdmans, 1992).

[6]For a good discussion, see Phillip L. Roberts and Duane Cady, *Humanitarian Intervention: Just War vs. Pacifism, Philosophers Debate Contemporary Issues,* ed. James P. Sterba and Rosemary Tong, (Lanham: Md.: Rowman and Littlefield, 1996), 45ff.

[7]See for example Jimmy Carter, *Talking Peace: A Vision for the Next Generation* (New York: Puffin Books, 1993).

[8]For an easy introduction to Bonhoeffer's life and thought, see *Bonhoeffer: Pastor, Pacifist, Nazi Resister,* a documentary film by Martin Doblmeier, Journey Films, www.firstrunfeatures.com

[9]My appreciation to Nancy Howell for this insight.

[10]Eberhard Bethge, *Dietrich Bonhoeffer: Man of Vision, Man of Courage* (New York: Harper and Row, 1970), 155.

[11]Greg Baker, *Ghosts of Rwanda,* WGBH Educational Foundation, PBS Home Video, 2004. Romeo Daillaire, *Shake Hands with the Devil: The Failure of Humanity in Rwanda* (New York: Carroll and Graf, 2005), 245.

[12]I use Romeo Dallaire's word *genocidaires* to refer to those who perpetrated the genocide in order to avoid referring to their ethnicity. The language of "Hutu extremists," like "Islamic fundamentalists," ignores the fact that most Hutus were not extremists in Rwanda, just as there are Muslims around the world who are not militant fundamentalists.

[13]Phillipe Guillard in Baker, *Ghosts of Rwanda.*

[14]For the risks and deaths of persons in humanitarian missions, see John S. Burnett, *Where Soldiers Fear to Tread: A Relief Worker's Tale of Survival* (New York: Bantam Books, 2005).

[15]Dallaire speaks of the lack of training of United Nations peacekeeping operations.

[16]Carl Wilkens in Baker, *Ghosts of Rwanda.*

[17]Romeo Dallaire in Baker, *Ghosts of Rwanda.*

[18]Dietrich Bonhoeffer, *Letters and Papers from Prison,* ed. Eberhard Bethge (New York: The Macmillan Company, 1953), 8.

[19]Romeo Dallaire in Baker, *Ghosts of Rwanda.*

[20]Phillipe Guillard in Baker, *Ghosts of Rwanda.*

[21]Dietrich Bonhoeffer, "Letter to Eberhard Bethge, Tegel, 21 July, 1944," in Bonhoeffer, *Letters,* 369–70.

[22]For alternatives, see Robert Seeley, *The Handbook of Non-Violence* (Westport, Conn.: Lawrence Hill, 1986); Barbara Stanford, ed., *Peacemaking: A Guide to Conflict Resolution for Individuals, Groups, Nations* (Bantam Books, 1976).

Chapter 10: Rhizomatic Ministry in a New Century of the Child

[1]Ellen Key, *The Century of the Child,* 9th Edition in English (New York: G.P. Putnam Sons, 1909). Originally published in Swedish in 1900. Last published in 1972, now available on the Web site of the Faculty of the Social Sciences, University of Nijmegen, http://www.socsci.kun.nl/ped/whp/histeduc/ellenkey/

[2]I have limited my attention to mainline denominations and Roman Catholicism and not considered independent evangelical organizations, largely because (1) I locate myself in the mainline church and (2) ministries of the mainline church have not captured media attention or been documented as have evangelical ministries such as James Dobson's "Focus on the Family."

[3]http://www.ncccusa.org/members/index.html

[4]www.uua.org/programs/justice/sjsb.pdf

[5]http://www.ncchuscc.org/cchd

[6]The metaphor of the rhizome in postmodernism is attributed to Gilles Deleuze and Felix Guittari. See Gilles Deleuze, *The Deleuze Reader,* ed. Constantin V. Boundas. (New York: Columbia University Press, 1993) See also Pamela D. Couture, "The Effect of the Postmodern on Pastoral/Practical Theology and Care and Counseling," *The Journal of Pastoral Theology* 13:1 (Spring 2003): 85-104.

[7]Keith Clements, *Learning to Speak: The Church's Voice in Public Affairs* (Edinburgh: T and T Clark, 1995), 157.

[8]Interview with Wanda Holcombe, Peace with Justice Educator for the General Board of Global Ministries in the Southwest Texas Annual Conference, The Bishops Initiative on Children and Poverty, January 17–18, 2003.

[9]Interview with Sandy Ferguson, Associate Council Director for the Baltimore-Washington Annual Conference, The Bishops Initiative on Children and Poverty. January 17–18, 2003.

[10]Interview with Gayle Davis, Area Coordinator for the Troy Annual Conference, The Bishops Initiative on Children and Poverty, January 17–18, 2003.

[11]Interview with Judy Lybeck, Area Coordinator for the Wisconsin Annual Conference, The Bishops Initiative on Children and Poverty, January 21, 2005.

[12]Interview with Joyce DeToni Hill, Area Coordinator for the Rocky Mountain Annual Conference, The Bishops Initiative on Children and Poverty, March 6, 2003.

[13]Interview with John F. Lacaria, Area Coordinator for the West Virginia Annual Conference, The Bishops Initiative on Children and Poverty, January 17-18, 2003.

[14]Interview with Sandy Ferguson, Associate Council Director, Baltimore-Washington Annual Conference, The Bishops Initiative on Children and Poverty, January 17-18,2003.

[15]Interview with Lin Stern and Peggy Eshelman, Dental Health Missionary and Area Coordinator for the Missouri Annual Conference, The Bishops Initiative on Children and Poverty, January 17–18, 2003.

[16]Ibid.

[17]Interview with Debra Rogosky, Area Coordinator for the Western Pennsylvania Annual Conference, The Bishops Initiative on Children and Poverty, January 17–18, 2003.

[18]Interview with Wanda Holcombe, January 17–18, 2003.

[19]Ibid.

[20]Interview with Libba Stinson, Area Coordinator for the Alabama-West Florida Annual Conference, January 17–18, 2003.

Chapter 11: Do Ministries with Children and Poverty Have a Role in Christian Disciplesip?

[1]See Sondra Higgins Matthaei, *Making Disciples: Faith Formation in the Wesleyan Tradition* (Nashville: Abingdon Press, 2000); Henry H. Knight III, *Eight Life-Enriching Practices of United Methodists* (Nashville: Abingdon Press, 2001).

[2]Warren Carter, *Matthew and the Margins: A Sociopolitical and Religious Reading* (Maryknoll, N.Y.: Orbis Books, 2000), 552–54.

[3]John P. Krentzman and John McKnight, *Building Communities from the Inside Out: A Path Toward Finding and Mobilizing a Community's Assets* (Chicago: ACTA Publications, 1993), 14.

[4]Interview with Maggie Rogers, Area Coordinator for the Northwest Texas Annual Conference, the Bishops Initiative on Children and Poverty, March 2003.

[5]Interview with Robert Harder, Area Coordinator for the Kansas East Annual Conference, The Bishops Initiative on Children and Poverty, February 27, 2003.

[6]Interview with Libba Stinson, Area Coordinator for the Alabama-West Florida Annual Conference, The Bishops Initiative on Children and Poverty, January 17–18, 2003.

[7]Interview with Sarah Wilke, Director of Urban Stategies for the North Texas Annual Conference, Bishops Initiative on Children and Poverty, March, 2003.

[8]Foundation Documents for the United Methodist Bishops Initiative on Children and Poverty, available at: http://archives.umc.org/initiative/cfagc/ http://archives.umc.org/frames.asp?url=http%3A//archives.umc.org/initiative/

[9]United Methodist German Annual Conference, *Kinder und Armut: Eine Initiative der Bischöfe*, EmK-Forum 12 (Stuttgart: Medienwerk der EmK, 1998).

[10]Interview with Charlotte Abrams, Area Coordinator for the Nebraska Annual Conference, The Bishops Initiative on Children and Poverty, January 6, 2005.

[11]Interview with Anita Henderlight, Area Coordinator for the Holston Annual Conference, The Bishops Initiative on Children and Poverty, February 10, 2005.

[12]Interview with Barbara Ross and Evelyn Althouse, Area Coordinator and Task Force Member, respectively, for the East Ohio Annual Conference, The Bishops Initiative on Children and Poverty, January 17–18, 2003.

[13]Interview with Ron Messer, Area Coordinator for the New England Annual Conference, The Bishops Initiative on Children and Poverty, January 17, 2003.

[14]Interview with Janet Hitch, Area Coordinator for the Western North Carolina Annual Conference, The Bishops Initiative on Children and Poverty, January 17–18, 2003.

[15]Interview with Angie Williams, Area Coordinator for the Mississippi Annual Conference, The Bishops Initiative on Children and Poverty, January 17–18, 2003.

[16]Interview with Debra Rogosky, Area Coordinator and Chair of Children's Ministry Team for the Western Pennsylvania Annual Conference, The Bishops Initiative on Children and Poverty, January 17–18, 2003.

[17]Interview with Barbara Ross and Evelyn Althouse, January 17–18, 2003.

[18]Interview with Anita Henderlight, February 10, 2005.

[19]Interview with Patricia Magyar, Area Coordinator for the Desert Southwest Annual Conference, The Bishops Initiative on Children and Poverty, March, 2003.

[20]Interview with Tina Whitehead, representative of Operation Sunday School of the Western Pennsylvania Annual Conference, The Bishops Initiative on Children and Poverty, January 17–18, 2003.

[21]Interview with Charlotte Abrams, January 6, 2005.

[22]Interview with Ed Folkwein, Area Coordinator for the Yellowstone Annual Conference, The Bishops Initiative on Children and Poverty, January 17–18, 2003.

[23]Interview with Ann Davis, Area Coordinator for the Virginia Annual Conference, The Bishops Initiative on Children and Poverty, January 17–18, 2003.

[24]Interview with Linda Kelly, Task Force Member for the California-Nevada Annual Conference, The Bishops Initiative on Children and Poverty, January 28, 2005.

[25]Bishop Michael Coyner, Dakotas Annual Conference, personal correspondence.

[26]Darrell L. Guder makes a similar point in *Missional Church: A Vision for the Sending of the Church in North America* (Grand Rapids: Eerdmans, 1998), 110 ff.

[27]Interview with Tina Whitehead, January 17–18, 2003.

Chapter 12: Renewing the Apostolate for Children and Poverty

[1]I thank Dr. Tom Haverly, who made this distinction in a sermon at Saint Paul School of Theology.

[2]Fred B. Craddock, *Luke: Interpretation: A Public Commentary for Teaching and Preaching* (Louisville: John Knox Press, 1990), 86.

[3]John Barton and John Muddiman, *The Oxford Bible Commentary* (Oxford: Oxford University Press, 2001), 934–35.

[4]See F. Klostermann, "Apostolate," in *New Catholic Encyclopedia*, Vol. I (Washington, D.C.: The Catholic University of America, 1967), 688; and Jan Kupka, "The chief points in the discussion about the apostolate of the laity in the Church today," in *Communio: The International Catholic Review* (Winter 1985): 408–24. See also "Dogmatic Constitution on the Church," *Lumen Gentium*, a document of the Second Vatican Council, promulgated by His Holiness Pope Paul VI, Nov. 21, 1964, http://www.vatican.va/archive/hist_councils/ii_vatican_council/documents/vat-ii_const_19641121_lumen-gentium_en.html

[5]Dorothy Day, "On Pilgrimage," *The Catholic Worker,* May 1948, www.catholicworker.org/dorothyday/

[6]Mary Milligan "Apostolic Spirituality," in *The New Dictionary of Catholic Spirituality,* ed. Michael Downey (Collegeville, Minn.: The Liturgical Press, 1993), 51–56.

[7]Ibid., 55.

[8]See chapter 3.

[9]Interview with Barbara Ross and Evelyn Althouse, Area Coordinator and Task Force Member, respectively, for East Ohio Conference, The Bishops Initiative on Children and Poverty, January 17–18, 2003.

[10]Sue Ellen Nicholson, Director of Children and Youth Ministries for the Eastern North Carolina Annual Conference, The Bishops Initiative on Children and Poverty, January 17, 2003.

[11]http://www.gbgm-umc.org/shalomzoneinc/intro.html

[12]Interview with Kathleen Stolz, Area Coordinator for the New Jersey Annual Conference, The Bishops Initiative on Children and Poverty, January 6, 2005.

[13]Interview with Patricia Magyar, Area Coordinator for the Desert Southwest Annual Conference, The Bishops Initiative on Children and Poverty, March, 2003.

[14]Interview with Wanda Holcombe, Peace with Justice Educator for the General Board of Global Ministries in the Southwest Texas Annual Conference, The Bishops Initiative on Children and Poverty, January 17–18, 2003.

[15]Interview with Ann Davis, Area Coordinator for the Virginia Annual Conference, The Bishops Initiative on Children and Poverty, January 17–18, 2003.

[16]Interview with Judy Lybeck, Area Coordinator for the Wisconsin Annual Conference, The Bishops Initiative on Children and Poverty, January 21, 2005.

[17]Interview with Peggy Eshelman and Lin Stern, Area Coordinator and Dental Health Missionary, respectively, for the Missouri Annual Conference, The Bishops Initiative on Children and Poverty, January 17, 2003.

[18]Interview with Barbara Garcia, Area Coordinator for the Tennessee Annual Conference, The Bishops Initiative on Children and Poverty, March 18, 2003.

Conclusion: Beyond "Cause du Jour"

[1]Based on UNICEF statistics, "Finance Development: Invest in Children," www.unicef.org/publications/pub_investchildren_ea.pdf

[2]Interview with Sarah Wilke in March 2003.

[3]Deb Smith, personal correspondence with the author, February 2, 2006.

Select Bibliography

Abraham, William. *The Logic of Evangelism*. Grand Rapids: William B. Eerdmans, 1989.

Abramovitz, Mimi. *Regulating the Lives of Women*. Boston: South End Press, 1996.

Abram, Charlotte, Nebraska Annual Conference Area Coordinator, The Bishops Initiative on Children and Poverty. Telephone interview by Ashley Cheung, January 6, 2005.

Althouse, Evelyn, Eastern Pennsylvania Area Coordinator, The Bishops Initiative on Children and Poverty, and Barbara Ross, Task Force member, The Bishops Initiative on Children and Poverty. Interview by Pamela D. Couture, January 17-18, 2003. Atlanta, Georgia.

Anderson, Herbert, and Susan B. Johnson. *Regarding Children: A New Respect for Children*. Louisville: Westminster/John Knox Press, 1994.

Anderson, Sarah, and John Cavanaugh. *A Field Guide to the Global Economy*. New York: The New York Press, 2000

Arendt, Hannah. *The Human Condition*. Chicago: University of Chicago Press, 1958.

Arias, Mortimer. *Announcing the Reign of God: Evangelism and the Subversive Memory of Jesus*. Philadelphia: Fortress Press, 1984.

Baker, Greg. *Ghosts of Rwanda*. WGBH Educational Foundation, PBS Home Video, 2004.

Barton, John, and John Muddiman. *The Oxford Bible Commentary*. Oxford: Oxford University Press, 2001.

Belkin, Lisa. "The Backlash Against Children." *The New York Times Magazine*, July 23, 2000.

Bethge, Eberhard. *Dietrich Bonhoeffer: Man of Vision, Man of Courage*. New York: Harper and Row, 1970.

Bevans, Stephen B., and Roger P. Schroeder. *Constants in Context: A Theology for Mission Today*. American Society of Missiologists, Vol. 3. Maryknoll: Orbis Press, 2004.

Blank, Rebecca M., and Ron Haskins. *The New World of Welfare.* Washington: Brookings Institution Press, 2001.

Bonhoeffer, Dietrich. *Letters and Papers from Prison.* Ed. Eberhard Bethge. New York: The Macmillan Company, 1953.

Bonhoeffer: Pastor, Pacifist, Nazi Resister, a documentary film by Martin Doblmeier, Journey Films, www.firstrunfeatures.com

Bons-Storm, Riet. *The Incredible Woman: Listening to Women's Silence in Pastoral Care and Counseling.* Nashville: Abingdon Press, 1996.

Boydston, Jeanne." The Pastoralization of Housework." In *Women's America: Refocusing the Past,* ed. Linda K. Kerber and Jane Sherron DeHart. 4th ed. New York: Oxford University Press, 1995.

Burnett, John S. *Where Soldiers Fear to Tread: A Relief Worker's Tale of Survival.* New York: A Bantam Book, 2005.

Cady, Duane, and Phillip L. Roberts, *Humanitarian Intervention: Just War vs. Pacifism.* Series: Philosophers Debate Contemporary Issues, ed. James P. Sterba and Rosemary Tong. Lanham, MD: Rowman and Littlefield Publishers.

Campbell, Alastair. *Paid to Care?* SPCK, 1985.

Carter, Jimmy. *Talking Peace: A Vision for the Next Generation.* New York: Puffin Books, 1993.

Carter, Warren. *Matthew and the Margins: A Sociopolitical and Religious Reading.* Maryknoll: Orbis Books, 2000.

Chanock, Martin. "'Culture' and human rights: orientalizing, occidentalizing, and authenticity." In *Beyond Rights Talk and Culture Talk: Comparative Essays on the Politics of Rights and Culture.* Mahmood Mamdani, ed. Capetown: David Philip Publishers, 2000.

Chin, Elizabeth. *Purchasing Power: Black Kids and American Consumer Culture.* Minneapolis: University of Minnesota Press, 2001.

Church, Leslie F. *More About the Early Methodist People.* London: The Epworth Press, 1949.

_____. *The Early Methodist People.* London: The Epworth Press, 1948.

Clebsch, William A., and Charles R Jaeckle. *Pastoral Care in Historical Perspective: An Essay with Exhibits.* Englewood Cliffs, New Jersey: Prentice-Hall, Inc., 1998.

Clements, Keith. *Learning to Speak: The Church's Voice in Public Affairs.* Edinburgh: T and T Clark, 1995.

Cornia, Giovanni Andrea and Sheldon Danziger. *Child Poverty and Deprivation in the Industrialized Countries, 1945-1995.* Oxford: Clarendon Press, 1997.

Couture, Pamela D. *Blessed Are the Poor? Women's Poverty, Family Policy, and Practical Theology.* Nashville: Abingdon Press, 1991.

_____. "The Blood the Tells (Knows) the Truth," in *Quarterly Review: Toward A Feminist Wesleyan Theology,* 23:4. Winter, 2003.

_____. "The Effect of the Postmodern on Pastoral/Practical Theology and Care and Counseling." In *The Journal of Pastoral Theology* 13:1. Spring, 2003.

_____. "The Fight for Children: Practical Theology and Children's Rights." In *Contact: The Interdisciplinary Journal of Pastoral Studies.* Edinburgh, Scotland. Issue 142 (2003).

_____. and Rodney J. Hunter. *Pastoral Care and Social Conflict: Essays in Honor of Charles V. Gerkin.* Nashville: Abingdon Press, 1995.

_____. "Public and Private Patriarchy." In *Religion, Feminism, and the Family,* ed. Anne Carr and Mary Stewart van Leewen. Louisville: Westminster/John Knox Press, 1996.

_____. *Seeing Children, Seeing God: A Practical Theology of Children and Poverty.* Nashville: Abingdon Press, 2000.

Coy, Patrick, ed. *A Revolution of the Heart: Essays on the Catholic Worker.* Philadelphia: Temple University Press, 1998.

Craddock, Fred B. *Luke: Interpretation: A Public Commentary for Teaching and Preaching.* Louisville: John Knox Press, 1990.

Campo, A., L. A. Hoedemaker, M.R. Spindler, and F. J. Verstraelen, gen. ed. *Missiology: An Ecumenical Introduction: Text and Contexts of Global Christianity.* Grand Rapids: William B. Eerdmans Publishing Company, 1995.

Dallaire, Romeo, and Samantha Power. *Shake Hands with the Devil: The Failure of Humanity in Rwanda.* New York: Carroll and Graf, 2005.

Davis, Ann, Virginia Annual Conference Area Coordinator, The Bishops Initiative on Children and Poverty. Interview by Ann Kemper, January 17-18, 2003. Atlanta, Georgia.

Davis, Gail, Troy Annual Conference Area Coordinator, The Bishops Initiative on Children and Poverty. Interview by Ann Kemper. January 17-18, 2003. Atlanta, Georgia.

Day, Dorothy. *The Eleventh Virgin.* Kansas City: Sheed and Ward, 1924.

Deleuze, Gilles. *The Deleuze Reader.* Constantin V. Boundas, ed. New York: Columbia University Press, 1993.

Dierks, Sheila Durkin, and Patricia Powers Ladley. *Catholic Worker Houses: Ordinary Miracles.* Kansas City: Sheed and Ward, 1988.

Drimmelen, Rob van. *Faith in a Global Economy: A Primer for Christians.* Geneva: WCC Publications, 1998.

Duncan, Greg J., and P. Lindsay Chase-Lansdale, eds. *For Better and For Worse: Welfare Reform and the Well-Being of Children and Families.* New York: Russell Sage Foundation, 2001.

Eilperin, Juliet. "Debate on Climate Change Shifts to Issues of Irreparable Change." In the *Washington Post*, January 29, 2006, Page A 01.

Erikson, Erik. *Gandhi's Truth: On the Origins of Militant Nonviolence.* New York: W.W. Norton and Company, 1969.

Eshelman, Peggy, Area Coordinator for the Missouri Annual Conference Bishops Initiative on Children and Poverty, and Lin Stern, Dental Health Missionary. Interview by Pamela D. Couture, January 17, 2003. Atlanta, Georgia.

Ferguson, Sandy, Associate Council Director, Baltimore-Washington Annual Conference. Interview by Ann Kemper, January 17-18, 2003.

Folkwein, Ed, Yellowstone Annual Conference Area Coordinator, The Bishops Initiative on Children and Poverty. Interview by Pamela D. Couture, March 11, 2003.

Forrester, Duncan B. "Health, Inequality and the Decent Society." In *Poverty, Suffering and HIV-AIDS: International Practical Theological Perspectives.* Cardiff: Cardiff Academic Press, 2002.

Garcia, Barbara, Area Coordinator, Tennessee Annual Conference, The Bishops Initiative on Children and Poverty. Interview by Ann Kemper, March 18, 2003. Atlanta, Georgia.

Gerkin, Charles. *Prophetic Pastoral Practice: A Christian Vision of Life Together.* Nashville: Abingdon, 1991.

Glendon, Mary Ann. *Rights-Talk: The Impoverishment of Political Discourse.* New York: The Free Press, 1991.

Gonzáles, Justo L. *Christian Thought Revisited: Three Types of Theology,* rev. ed. Maryknoll, N.Y.: Orbis Books, 1999.

Guder, Darrell L. *Missional Church: A Vision for the Sending of the Church in North America.* Grand Rapids: W. B. Eerdmans, 1998.

Harder, Robert, Area Coordinator, Kansas East Annual Conference, The Bishops Initiative on Children and Poverty. Interview by Pamela D. Couture, February 27, 2003.

Heitzenrater, Richard P. "John Wesley and Children." In *The Child in Christian Thought*, ed. Marcia Bunge. Grand Rapids: William B. Eerdmans Publishing Company, 2001.

Henderlight, Anita, Area Coordinator, Holston Annual Conference, The Bishops Initiative on Children and Poverty. Interview by Pamela D. Couture, February 10, 2005.

Herzog, Kristen. *Children and Our Global Future: Theological and Social Challenges*. Cleveland: The Pilgrim Press, 2005.

Hill, Joyce DeToni, Rocky Mountain Annual Conference, The Bishops Initiative on Children and Poverty. Interview by Ann Kemper, January 17-18, 2003.

Hitch, Janet, Area Coordinator, Western North Carolina Annual Conference, The Bishops Initiative on Children and Poverty. Interview by Ann Kemper, January 17-18, 2003.

Hochschild, Adam. *King Leopold's Ghost: A Story of Greed, Terror, and Heroism in Colonial Africa*. New York: A Mariner BookHoughton Mifflin Company, 1998.

Holcombe, Wanda, Area Coordinator of the Southwest Texas Annual Conference, The Bishops Initiative on Children and Poverty. Interview by Ann Kemper. January 17-18, 2003. Atlanta, Georgia.

Howell, Nancy R. *A Feminist Cosmology: Ecology, Solidarity, and Metaphysics*. Amherst: Humanity Books, 2000.

_____. "The Importance of Being Chimpanzee," *Theology and Science* 1.2 (October, 2003).

In Defense of Creation: the Nuclear Crisis and a Just Peace, The United Methodist Council of Bishops. Nashville: The Graded Press, 1986.

Jackson, Thomas. *Centenary of Wesleyan Methodism*. London: Mason, 1839.

James, Harold. *The End of Globalization: Lessons from the Great Depression*. Cambridge: Harvard University Press, 2001.

Jennings, Theodore. *Good News to the Poor: John Wesley's Evangelical Economics*. Nashville: Abingdon Press, 1990.

Johnson, Ben Campbell. *Rethinking Evangelism: A Theological Approach*. Philadelphia: The Westminster Press, 1987.

Johnson, Suzanne. "Women, Children, Poverty and the Church: A Faith-Based Community Revitalization Approach to Addressing Poverty." In *Poverty, Suffering, and HIV-AIDS*, ed. Pamela Couture and Bonnie Miller-McLemore. Cardiff Academic Press, January, 2003.

Jones, Scott J. *The Evangelistic Love of God and Neighbor: A Theology of Witness and Discipleship.* Nashville: Abingdon Press, 2003.

Jung, Shannon. "Eating Intentionally." In *Justice in a Global Economy,* ed. Pam Brubaker, Rebecca Todd Peters, and Laura Stivers. Louisville: Westminster / John Knox, 2006.

Kelly, Linda, Task Force member, California-Nevada Annual Conference, the Bishops Initiative on Children and Poverty. Interview by Ashley Cheung, January 28, 2005.

Key, Ellen. *The Century of the Child,* 9th Edition in English. New York: G.P. Putnam Sons, 1909.

Kimbrough, ST, Jr. , *A Song for the Poor: Hymns by Charles Wesley.* Singer's edition. New York: GBGMusik, The General Board of Global Ministries, 1997.

King, Martin Luther, Jr. *Strength to Love.* Philadelphia: Fortress Press, 1981.

Klostermann, F. "Apostolate." In *New Catholic Encyclopedia,* Vol. I. Washington, D.C.: The Catholic University of America, 1967.

Knight, Henry H. III. *Eight Life-Enriching Practices of United Methodists.* Nashville: Abingdon Press, 2001.

Krentzman, John P., and John McKnight. *Building Communities from the Inside Out: A Path Toward Finding and Mobilizing a Community's Assets.* Chicago: ACTA Publications, 1993.

Kupka, Jan. "The chief points in the discussion about the apostolate of the laity in the Church today." In *Communio: The International Catholic Review,* Winter 1985.

Lacaria, John F., Area Coordinator, West Virginia Annual Conference Bishops Initiative on Children and Poverty. Interview by Pamela D. Couture, March 18, 2003.

Lamphear, Bruce MD, MPH, Kim Deitrich, PHD, and Peggy Auginer, MS, Christopher Cox, PHD. "Cognitive Deficits Associated with Blood Level Concentrations < Ug / Dl in US Children and Adolescents." *Public Health Reports* 115 (December 2000).

Lartey, Emmanuel. *In Living Colour: An Intercultural Approach to Pastoral Care and Counselling.* London: Wellington House, 1997.

Lendvai, Paul. *The Hungarians: A Thousand Years of Victory in Defeat,* tr. Ann Major Princeton: Princeton University Press, 2003.

Lester, Andrew. *Hope in Pastoral Care and Counseling.* Louisville: Westminster / John Knox Press, 1995.

Long, Stephen. *Living the Discipline: United Methodist Theological Reflections on War, Civilization and Holiness*. Grand Rapids: William B. Eerdmans Publishing Company, 1992.

Louv, Richard. *Last Child in the Woods: Saving Our Children from Nature-Deficit Disorder*. Chapel Hill N.C.: Algonquin Books of Chapel Hill, 2005.

Lybeck, Judy, Area Coordinator, Wisconsin Annual Conference Bishops Initiative on Children and Poverty. Interview by Pamela D. Couture, January 20, 2005.

Magyar, Patricia, Area Coordinator, Desert Southwest Annual Conference Bishops Initiative on Children and Poverty. Interview by Pamela D. Couture, January 17-18, 2003. Atlanta, Georgia.

Marshall, Kathleen, and Paul Parvis. *Honouring Children*. Edinburgh: Saint Andrew Press, 2004.

Matthaei, Sondra Higgins. *Making Disciples: Faith Formation in the Wesleyan Tradition*. Nashville: Abingdon Press, 2000.

Maurin, Peter. *The Catholic Worker*. Vol. I, no. 5 (October, 1933).

McLean, Bethany, and Peter Elkind. *The Smartest Guys in the Room: The Amazing Rise and Scandalous Fall of Enron*. New York: Penguin Books, 2003.

McCleary, Paul, to Pamela D. Couture, July 25, 2005. Transcript in the hands of Pamela D. Couture.

McKoen, Richard. *Introduction to Aristotle*. "Nichomachean Ethics," Book VII. Chicago: University of Chicago Press, 1973.

McNeal, James U. "An Exploratory Study of the Consumer Behavior of Children." In *Dimensions of Consumer Behavior*, ed. James U. McNeal. New York: Appleton-Century Corfts,1969.

Menon, Nivedita. "State, community and the debate on the uniform civil code in India." In *Beyond Rights and Culture Talk*, ed. Mahmood Mamdani. Capetown: David Philip Publishers, 2000.

Mercer, Joyce. *Welcoming Children: A Practical Theology of Childhood*. St. Louis: Chalice Press, 2005.

Messer, Ron, Area Coordinator, New England Annual Conference Bishops Initiative on Children and Poverty. Interview by Pamela D. Couture, January 17, 2003.

Miller, William D. *All is Grace: The Spirituality of Dorothy Day*. New York: Doubleday and Company, 1987.

Miller-McLemore, Bonnie J. *Let the Children Come: Reimagining Childhood from a Christian Perspective.* San Francisco: Jossey-Bass, 2003.

Milligan, Mary R.S.H. M, "Apostolic Spirituality." In *The New Dictionary of Catholic Spirituality,* ed. Michael Downey. Collegeville: The Liturgical Press, 1993.

Moore, Mary Elizabeth. *Ministering with the Earth.* St. Louis: Chalice Press, 1998.

Nhlapo, Thandabantu. "The African customary law of marriage and the rights conundrum." In *Beyond Rights and Culture Talk,* ed. Mahmood Mamdani. Capetown: David Philip Publishers, 2000.

Nicholson, Sue Ellen, Director of Children and Youth Ministries, Eastern North Carolina Annual Conference. Interview by Ann Kemper, January 17-18, 2003.

Nussbaum, Martha C. *Women and Human Development: The Capabilities Approach.* Cambridge: Cambridge University Press, 2000.

O'Brien, Timothy. *The Bad Bet: the Inside Story of the Glamour, Glitz and Danger of America's Gaming Industry.* New York: Random House, 1998.

O'Gorman, Angie, and Patrick G. Coy. "Houses of Hospitality: A Pilgrimage into Nonviolence." In Patrick G. Coy., ed., *A Revolution of the Heart: Essay on the Catholic Worker.* Philadelphia: Temple University Press, 1988.

Outler, Albert, ed. *The Works of John Wesley,* Vol. I. Nashville: Abingdon Press, 1985.

Parachin, Janet W. "Educating for an Engaged Spirituality: Dorothy Day and Thich Nhat Hanh as Spiritual Exemplars." In *Religious Education* 95 (2003): 250-268.

Pattison, Stephen A. *Critique of Pastoral Care* . St. Albans Place: SCM Press, 2000.

Peters, Rebecca Todd. *In Search of the Good Life: The Ethics of Globalization.* New York: Continuum, 2004.

Poling, James Newton. *Render Unto God: Economic Vulnerability, Family Violence and Pastoral Theology.* St. Louis: Chalice Press, 2002.

Ramsay, Nancy. "Metaphors for Ministry: Normative Images for Pastoral Practice." Installation address, Caldwell Chapel, Louisville Seminary, September 13, 1993.

Ramsay, Paul, and Stanley Hauerwas. *Speak Up for Just War or Pacifism: A Critique of the United Methodist Bishops' Pastoral Letter "In Defense of Creation."* University Park: The Pennsylvania State University Press, 1988.

Rasmussen, Larry. *Earth Community Earth Ethics*. Maryknoll: Orbis Press, 2001.

Report of the General Secretary Kofi Anan, "We the Children: End-decade review of the follow-up to the World Summit for Children," United Nations General Assembly, A/S-27/34, May 2001.

Rogers, Maggie. Area Coordinator for Northwest Texas Annual Conference. Interview by Pamela D. Couture, March 2003.

Rogosky, Debra, Area Coordinator Western Pennsylvania Annual Conference, the Bishops Initiative on Children and Poverty. Interview by Pamela D. Couture, January 17-18,2003. Atlanta, Georgia.

Roseland, Mark. *Toward Sustainable Communities: Resources For Citizens and Their Government*. Gabrioloa Island, British Columbia, Canada: New Society Publishers, 1998.

Ross, Barbara, Task Force member, and Evelyn Althouse, Area Coordinator, East Ohio Annual Conference of the Bishops Initiative on Children and Poverty. Interview by Pamela D. Couture, January 17-18, 2003. Atlanta, Georgia

Roy, Joseph-Edmond. *Guillaume Couture: Premier Colon de la Pointe-Lev.* Montreal: Mercier & Cie., Libraires-Imprimateurs, 1884.

Runyon, Theodore. *The New Creation: John Wesley's Theology Today*. Nashville: Abingdon Press, 1998.

Schultz, William. *In Our Own Best Interests: How Defending Human Rights Benefits Us All*. Boston: Beacon Press, 2001.

Schwab, Peter. *Africa: A Continent Self-Destructs*. New York: Palgrave Macmillian, 2001.

Second Vatican Council. Dogmatic Constitution on the Church, *Lumen Gentium*, Nov. 21, 1964.

Seeley, Robert. *The Handbook of Non-Violence*. Westport: Lawrence Hill and Company, 1986.

Senior, Donald C.P., and Carroll Stuhlmuehler, C.P. *The Biblical Foundations for Mission*. Maryknoll: Orbis Press, 1983.

Sennett, Richard. *The Fall of Public Man*. New York: Alfred A. Knopf, 1977.

Skocpol, Theda. *Protecting Soldiers and Mothers: The Political Origins of Social Policy in the United States*. Cambridge: The Belknap Press of Harvard University Press, 1992.

Smith, Deb. Personal correspondence with Pamela Couture, Feb. 2, 2006.

Stanford, Barbara, ed. *Peacemaking: A Guide to Conflict Resolution for Individuals, Groups, Nations*. New York: Bantam Books, 1976.

SteinhoffSmith, Roy Herndon. *The Mutuality of Care*. St. Louis: Chalice Press, 1999.

Stern, Lin, Dental Health Missionary, and Peggy Eshelman, Area Coordinator Missouri Annual Conference Bishops Initiative on Children and Poverty. Interview by Pamela D. Couture, January 17-18, 2003. Atlanta, Georgia.

Stinson, Libba, Area Coordinator of the Alabama-West Florida Annual Conference Bishops Initiative on Children and Poverty. Interview by Pamela D. Couture, January 17-18, 2003. Atlanta, Georgia.

Stolz, Kathleen, Area Coordinator of the New Jersey Annual Conference Bishops Initiative on Children and Poverty. Interview by Ashley Cheung, January 6, 2005.

Strange, Susan. *Casino Capitalism*. New York : Manchester University Press, 1986.

Swinton, John. *Resurrecting the Person: Friendship and Care of People with Mental Health Problems*. Nashville: Abingdon Press, 2000.

Temple-Raston, Dina. "Analysis: New York Could Become First State to Protect Teen Prostitutes." National Public Radio, July 22, 2005.

The Human Development Report 2000, Published for the United Nations Development Programme, New York: Oxford University Press.

Thomas, James. "Black Methodism: Legacy of Faith," special session of *Catch the Spirit*, distributed by Ecufilms, 610 Twelfth Ave., Nashville, Tennessee 37203, 1993.

Washington, James M., ed. *A Testament of Hope: The Essential Writings and Speeches of Martin Luther King, Jr.*, San Francisco: Harper, 1991.

Weaver, Jace, ed. *Defending Mother Earth: Native American Perspectives on Environmental Justice*. Maryknoll: Orbis Books, 1996.

Weigel, George. "Re-reading Cairo: Moral Argument and Universal Human Rights." In *The Challenge of Global Stewardship: Roman Catholic Responses*, ed. Todd David Whitmore and Maura A. Ryan. Notre Dame: University of Notre Dame Press, 1997.

Wesley, Charles, author, John Wesley, editor. "A Collection of Hymns for the use of the People Called Methodist," in *The Works of John Wesley*, Vol. 1. Hymn 461. Richard Heitzenrater, general editor; Franz Hildebrandt and Oliver A Beckerlegge, editors. Oxford: Oxford University Press, 1983.

Whitehead, Tina, Eastern Pennsylvania Annual Conference representative of Operation Sunday School to Consultation on Bishops Initiative on Children and Poverty. Interview by Pamela D. Couture, January 17-18,2003. Atlanta, Georgia.

Wilke, Sarah, Director of Urban Strategies for North Texas Annual Conference, Bishops Initiative on Children and Poverty. Interview by Pamela D. Couture, March, 2003. Atlanta, Georgia.

Williams, Angie, Area Coordinator Mississippi Annual Conference Bishops Initiative on Children and Poverty. Interview by Pamela D. Couture, January 17-18,2003. Atlanta, Georgia.

Wilson, William Julius. *The Truly Disadvantaged: The Inner City, the Underclass, and Public Policy.* Chicago: University of Chicago Press, 1987.

Wink, Walter. *Jesus and Nonviolence: A Third Way.* Minneapolis: Fortress Press, 2003.

Wolfe, Alan. *Whose Keeper? Social Science and Moral Obligation.* Berkeley: University of California Press, 1989.

Yergin, Daniel, and Joseph Stanislaw. *The Commanding Heights: The Battle for the World Economy.* New York: Touchstone, 1998.

Yoder, John H. *If a Violent Person Threatened to Harm a Loved One...What Would You Do?"* Scottdale, Pa.: Herald Press, 1983.

_____. *Nevertheless: The Varieties of Religious Pacifism.* Scottdale, Pa.: Herald Press, 1971.

Web Sites of General Interest

Annie E. Casey Foundation: http://www.aecf.org/initiatives/mc

Coalition to Prevent Lead Poisoning in Rochester: www.leadsafeby2010.org

ESRC Research Center for the Analysis of Social Exclusion in Great Britain: http://sticerd.lse.ac.uk/case/

Global Issues Forum: http://globalissues.org/Geopolitics/Africa/DRC.asp

Environmental Protection Agency: www.epa.gov/lead

National Center for Children and Poverty: www.nccp.org

National Council of Churches, http://ncccusa.org/

Shalom Zone, Inc.:http://www.gbgm-umc.org/shalomzoneinc/intro.html

UNICEF: www.unicef.org

Unitarian Universalist Association: www.uua.org/programs/justice/
The United Church of Christ, http://www.ucc.org/justice/children.
htm
United Methodist Bishops Initiative on Children and Poverty: http://
archives.umc.org/initiative
United States Conference of Catholic Bishops Campaign for Human
Development: http://www.nccbuscc.org/cchd
Women's Division of the General Board of Global Ministries, http://
gbgm-umc.org/umw/

Web Sites Identified by Author

Danziger, Sandra K., and Sheldon Danziger. "The U.S. Social
Safety Net and Poverty: Lessons Learned and Promising
Approaches." www.fordschool.umich.edu/research/pdf/
Mexico-Danzigers-Jul05.pdf., 6.

Fisher, George M. "Relative or Absolute—New Light on the Behavior
of Poverty Lines over Time," http://aspe.hhs.gov/poverty/
papers/relabs.htm

_____. "Enough for a Family to Live On? Questions from Members
of the American Public and New Perspectives from British
Social Scientists," http://www.census.gov/hhes/poverty/
povmeas/papers/ndqppr1c.nnt.pdf

Gennetian, Lisa A., Cynthia Miller, and Jared Smith, "Minnesota's
Family Investment Program Evaluation: Turning Welfare into
Work: Six Year Impacts on Parents and Children from MFIP,"
July 2005. http://www.mdrc.org/publications/411/overview.
html; Rebecca Blank, "Evaluating Welfare Reform."

Haider, Steven J. , Alison Jacknowitz, Robert F. Schoeni, "Welfare
Work Requirements and Child Well-Being: Evidence from the
Effects of Breastfeeding," May 2003. http://www.npc.umich.
edu/ publications/working_papers/paper3/

Hall, Ayana Douglas, and Heather Koball, "Children of Recent
Immigrants: National and Regional Trends," December, 2004,
www.nccp.org/pub_cri04.html

Kenney, George. "The Bosnian Calculation: How Many Have Died?
Not As Many as You Would Think," *The New York Times
Magazine*, April 23, 1995. http://www.balkan-archive.org.
yu/politics/war_crimes/srebrenica/bosnia_numbers.html

"Key, Ellen, *The Century of the Child*, 9th Edition in English (New York:
G.P. Putnam Sons, 1909). Originally published in Swedish in

1900. Last published in 1972; now available on the website of the Faculty of the Social Sciences, University of Nijmegen, http://www.socsci.kun.nl/ped/whp/histeduc/ellenkey/

Korfmacher, Katrina Smith. "Rochester Moves to Make Lead History," Lead and Environmental Hazard Association, http://www.leadmoldcommunity.com/index.php.

Lawrence, Sharmila, Michelle Chau, and Mary Clare Lennon, "Depression, Substance Abuse, and Domestic Violence: Little Is Known About Co-Occurance and Combined Effects in Low Income Families," and related articles, June, 2004. http://www.nccp.org/media/dsd04-text.pdf

Quigley, William P. "Five Hundred Years of English Poor Laws, 1349-1834: Regulating the Working and Nonworking Poor," 30 Akron L. Rev. 73-128 (1996). http://www3.uakron.edu/lawrev/quigley1.html.

Williamson, John. "What Should the World Bank Think About the Washington Consensus?" *The World Bank Research Observer* 15:2 (August, 2002), 7. Available at http://www.worldbank.org/research/journals/wbro/absaug00/pdf/(6)Williamson.pdf.

Web Sites Identified by Source

A particularly comprehensive literature review by Rebecca Blank points out that as of 2002, immigrants and children were unrepresented in the literature. Rebecca Blank, "Evaluating Welfare Reform in the United States," May, 2002. http://www.fordschool.umich.edu/research/papers/PDFfiles/02-003.pdf

Center for Children of Incarcerated Parents, http://www.e-ccip.org/ and a number of camps for children of incarcerated parents that have developed in response to the United Methodist Bishops Initiative on Children and Poverty.

"Community Ministries and Government Funding," a report jointly written by the General Council on Finance and Administration, the General Board of Global Ministries, and the General Board of Church and Society, http://gbgm-umc.org/news/2001/june/faith.htm

Convention on the Rights of the Child (CRC) and the Optional Protocols can be found at www.unicef.org/crc

Dogmatic Constitution of the Church, "Lumen Gentium," a document of the Second Vatican Council, promulgated by Holiness Pope

Paul VI, Nov. 21, 1964. http://www.vatican.va/archive/hist_councils/ii_vatican_council/documents/vat-ii_const_19641121_lumen-gentium_en.html

"Early Childhood Poverty: A Statistical Profile," The National Center for Children and Poverty, http://www.nccp.org/pub_ecp02.html

Environmental Protection Agency: www.epa.gov/agriculture/ag101/demographics, quoted in Shannon Jung, "Eating Well," in *Justice in a Global Economy* (Knoxville: Westminster/John Knox Press, 2006.

"Five Million Children: 1991 Update," The National Center for Children and Poverty, http://www.nccp.org/media/fmc91-text.pdf

Foundation Documents for the United Methodist Bishops Initiative on Children and Poverty: http://archives.umc.org/initiative/cfagc/ http://archives.umc.org/frames.asp?url=http%3A//archives.umc.org/initiative/

New York Assembly Bill A 6597, Sponsored by William Scarborough of St. Albans, New York.

United Nations Security Council report, "Letter dated 15 October 2003 from the Chairman of the Panel of Experts on the Illegal Exploitation of Natural Resources and Other Forms of Wealth of the Democratic Republic of the Congo addressed to the Secretary-General," see http://globalpolicy.org/security/issues/kongidx.htm.

"Young Children in Poverty: A Statistical Update," June, 1999, The National Center for Children and Poverty, http://www.nccp.org/pub_ycp99.html

Index